Self-Instruction Materials on Non-Narrative Discourse Analysis

Editor-in-Chief
Sue McQuay, Managing Editor

Managing Editor
Eugene Burnham

Proofreader
Eleanor J. McAlpine

Production Staff
Priscilla Higby, Production Manager
Judy Benjamin, Compositor
Barbara Alber, Graphics Designer

Self-Instruction Materials
on Non-Narrative Discourse Analysis

Stephen H. Levinsohn

SIL International®
Dallas, Texas

© 2023 by SIL International®
Library of Congress Control Number: 2022943378
ISBN: 978-1-55671-462-7 (pbk)
ISBN: 978-1-55671-497-9 (ePub)

All rights reserved

No part of this publication may be reproduced, stored in a retrieval system, or transmitted in any form or by any means – electronic, mechanical, photocopy, recording, or otherwise – without the express permission of SIL International®. However, short passages, generally understood to be within the limits of fair use, may be quoted without permission.

Copies of this and other publications of SIL International® may be obtained through distributors such as Amazon, Barnes & Noble, other worldwide distributors and, for select volumes, www.sil.org/resources/publications:

SIL International Publications
7500 W. Camp Wisdom Road
Dallas, TX 75236-5629 USA

General inquiry: publications_intl@sil.org
Pending order inquiry: sales_intl@sil.org

Scripture quotations identified as *NIV* are from the *Holy Bible, New International Version*®, *NIV*®, © 1973, 1978, 1984, Biblica, Inc.® All rights reserved worldwide. Used by permission.

Scripture quotations identified as *NRSV* are from the *New Revised Standard Version Bible*, copyright © 1989, National Council of the Churches of Christ in the United States of America. Used by permission. All rights reserved.

Greek examples and word-by-word translations were adapted from *The New Greek-English Interlinear New Testament* by Brown, Comfort and Douglas, copyright © 1990. Used by permission of Tyndale House Publishers. All rights reserved.

Contents

Tables	**xi**
0 Introduction	**1**
0.1 Mismatches	1
0.2 Reading in preparation for this course	2
0.3 Overview of chapter topics	2
0.4 Assignments and consulting	3
0.5 Abbreviations	4
1 Preparation and Charting of Non-Narrative Texts	**5**
1.1 Why analyse texts?	5
1.2 Types of text	5
1.3 Text selection: What sort of text should I begin with?	5
1.4 Preparing your texts for charting and analysis	6
1.5 Displaying a text in simplified chart form	6
2 Types of Information and Reasoning Types	**13**
2.1 Articulations of the sentence	13
2.2 Theme-line versus supportive material	14
2.2.1 Characteristics of theme-line information in the four broad text genres	14
2.2.2 The message framework	15
2.2.3 Distinguishing theme-line and supportive information in hortatory texts	15
2.2.4 Supportive exhortations	16
2.3 Inductive style versus deductive style	17
2.4 Deductive versus inductive reasoning and instruction versus persuasion	19
2.5 Types of supportive information	21
2.6 Distribution of different types of supportive information in VO and OV languages	23
3 Connectives, Counterpoints and Propositional Order	**27**
3.1 The default way of intersentential coordination in different genres	27
3.1.1 The default way of intersentential coordination in non-narrative texts	28
3.1.2 The function in non-narrative texts of the default form of coordination in narrative	29
3.1.3 Leaving a coordinative relation implicit in non-narrative	30
3.2 Encoding countering relations	30
3.2.1 Factors that may determine when a countering relation is marked or left implicit	30
3.2.2 Application to Koine Greek	31
3.2.3 Countering in the hortatory text in Kalinga (VS/VO)	32

3.2.4 Countering in the hortatory text in Bariai (SV/VO)	32
3.2.5 Countering in the hortatory text in Dungra Bhil (SV/OV)	32
3.3 Counterpoints	33
3.4 Constituent order and the order of propositions	34
3.4.1 Verb-object order and the ordering of unequal prominence relations	35
3.4.2 Observations	37
3.5 Encoding logical relations	38
3.5.1 Encoding logical relations in specific contexts	38
3.5.2 Factors that may determine when a logical relation is marked or left implicit	39
3.5.3 Logical relations in the letter to Philemon in Koine Greek	39
3.5.4 Logical relations in the hortatory text in Kalinga (VS/VO)	40
3.5.5 Logical relations in the hortatory text in Bariai (SV/VO)	40
3.5.6 Logical relations in the hortatory text in Dungra Bhil (SV/OV)	40
3.6 Resuming an argument line	41
4 Intersentential Progression within a Paragraph; Variations in Constituent Order	**43**
4.1 Intersentential and interclausal progression within a paragraph	43
4.2 Variations in constituent order: an overview	46
4.3 Points of departure in non-narrative	47
4.3.1 Points of departure in Koine Greek	48
4.3.2 Preverbal subjects in Koine Greek	49
4.3.3 Points of departure in the Kalinga (VS/VO) text	52
4.3.4 Points of departure in the Bariai (SV/VO) text	53
4.3.5 Points of departure in the Dungra Bhil (SV/OV) text	53
4.4 Constituent order changes and the Principle of Natural Information Flow	55
5 Focal and Emphatic Prominence	**57**
5.1 Two technical terms: focus and prominence	57
5.2 Violating the Principle of Natural Information Flow	59
5.2.1 Violations of the Principle of Natural Information Flow in the Greek of Philemon	59
5.2.2 Violations of the Principle of Natural Information Flow in Kalinga (VS/VO)	61
5.2.3 Violations of the Principle of Natural Information Flow in Dungra Bhil (SV/OV)	62
5.3 Postposing or isolating the DFE	63
5.4 Other devices used to give prominence to a focal constituent	64
5.5 Giving prominence to part of a constituent	66
5.6 Markers of emphasis	69
6 Determiners and Thematic Prominence	**71**
6.1 Determiners and thematic prominence in Koine Greek	71
6.1.1 The distal demonstrative ἐκεῖνος 'that'	71
6.1.2 The proximal demonstrative οὗτος 'this'	72
6.1.3 The article	72
6.2 Determiners in languages of the Philippines, including Kalinga	73
6.3 Determiners and thematic prominence in the Bariai text	74
6.4 Determiners and thematic prominence in the Dungra Bhil text	74
6.5 Relative clauses in non-narrative material in African languages and Hebrew	76
7 Backgrounding and Highlighting Devices	**81**
7.1 The relative potency of different forms of exhortation	81
7.1.1 What makes an exhortation potent?	82
7.1.2 Factors influencing the form of exhortation chosen	82
7.2 Different forms of exhortation in Koine Greek	84
7.2.1 Exhortations that are directed to the exhortee(s)	84
7.2.2 Exhortations that the exhortee is to pass on to others	87
7.2.3 Exhortations expressed or implied in an anarthrous participial clause	88
7.2.4 Application to the letter to Philemon	89

7.3 Different forms of exhortation in the Kalinga text	90
7.4 Different forms of exhortation in Bariai	91
7.5 Different forms of exhortation in the Dungra Bhil text	91
7.6 Devices used to background propositions in non-narrative texts	92
7.6.1 Application to the Kalinga text	93
7.6.2 Application to the Dungra Bhil text	94
7.7 Highlighting propositions in non-narrative texts	94
7.7.1 The presentation of established information immediately prior to an important THESIS	95
7.7.2 Repetitions or paraphrases of important THESES	96
7.7.3 Presentative particles	96
7.7.4 Rhetorical questions that are answered immediately by the exhorter	97
7.7.5 Other marked patterns or structures	97
8 Boundary Features	**99**
8.1 Problems in identifying boundaries	99
8.1.1 The paragraph or section is a semantic unit	99
8.1.2 Surface features do not exclusively indicate boundaries	99
8.2 The presence of a point of departure	101
8.3 Connectives and juxtaposition	102
8.4 Summarising expressions and cataphoric demonstratives	105
8.5 *Inclusio* structures	106
8.6 Chiastic and parallel structures	107
8.7 Rhetorical questions	109
8.8 Referent identification by means of a seemingly redundant NP	110
8.9 Vocatives	110
8.10 Orienters	111
8.11 Shifts of verb tense-aspect, mood and person	113
8.12 Back reference	114
8.13 Application to the letter to Philemon	115
8.14 Application to the Kalinga text	116
8.15 Application to the Bariai text	117
8.16 Application to the Dungra Bhil text	117
Appendix A: Letter to Philemon (Koine Greek)	**119**
Appendix B: Advice to a Student (Lower Tanudan Kalinga)	**125**
Appendix C: Banana Beer and Marijuana (Bariai)	**131**
Appendix D: Liquor Text (Dungra Bhil)	**135**
References	**143**
Index of Languages	**147**
Index of Scripture References	**149**

Tables

Table 1. Supportive information in VO and OV languages	24
Table 2. Intersentential connectives in the letter to Philemon	28
Table 3. Constituent order and propositional order correlations	31
Table 4. Propositional order and means of conjoining correlations	31
Table 5. HEAD-dependent ordering correlations	35
Table 6. Verb-object order and NUCLEUS-support propositions correlations	35
Table 7. Examples of ordering of propositions	35
Table 8. Chiastic and parallel structures of Acts 28:27	109
Table 9. Features supporting paragraph breaks in the NRSV	115
Table 10. Features supporting section breaks in the Kalinga text	116
Table 11. Features supporting section breaks in the Bariai text	117
Table 12. Features supporting section breaks in the Dungra Bhil text	118

0

Introduction

This course is designed for linguists who are interested in translating hortatory and expository texts from one language to another. Like the "Self-Instruction Materials on Narrative Discourse Analysis" course on which it builds (Levinsohn 2015), it concentrates on those text-related features that have been found to present particular problems in translation.

0.1 Mismatches

Many problems in translation arise because of **mismatches** between the way the features are handled in the source language (SL) and the receptor language (RL).

Dryer (1997) distinguishes languages on the basis of two variables: whether or not the object (O) follows the verb (V) (VO versus OV) and whether or not the subject (S) commonly follows the verb (VS versus SV). A number of discourse features tend to correlate with these variables, including the following (see Levinsohn 2006a for further examples):

VO versus OV. While working on OV languages of Papua New Guinea, Terry Borchard (1991) and John Roberts (1997) identified a number of significant mismatches with VO languages, particularly in the area of NUCLEUS-support relations. They concluded that it is often necessary to reorder propositions to ensure that the supporting proposition supports the correct NUCLEUS (see 2.6 for detailed discussion of this point). Such reordering may also be necessary to ensure that it is the NUCLEUS proposition, rather than the supporting one, that is more prominent (3.4.2).

VS versus SV. A common mismatch between languages in which it is common for the verb to precede the subject (VS) (Ancient Hebrew [hbo],[1] Koine Greek [grc], N. W. Austronesian and Mixtec) and those in which such an order is rare (SV) involves **conjunctions**. For example:

- A number of VS languages use a **conjunction** (usually glossed "for") whose function is to indicate that what follows **strengthens** a previous assertion, without specifying the logical relation between the two (e.g. γάρ in Koine Greek, *kî* in Ancient Hebrew, *te* in Lower Tanudan Kalinga [kml], *chi* in Southeastern Nochixtlán Mixtec [mxy].[2]

- In contrast, strengthening conjunctions like "for" are used relatively infrequently in natural text in SV/VO languages and very rarely in SV/OV languages.

---

[1] ISO 639-3, *Codes for the representation of names of languages*, are incorporated into this volume in square brackets following the language name, when known. For example, Inga [inb], Jóola [dyo], Chichicapan Zapotec [zpv]. For further information see www.ethnologue.com/codes

[2] See Levinsohn 2015, 0.3, on how I recognise that a language is of the VS type.

Other mismatches are specific to particular languages or groups of languages. For example, **relative clauses** have been found to be associated with **prominence** in large numbers of languages in Africa, as well as Ancient Hebrew (see Levinsohn 2015, 10.3.6–7). No such association is found in Indo-European languages like Koine Greek.

0.2 Reading in preparation for this course

As indicated above, this course builds on the "Self-Instruction Materials on Narrative Discourse Analysis" course. Consequently, concepts that have already been introduced in that course will not be repeated here. Instead, the reader will be directed to the section(s) in the course text (Levinsohn 2015) where the concepts were originally presented.

At this point, you should study the following introductory sections of the narrative course:

0.1 The nature of text-related explanations

0.2 Some key concepts in textlinguistics

    0.2.1   Choice implies meaning

    0.2.2   Semantic meaning and pragmatic effects

    0.2.3   Default versus marked phenomena

0.3 Overview of chapter topics

This section outlines the contents of the remaining chapters of this course.

Chapter 1 deals with the selection, preparation and charting of non-narrative texts. It identifies those texts that are most suitable for beginning the analysis of expository and hortatory material. It describes how to prepare a text for charting and then presents a method of charting texts in a systematic way. This is illustrated by sample charts for the three major language types (VS/VO, SV/VO and SV/OV).

Chapter 2 distinguishes two types of reasoning (instruction and persuasion) and notes a correlation with inductive versus deductive reasoning. This leads to a description of the types of supportive information that Breeze (1992) identifies for hortatory discourses, and to where mismatches are most likely to occur when translating from a verb-object (VO) language to an object-verb (OV) language.

Chapter 3 concerns the use and nonuse of connectives to signal relations between propositions and groups of propositions in non-narrative texts. The default way of coordinating sentences in narrative and non-narrative may differ. The order of propositions may affect the connective used. Countering and logical relations may be expressed in different ways in the source and receptor languages. Some logical connectives may signal the resumption of the theme line of a non-narrative discourse. In some languages, a "counterpoint" is a useful concept: "a contrasting … idea, used to set off the main element" (*Oxford English Dictionary – OED*).

Chapter 4 begins with different types of intersentential progression within a paragraph. It then gives an overview of factors underlying variations in constituent order, before dealing with two of these factors: the role of "points of departure" (topicalised constituents) in non-narrative discourse and conformity to Comrie's (1989:127–128) "Principle of Natural Information Flow". The chapter also considers the presence of the subject in pro-drop languages and its position in languages like Koine Greek and Kalinga that allow it to either precede or follow the verb.

Chapter 5 considers violations of the Principle of Natural Information Flow. These occur not only in identificational sentences, but also in connection with contrastive and emphatic prominence, and when a foil (a constituent that serves to set off a later constituent to advantage by contrast) is preposed. Other devices that give prominence to a focal constituent include the postposing or isolation of the dominant focal element (DFE – Levinsohn 2015, 4.2.4) and dedicated prominence markers. Prominence may also be given to only part of a constituent.

Chapter 6 is concerned particularly with devices used to draw attention to a referent because of the significant role it will have to play in the subsequent discourse. Such devices include so-called 'emphatic' pronouns, one or more of the sets of demonstratives found in the language and, especially in Ancient Hebrew and many African languages, those relative clauses that contain information which is not really needed to establish the identity of the referent. In addition, some of the devices that give prominence to a focal constituent (ch. 5) may also be employed to give prominence to a point of departure or connective, thereby highlighting the material that follows.

Chapter 7 considers the relative potency of different forms of exhortation and when each form is appropriate. It also reviews and illustrates the backgrounding devices that were presented in chapter 5 of Levinsohn 2015, before discussing devices that commonly highlight propositions or groups of propositions in non-narrative material.

Chapter 8 concerns criteria that enable a reader or hearer to recognise boundaries between paragraphs and larger units such as episodes of a narrative or sections of a book.

0.4 Assignments and consulting

As you work through each chapter, you will find paragraphs entitled "Application". These paragraphs suggest how you should apply what you have read to the analysis of your texts.

Questions may well arise as you try and apply what you have read to your texts. If you would like to direct such questions to me, send an email to stephen_levinsohn@sil.org. If you wish to discuss how to analyse any feature of your texts, I will invite you to send me a copy of your charted text(s), together with a free translation (see ch. 1).

You are encouraged to record the results of your research. Various people will benefit if you record your findings (e.g. in the form of answers to the Application questions):

1. you (it is common in workshops to find that consultees have later forgotten what they have already discovered about the feature being analysed);
2. your translation consultant (if you have explained how different text-related features function, your consultant may not have to ask you how they function, but will be able to read your description!);
3. people working in related languages (there is no value in rediscovering the wheel!).

0.5 Abbreviations

The following abbreviations are used throughout this course (additional ones peculiar to a particular text will be interpreted as needed):

ABS	absolutive	NM	preposed noun marker (ABS) (in Kalinga)
ACC	accusative		
ADD	additive	NOM	nominaliser
AG	agentive, agent of nominalised verb	NP	noun phrase
AJR	adjectiviser	*NRSV*	*New Revised Standard Version*
ANA	anaphoric marker	O	object
AUX	auxiliary	OBL	oblique
COMP	completive	OCC	occasion (in Kalinga)
d	dual	*OED*	*Oxford English Dictionary*
DEM	demonstrative	p, PL	plural
DFE	dominant focal element	PASS	passive, passive-like
DM	development marker	PER	perfect
DUR	durative	PF	perfective
EMP	marker of emphasis	PoD	point of departure
ex	exclusive (1st person)	POS	possessive
EXC	exclusive prominence	POT	potential
EXIS	existential	PRE	present tense
EXP	experiencer of nominalised verb	PRO	prohibitive
FOC	focus	PTC	participle
FUT	future	PUR	purpose
GEN	genitive	QUES	question
GER	gerund	REC	recipient
GP	general preposition (in Bariai)	REL	relative marker, anaphoric relativiser
IMP	imperative	s	singular
IMPF	imperfective aspect	S	subject
in	inclusive (1st person)	SR	switch reference
INF	infinitive	SS	same subject
IRR	irrealis	ST	stative
LK	linker	TH	theme (transitive with 'O' orientation in Kalinga)
LOC	locative		
m	masculine	TOP	topic, topicalised constituent
NEG	negative	V	verb
NIV	*New International Version*	1, 2, 3	1st, 2nd, 3rd person

1

Preparation and Charting of Non-Narrative Texts

1.1 Why analyse texts?

To prepare for charting of non-narrative texts, review section 1.1 in the narrative course textbook (Levinsohn 2015:9–11).

1.2 Types of text

The following sections of this chapter concern the sort of text you should begin with (1.3), matters you should take care of before charting the text (1.4) and how to display the text in chart form (1.5).

1.3 Text selection: What sort of text should I begin with?

Section 1.3 of the narrative course explains why you should begin text analysis with narratives and which sorts of narrative text you should work on. Once you have studied some narrative, I suggest you obtain hortatory texts of the following two types:[1]

- **INSTRUCTION:** A speaker or writer (exhorter) considers him- or herself to have the right or authority to instruct the exhortee how to behave (apostolic authority, in the case of the Pauline epistles). Directives from employers to employees are typically of this type. In some cultures, parents have the right to instruct their adult children how to behave once married, etc., too. This category may also include strong rebukes of existing behaviour, as when someone "instructs" a friend to stop maintaining enmity with another person or to stop being lazy.

- **PERSUASION:** The exhorter appeals to the reasoning logic of the recipient and seeks to convince him or her to follow a course of action. Typically, the exhorter uses persuasion because he or she cannot make the exhortee pursue such a course of action. However, there are occasions, too, when a person in authority chooses to persuade rather than instruct.

Application to the language you are analysing

Which type of text are you planning to translate first: instruction or persuasion? Then select from your corpus a hortatory text of the same type.

---

[1] See further in 2.4.

1.4 Preparing your texts for charting and analysis

Although section 1.4 of the narrative course concerns narratives, the same principles apply to non-narrative texts, so please read sections 1.4.1–1.4.3. (If you have already analysed narrative texts, then you will not need to answer the questions of 1.4.4 again.)

Application to the language you are analysing

1. If you are in a position to do so, check that the text you have selected for charting is well formed and that you control the facts. Obtain a free translation of the text.
2. Take a glossed copy of the text and mark tentative divisions into sentences, clauses and phrases. Number the sentences consecutively and give simple labels to the constituents.

1.5 Displaying a text in simplified chart form

In section 1.5 of the narrative course, you were asked to chart a text in a way that allocated each clause constituent to a separate column. If you charted one or more narratives in this way, then there should be no need for you to display your non-narrative texts in such a detailed way (though some analysts like to do so). Instead, it should be sufficient to display your texts clause by clause.

General conventions for a simplified chart

1. Start a new line for every new clause.
2. Start each clause at the appropriate tab on the page and continue for as long as necessary. The tabs in the following charts are set at 0.35" (0.89 cm), 0.75" (1.9 cm) and then every 0.25" (0.63 cm). The columns are as follows:

    | 0.0" | **Ref**: sentence number |
    | 0.35" | **Con**: Connectives and any initial vocatives |
    | 0.75" | **Prenuclear**: left-dislocated and preposed constituents (depending on the language type), plus prenuclear subordinate clauses. |
    | 1.75" | **Nucleus**: verb, subject, objects and oblique constituents (when not preposed or postposed) |
    | 3.5" | **Postnuclear**: right-dislocated and postposed constituents, plus postnuclear subordinate clauses. |

3. Put a line across the page before each new sentence.[2]
4. Do NOT reorder material to get it in the correct column. The text should read in its original order from left to right, then down to the next line. When a constituent is too long to fit on one line, go on to the next line.
5. Set up different styles for the language, the gloss, and the free translation. The free translation can either go after each sentence or at the end of the chart.[3]
6. Use square brackets to mark the boundaries of a complex constituent. (In Kalinga clause 3b, for example, *many who are delayed in their studies* is treated as a single prenuclear constituent.)
7. In the connectives column, use curly brackets to note any potential connectives that occur in non-initial position (e.g. {kad} in Kalinga clause 3c).

On the following pages, you will find sample charts for the three major language types: VS/VO (Lower Tanudan Kalinga), SV/VO (Bariai [bch]) and SV/OV (Dungra Bhil [duh]). Select as your model the language type that is closest to the language you are analysing. Study the chart, then read the comments about the display.

---

[2] I view a sentence as a main CLAUSE together with those clauses that are subordinate to it. Very often, as a result, each sentence will contain only one main clause.

[3] For users of the Shoebox program, you do not need both the \t and \m lines for discourse purposes. I combine the two, as I like to include the morpheme breaks.

1.5 Displaying a text in simplified chart form

Sample page of a charted text in a VS/VO language (Lower Tanudan Kalinga)

Ref.	Con.	Prenuclear-V		Nucleus	Postnuclear				
01		*Abeng*	*annaya*	*[ma-sapul]*	*e*	*ko-on-yu*	*e*	*um-oy an-uswila*	*si adayul.*
		child	this.EMP	PASS.IMPF-need	LK	do-TH.IMPF-2p.GEN	LK	AG-go AG-study	LOC far
		Children, this (is) what you need to do when you go to school in a far place.							
02a		*Sa*	*um-una,*	*sosomk-on-yu*					
		the	AG-first	DUR.think-TH.IMPF-2p.GEN					
02b						*ta*	*siya*	*iy-enrol-yu*	*de makwa e pion-yu*
						PUR	that.which	TH-enrol-2p.GEN	ABS POT.know LK like-2p.GEN
02c						*kan*	*ma-kaya-yu*	*e courso.*	
						and	PASS-carry-2p.GEN	LK course	
		The first thing (is) to think hard, so that what you enrol in is a course you know you like and one you can afford.							
03a	*Te*				*igammu-yu*	*kamman*			
	for				know-2p.GEN	QUES			
03b		*[ka-adu-wan'*	*e*	*maka-taktak*	*si*	*an-uswila],*			
		REC-many-REC	LK	POT-delay	OBL	AG-study			
03c	{*kad*}	*adi-na*	*pun*	*kad*	*pion*	*awa illus-na*	*iy-enrol*		
		NEG-3s	NEG	then/then	want	EXIS TH.start-3s	TH-enrol		
03d					*i-kasin-na*	*bos ang-ala*	*'k osa*	*'k courso.*	
					TH-repeat-3s	also AG-take	OBL one	OBL course	
		After all, don't you know, many (who) are delayed in their studies, when/then they don't like what it is they enrolled in, again take another course.							
04	*Kad*	*sadi*			*osa*	*e*	*ma-gastu*	*lawa pilak*	
	Then	that			one	LK	PASS.IMPF-spend	no.reason money	
	then	that is one way money is spent for nothing/senselessly.							
05a	*[Sa*	*osa*	*e*	*mi-baga*	*kan dikayu,*	*e*	*abeng'*	*e um-adayul,*	
	the	one	LK	PASS-tell	OBL2p.TOP	LK	child	LK AG-far	
05b					*adi-kayu*	*okyan*	*al-lasu*	*e um-ayu,*	
					NEG-2p.ABS	should	AJR-easy	LK AG-homesickness	
05c						[*te*	*sadi*	*osa e*	*angi-agay-an da udum' e an-uswila,*
						for	that	one LK	OCC-stop-OCC PL other LK AG-study
05d						*adi-da*	*pun*	*maka-kwa si*	*ayu-da].*
						NEG-3p	NEG	POT-do OBL	homesickness-3p
		The one thing I'm telling you, children that go far, you should not easily be homesick, because that is one thing that stops others that go away to school, not being able to bear their homesickness.							

Comments on charting the Lower Tanudan Kalinga (VS/VO) text

The text displayed on the previous page is the first part of a letter in Kalinga written in 1997 by Mary Dunol to children who had just been sent away for school. It is of the Instruction type of exhortation. Jewell Machlan (p.c.) translated the text into English [eng] and kindly made it available to me.

   Convention 2. The Prenuclear-V column of the chart is used for all constituents that precede the **verb** other than connectives and initial vocatives.

   Convention 6. Square brackets used to mark the boundaries of complex constituents. In 5c–d, the reason for 5b extends over two clauses (5d is further indented).

   Note: You will find a chart of the full text in Kalinga in Appendix B.

1.5 Displaying a text in simplified chart form

Sample page of a charted text in an SV/VO language (Bariai)

Ref.	Con.	Prenuclear-V	Nucleus	Postnuclear
01			[Iaba ga mariuana] ein danga paeamao. banana.sp & marijuana this thing bad Banana [beer] and marijuana, this is a bad thing.	
02a			Kapeipei ga kakau, gau na-keo tautaunga pa-gimi, elders & youth I 1s-speak truly at-2p	
02b		[kado-nga do-NOM	ngan un-nga iaba ga ean-nga GP drink-NOM banana.sp & consume-NOM	guas mariuana] ein danga paeamao. tobacco marijuana this thing bad
02c			ngansa i-paeabu ngan le-da mado-nga tuanga-i. because 3s-destroy GP AG-1in sit-NOM village-LOC
			Elders and young people, I speak truly to you, the behaviour with regard to drinking banana [beer] and consuming marijuana tobacco, this is a bad thing. because it destroys our living in the village.	
03a	be ADD	[oangga if	sai i-longo linge-g mao, who 3s-hear voice-1s NEG	
03b	be ADD	i-an 3s.consume	guas paeamao tobacco bad	
03c	ga &	i-un iaba,] 3s-drink banana.sp		
03d	eine ga this IRR		i-paeabu ngan i-uae ede pade 3s-destroy GP 3s-companion one ADD	
03e			ga i-mate. IRR 3s-die	
			Yes, if anyone doesn't listen to my voice, but consumes bad tobacco and drinks banana [beer], he will destroy his fellow companion so that he dies.	
04a			Na-keo tautaunga pa-gimi, 1s-speak truly at-2p	
04b		[kado-nga do-NOM	toa bedane] eine paeamao ANA like.this this bad	
04c			[ngansa {oangga kado-nga toa bedane i-uotot somisomi tuanga-i,} because if do-NOM ANA like.this 3s-happen.IMPF always village-LOC
04d	eine ga this IRR		panua busa ga ti-matemate ngan kado-nga toa beda-oa]. people many IRR 3p-die.IMPF GP do-NOM ANA like.that
	then		I speak truly to you, behaviour like this is bad because, if behaviour like this is always coming about in the village, many people will be dying from such behaviour.	

Comments on charting the Bariai (SV/VO) text

The text displayed on the previous page is the first part of a text written in Bariai by the late Peter Biriu in 2004. It is of the Persuasion type of exhortation. Steve Gallagher (p.c.) translated the text into English and kindly made it available to me.

Convention 2. The Prenuclear column of the chart is used for all constituents that precede the **subject** other than connectives and initial vocatives.

Convention 6. Square brackets mark the boundaries of complex constituents. In 2b, *the behaviour with regard to drinking banana [beer] and consuming marijuana tobacco* is treated as a single left-dislocated, prenuclear constituent. In 3, the prenuclear conditional clauses *if anyone doesn't listen to my voice, but consumes bad tobacco and drinks banana [beer]* extend from 3a–c. In 4c–d, the reason for 4b extends over two clauses (a prenuclear conditional clause [4c] and a main clause [4d, further indented]).

Note: You will find a chart of the full text in Bariai in Appendix C.

1.5 Displaying a text in simplified chart form

Sample page of a charted text in an SV/OV language (Dungra Bhil, Indo-Aryan, India)

Ref.	Con.	Pre-S	Nucleus				(Post-V)		
01		*o maa pujra*	*tumi*	*horu*	*ma*	*piha.*			
		oh my children	2p	liquor	PRO	drink.be.PL			
		Oh, my children, you shouldn't be drinking liquor.							
02			*horu*	*to*	*ek*	*dʒer*	*hudu*	*hoje.*	
			liquor	SPACER	one	poison	like	be	
			Liquor is like a poison.						
03a			[*horu*	*pi-nara*	*mahõ-õ̃*	*ɖua*]	*tumi*	*pala,*	
			liquor	drink-AGENT	man-POS	eye.OBL	2p	see.IMP	
03b			*tijaa*	*ɖua*	*ekdom*	*rata*	*rata*	*dekh-a.*	
			3ms.POS	eye.OBL	complete	red	red	see-PASSIVE	
			Look at the eyes of a liquor-drinking person; his eyes appear completely red.						
04	*ono*		[*tijaa*	*dʒĩgi*]	*tumi pala,*				
	&		3ms.POS	life	2p see.IMP				
	And		look at his life;						
05a			*tuʔu ek*	*vaʔa*	*horu*		*pit-neje,*		
			3ms one	time	liquor		drink-COMP		
05b	*tahã*			*tija-ha*		*horu*	*pi-va*	*nag-e.*	
	then			3ms.OBL-ACC		liquor	drink-INF	feel-FUT	
			(if) he liquor-drinks all at one go, then he will acquire a desire for liquor-drinking.						
06a	*ono*		[*tuʔu*	*tijaa*	*phaje*	*dʒetihi*	*modʒuri*	*koʔ-e*],	
	&		3ms	3ms.POS	with	how.much	work	do-FUT	
06b				*tetaha*		*horu*	*pi*	*dʒa-je.*	
				that.much		liquor	drink	go-FUT	
	And	whatever work he may do, he will drink liquor with it (that will be completed in liquor-drinking).							
07	*tahã*		[*tuʔu*	*tijaa*	*bujeʔẽ*	*ono*	*pujre*]	*kihĩ*	*koʔ-e?*
	then		3ms	3ms.POS	lady	&	children	what	do-FUT
	Then		what will his wife and children do?						
08			*phuko*		*moʔ-e.*				
			hunger.OBL		die-FUT				
			They will die of hunger.						

Comments on the charting the Dungra Bhil (SV/OV) text

The text displayed in the chart is the first part of an exhortation by a man from Mathwad village in Madhya Pradesh State to his children, because they are lazy and do not work in the fields. It is of the Instruction type of exhortation. Sunil K. Mathew translated the text into English and kindly made it available to me. The original form of the text appears in Mathew 2004. I have modified the translation to make it more natural.

Convention 2. The Pre-S column of the chart is used for all constituents that precede the subject other than connectives and initial vocatives. The Post-V column would be used for any postverbal constituents.

The Post-V column would be used for any postverbal constituents.

Convention 6. Square brackets mark the boundaries of complex or preposed constituents. In 7, *his wife and children* is a complex subject. In 3a, *the eyes of a liquor-drinking person* is a preposed object (see also 4). In 6a, *whatever work he may do* is a left-dislocated constituent.

Note: You will find a chart of the full text in Dungra Bhil in Appendix D.

Application to the language you are analysing

1. Base your chart on the model that is closest to the language you are analysing (VS/VO, SV/VO or SV/OV).
2. Start inserting the text you have selected into your chart, following the conventions given earlier.
3. When you have completed two pages of your chart, send it to your consultant or myself (stephen_levinsohn@sil.org) for checking.

2

Types of Information and Reasoning Types

This chapter begins by reviewing three ways in which information is arranged functionally within sentences (2.1). It then considers what characterises theme-line information for each broad text genre (2.2). Sections 2.3–4 discuss some implications of using inductive versus deductive reasoning in an exhortation. This leads to a description of the types of supportive information that Breeze (1992) identifies for hortatory discourses, and to where mismatches are most likely to occur when translating from a verb-object (VO) language to an object-verb (OV) language (2.5–2.6).[1]

Materials which will be needed while studying this chapter include charted hortatory texts in Kalinga (VS/VO), Bariai (SV/VO), Dungra Bhil (SV/VO), and Koine Greek.

Each of the above sections is illustrated from hortatory texts in Kalinga (VS/VO), Bariai (SV/VO) and Dungra Bhil (SV/OV), as well as the letter to Philemon in Greek. The reader should pay particular attention to those texts that are of the same language type as the one he or she is analysing.

2.1 Articulations of the sentence

Many linguists recognise different functional or "pragmatic" sentence structures (Comrie 1989:64); in other words, different ways that the information in a sentence is arranged.[2] Andrews (1985:77–80) distinguishes three principal "articulations" of the sentence or proposition, which I will refer to as topic-comment, identificational and thetic (see Lambrecht 1994:122, 144).[3]

The following proposition (Dungra Bhil 3b) is an example of **topic-comment** articulation. It has a topic (in this case, *his eyes*)[4] and a comment giving information about the topic *his eyes*.[5]

3b	*tijaa*	*ḍua*	/	*ekdom*	*rata rata*	*dekh-a.*
	3ms.POS	eye.OBL		complete	red red	see-PASS
	'his eyes			appear completely red.'		

---

[1] These sections are taken from Levinsohn 2006a.
[2] For a more comprehensive discussion of sentence articulations, see Levinsohn 2015, 2.1.
[3] Andrews uses the terms "focus-presupposition" for identificational, and "presentational" for thetic.
[4] The topic of a topic-comment proposition is usually, but not necessarily, the subject of the proposition.
[5] Care must be taken not to confuse the term "(propositional) topic" with the topic (theme) of a paragraph or longer stretch of speech or writing. "A referent is interpreted as the topic of a proposition if in a given situation the proposition is construed as being about this referent, i.e., as expressing information that is relevant to and that increases the addressee's knowledge of this referent" (Lambrecht 1994:131). The topic of a proposition is of *current interest*; the referent must either be already established in the discourse or easily related to one that is already established (p. 164).

The following Greek proposition (1 Corinthians 1:13) illustrates **identificational** articulation. Except for one element, the information it conveys is assumed to be known ([someone] *was crucified for you*. The focus ("the most important ... information in the given setting" – Dik 1978:19) is on the element that is lacking in the presupposed proposition (who the someone was – or wasn't, in this case).

13 μὴ   Παῦλος   ἐσταυρώθη   ὑπὲρ   ὑμῶν,
   [surely].not Paul   was.crucified   for   you.PL

   'Was Paul crucified for you?' (expected answer: No!)

The following proposition (Dungra Bhil 17) illustrates **thetic** articulation. It presents or introduces a new entity or event (in this instance, the absence of *peace*) into the text.

17 *ihĭkojite   horu   pi-nara-a   koʔ-me   kedihi   sãti   naj   uve.*
   likewise   liquor   drink-AG-POS   house-in   never   peace   NEG   become

   'Similarly, in the house of a liquor-drinking person, there will never be any peace.'

Identifying the articulation of individual sentences or propositions helps to identify the domain of its focus (see 5.1). It also explains certain deviations from the default order in which their constituents are presented (see 5.2–5.3).

2.2 Theme-line versus supportive material

The theme line is distinguished from supportive material. The theme line

> presents the backbone of the discourse—whether this be the main events of a narrative, the main steps of a procedure, the main points of an argument or the main commands of an exhortation—while the supportive material provides all that is necessary as a background for understanding the story, procedure, or argument as a whole. These different types of information, which work together to communicate the total message of a discourse, can be distinguished from each other by certain language-specific surface features, such as tense and aspect markers, verb forms, conjunctions, special particles, and word order. (Breeze 1992:314)

2.2.1 Characteristics of theme-line information in the four broad text genres

In all text genres, the default way of presenting theme-line information is with **topic-comment** articulation (2.1).

In a NARRATIVE, sentences that present theme-line events typically have **perfective** aspect (the aspect that portrays events or states as a whole – Levinsohn 2015, 5.3.2). When no discontinuity is signalled (e.g. with a prenuclear adverbial constituent like *the next day* – Levinsohn 2015, 3.1), a distinctive verb form is often used (a "narrative" or "neutral" form in many African languages, the aorist in Greek, the *wyyqtl* form in Hebrew).

In a PROCEDURE, sentences that present the main steps typically have **imperfective** aspect (the aspect that portrays events or states as not completed at the point of reference – Levinsohn 2015, 5.3.2). When no discontinuity is signalled, a distinctive verb form is often used (e.g. a future infinitive in Inga [inb], the *wqtl* form in Hebrew).

In an EXHORTATION, we can expect the main commands to be presented with a distinctive verb form, too (e.g. with imperatives rather than a more mitigated form such as *I would like you to …*).

In an EXPOSITION, "the most static clauses of the language [constitute] its mainline" (theme line). Static clauses have as their main verb "'be', 'have', or null in place of 'be', or the verb 'remain/stay'" (Longacre 1983:4).

2.2.2 The message framework

In her analysis of Ephesians (a basically hortatory text), Breeze excludes the "message framework" – "material that provides a framework for the message without being part of the message itself" (1992:314). This framework comprises:

- the **introduction**, which "relates the author to the recipients and gives a greeting" (e.g. Ephesians 1:1–2)
- the **closure**, which "consists of personal notes and a benediction" (e.g. Ephesians 6:23–24).[6]

The rest of the book constitutes the "**main body**".

Application to the letter to Philemon in Koine Greek

First, familiarise yourself with this charted text (in Appendix A).
Now identify the message framework. In particular:

- Which verse(s) constitute the **introduction**?
- Which verse(s) constitute the **closure**?[7]

Application to the hortatory text in Kalinga (VS/VO)

First, familiarise yourself with the rest of this charted text (in Appendix B).
Now identify the message framework. In particular:

- Which sentence(s) constitute the **introduction**?
- Which sentence(s) constitute the **closure**?[8]

Note: Some texts do not have a message framework. Such appears to be the case for the hortatory texts in Bariai (SV/VO) and Dungra Bhil (SV/OV).

2.2.3 Distinguishing theme-line and supportive information in hortatory texts

Within the main body, Breeze's primary distinction is between the theme-line hortatory THESES[9] and the **supportive** information. On this basis, the main body of the letter to **Philemon** (4–22) may be divided as follows (see 2.2.4 on the supportive nature of the exhortations of 20):

4–7 supportive   *I always thank my God when I remember you in my prayers, because I hear of your love for all the saints and your faith toward the Lord Jesus. I pray that the sharing of your faith may become effective when you perceive all the good that we may do for Christ. I have indeed received much joy and encouragement from your love, because the hearts of the saints have been refreshed through you, my brother.*

---

[6] In her article, Breeze treats 6:21–24 as the closure, but agrees (p.c.) that it is better to limit the closure to 23–24.
[7] **Suggested answers**: Philemon 1–3 constitute the introduction. Philemon 23–25 constitute the closure. Russell (1998:22–23) describes these verses as "Epistolary Conventions".
[8] **Suggested answers**: Sentence 23 of the Kalinga text constitutes the closure. If Breeze's definition is followed, then the text has no introduction.
[9] Throughout these chapters, the label in small caps is the HEAD or NUCLEUS relation; the other label is the support relation. The *OED* defines a THESIS as 'a statement ... that is put forward as a premise to be maintained or proved'.

8–16 supportive	*Therefore (Διό), though I am bold enough in Christ to command you to do your duty, yet I would rather appeal to you on the basis of love—I, Paul, do this as an old man, and now also a prisoner of Christ Jesus. I am appealing to you for my child, Onesimus, whose father I have become during my imprisonment; one formerly useless to you, but now indeed useful both to you and to me, whom I am sending, that is, my own heart, back to you; whom I was wanting to keep with me, so that he might be of service to me in your place during my imprisonment for the gospel; but I preferred to do nothing without your consent, in order that your good deed might be voluntary and not something forced. Perhaps this is the reason he was separated from you for a while, so that you might have him back forever, no longer as a slave but more than a slave, a beloved brother – especially to me but how much more to you, both in the flesh and in the Lord.*
17–18 HORT. THESES	*If, then (οὖν), you consider me your partner, welcome him as you would welcome me.*
	And (δέ) if he has wronged you in any way, or owes you anything, charge that to my account.
19–21 supportive	*I, Paul, am writing this with my own hand: I will repay it. I say nothing about your owing me even your own self.*
	²⁰Yes, brother, let me have this benefit from you in the Lord! Refresh my heart in Christ.
	²¹Confident of your obedience, I am writing to you, knowing that you will do even more than I say.
22a HORT. THESIS	*One thing more – prepare a guest room for me,*
22b–c supportive	*for I am hoping through your prayers to be restored to you.*

Paul's prayer of thanksgiving (4–7) "lays a foundation for the rest of the letter" and may be "viewed as motivational information, designed to evoke in the readers a sense of joy and gratitude to God that will prepare them to receive the forthcoming commands with a proper attitude" (Breeze 1992:322, commenting on the prayer of thanksgiving in Ephesians 1:3–14). In other words, 4–7 **lead up** to 8–16, which in turn lead up to the hortatory THESES of 17–18. This is confirmed by the connectives used: inferential Διό 'therefore' in 8 and inferential-resumptive οὖν 'then' in 17 (see further in 3.5.3 and 3.6).

In contrast, 19 provides support for the **preceding** hortatory THESIS (18). Similarly, 21 provides support for the preceding hortatory THESES. Finally, 22b–c provide support for the preceding hortatory THESIS of 22a.

2.2.4 Supportive exhortations

We turn now to the exhortations of 20, which Banker (1999) correctly identifies as supporting the appeal of 17. In other words, these exhortations are not theme-line hortatory THESES in the text. Rather, they are used to **reinforce** preceding theme-line THESES.[10]

Other exhortations, such as 'Listen!', function as attention getters for following THESES. Consider sentences 3–5 of the Dungra Bhil text:

3a	[*horu*	*pi-nara*	*mahõ-õ*	*ḍua*]	*tumi*	*pala,*
	liquor	drink-AG	man-POS	eye.OBL	2p	see.IMP
3b	*tijaa*	*ḍua*	*ekdom*	*rata rata*	*dekh-a.*	
	3ms.POS	eye.OBL	complete	red red	see-PASS	

'Look at the eyes of a liquor-drinking person; his eyes appear completely red.'

---

[10] Russell also treats the imperative of 18 as supportive, calling 18–22 a "motivated appeal" (1998:10).

4	ono	[tijaa	dʒĩgi]	tumi	pala,	
	&	3ms.POS	life	2p	see.IMP	

'And look at his life;'

5a		tuʔu	ek	vaʔa	horu	pit-neje,
		3ms	one	time	liquor	drink-COMP
5b	tahã	tija-ha		horu	pi-va	nag-e.
	then	3ms.OBL-ACC		liquor	drink-INF	feel-FUT

'(if) he liquor-drinks all at one go, then he will acquire a desire for liquor-drinking.'

Although propositions 3a and 4 of the above extract are imperatives (*Look at ...*), their function is to draw attention to the following assertions (expository THESES).

Supportive exhortations typically occur at the beginning or at the end of the unit they support.

Application to the hortatory text in Kalinga (VS/VO)

1. Identify the sentence(s) that contain exhortations.
2. Do any of these exhortations appear to be supportive, rather than theme-line THESES?[11]

Application to the hortatory text in Bariai (SV/VO)

Identify the sentence(s) that contain exhortations.[12]

Application to the hortatory text in Dungra Bhil (SV/OV)

The imperatives of 3 and 4 have been identified as attention getters (see above).
   Identify the other sentences that contain exhortations.[13]

Application to the language you are analysing

1. Identify any sentences of the text that provide the message framework (2.2.2).
2. Classify each remaining sentence as an exhortation or as supportive material.
3. Identify any exhortations that are supportive (reinforcing previous theme-line THESES or drawing attention to following THESES). Note: Treat exhortations that restate or paraphrase a theme-line THESIS as further theme-line THESES, **not** as supportive ones.

2.3 Inductive style versus deductive style

Inductive writing is characterised as having the THESIS statement in the **final** position.
Deductive writing has the THESIS statement in the **initial** position (see Connor 1996:42).

In one text in Dungra Bhil, a request was directed to a government official. After greeting him, the speaker set out the need for a good road in 33 sentences, none of which contained an exhortation. Only

---

[11] **Suggested answers** for the Kalinga text:
1. The following sentences contain exhortations: 2, 5–8, 10–11, 13, 16–18, 20, 22; plus 1 (pointing forward to later exhortations).
2. The exhortation of 22 appears to be supportive, reinforcing the preceding hortatory THESES. Sentence 1 could be an attention getter for the following hortatory THESES.

[12] **Suggested answer** for the Bariai text: The only sentence that contains an actual exhortation is 15, although earlier ones have implied that the hearers should avoid *banana [beer] and marijuana* (1, 9) and instead *get knowledge of God's book's talk* (8a).

[13] **Suggested answer** for the Dungra Bhil text: The following sentences contain exhortations: 1, 21, 23–24, 27–29, 34–38 and, possibly, the rhetorical question of 30 (plus, in reported speeches, 19b–20).

then did he spell out his request for the road. The text therefore has **inductive** style; sentences 1–34 lead up to the hortatory THESES of 35ff.

1–34 supportive	*And he was so hurt that he could not walk. How could we take those two sick people [to hospital]? (If) the road to our village were good, we would not suffer this much difficulty.*
35ff. HORT. THESES	*So, Tahasil officer, please help us. Please build a good road for us poor people.*

We noted in 2.2.3 that Philemon 4–16 **lead up** to the hortatory THESES of 17–18. Verses 4–18 could therefore be said to have inductive style, with the hortatory THESIS in the final position.

However, the THESES of 17–18 are also followed by supportive material, as is the THESIS of 22a. In other words, this part of the text has **deductive** style.

Application to the hortatory text in Kalinga (VS/VO)

What style does this text have?[14]

Application to the hortatory text in Bariai (SV/VO)

This text has 16 sentences and contains only one exhortation (sent. 15). What, then, is the dominant style in this text?[15]

The style of the hortatory text in **Dungra Bhil** will be discussed in 2.4.

Now some examples from **Ancient Hebrew**.

When the LORD gives commands to the people of Israel through Moses, He typically uses **deductive** style. Exodus 20:5 provides an example.

5a HORT. THESIS	*You shall not bow down to them or worship them;*
5b supportive	*for (kî) I, the LORD your God, am a jealous God.*

Similarly, when David appeals to God in Psalm 54:1–3, he uses deductive style:

1–2 HORT. THESIS	*Save me, O God, by your name and vindicate me by your might. Hear my prayer, O God; listen to the words of my mouth.*
3 supportive	*for (kî) strangers attack me and ruthless men seek my life; they give no thought to God. Selah.*

When the daughters of Zelophehad present a request to Moses, in contrast, they use **inductive** style (Numbers 27:3–4):

3–4a supportive	*Our father died in the desert. He was not among Korah's followers, who banded together against the LORD, but he died for his own sin and left no sons. Why should our father's name disappear from his clan because he had no son?*
4b HORT. THESIS	*Give us property among our father's relatives.*

---

[14] **Suggested answer**: The Kalinga text has deductive style. The exhortation of 2 is supported by 3–4, that of 8 is supported by 9, that of 11 is supported by 12, that of 13 is supported by 14–15 and that of 18 is supported by 19–21.

[15] **Suggested answer**: The dominant style in the Bariai text is inductive.

Similarly, when the LORD speaks to Moses in Exodus 3:7–10, He uses inductive style:

7–9 supportive	*I have indeed seen the misery of my people in Egypt. I have heard them crying out because of their slave drivers, and I am concerned about their suffering. I have come down to rescue them from the hand of the Egyptians and to bring them up out of that land into a good and spacious land. … Now the cry of the Israelites has reached me, and I have seen the way the Egyptians are oppressing them.*
10 HORT. THESIS	*And now, go. I am sending you to Pharaoh to bring my people the Israelites out of Egypt.*

2.4 Deductive versus inductive reasoning and instruction versus persuasion

Kompaoré proposes classifying hortatory discourses according to four parameters. The most significant parameter appears to be what she calls the "volitive weight" of the exhortation (2004:40).[16] A basic distinction is between **instruction** (Longacre 1995:18–20)[17] and **persuasion**.[18]

- **INSTRUCTION**: A speaker or writer (exhorter) considers him- or herself to have the right or authority to tell the exhortee how to behave (apostolic authority, in the case of Paul's epistles). The Ten Commandments (Exodus 20:2–17) are instructional (one is cited in 2.3). As noted in 1.3, directives from employers to employees are typically of this type. In some cultures, parents have the right to instruct their adult children how to behave once married, etc., too. This category may even include strong **rebukes** of existing behaviour, as when someone "instructs" a friend to stop maintaining enmity with another person or to stop being lazy. **Demands** to act in a certain way seem to fit here, too, such as when the Israelites call on Aaron to make them an idol (Exodus 32:1).

- **PERSUASION**: The exhorter "appeals to the **reasoning logic** of the recipient, seeks to convince" (Longacre 1995:18–20). Examples include the request of the daughters of Zelophehad to Moses (cited in 2.3), David's speech to Solomon (1 Chronicles 22:7–16 – cited below in 2.5) and Paul's speech to the philosophers in Athens (Acts 17:22–31). Typically, the exhorter uses persuasion because he or she cannot make the exhortee pursue the desired course of action. However, a person in authority may choose to persuade rather than instruct (e.g. the LORD to Moses in Exodus 3:7–10 – cited in 2.3).

Both major language types (VO and OV) typically use **inductive** reasoning for PERSUASION. However, problems arise when translating an INSTRUCTION from a VO language like Greek, Hebrew or English into an OV language.

In **VO** languages, it is normal for an exhorter to use **deductive** reasoning for INSTRUCTIONS. In contrast, in natural texts in **OV** languages, such texts tend to begin with the THESIS, follow it with supportive material, then close it with a reiteration of the THESIS (an '*inclusio*').[19]

This is illustrated by the following extract from a hortatory text in Menya [mcr].[20] The sentences that introduce the theme (see 2.5) are followed immediately by the first exhortation of the text (3), which is then supported (4–5), before being repeated in 6:

---

[16] The other three parameters proposed by Kompaoré are:
- social relationships between the "exhorter and the exhortee" (p. 24): power, authority, eldership, knowledge and wisdom superiority
- "action for the benefit of" (p. 25): exhorter, exhortee, third party, not pertinent
- "directive validity" (p. 40): incontestable, contestable, open to judgment.

[17] Kompaoré uses the term "imposition" (p. 27).

[18] Appeals such as that of Psalm 54:1–3 are discussed at the end of this section.

[19] *Inclusio* structures involve the "bracketing of a pericope by making a statement at the beginning of the section, an approximation of which is repeated at the conclusion of the section" (Guthrie 1998:14).

[20] The text was written by John Manggo in preparation for a National Translators Course in 1996 and was translated by Carl Whitehead (p.c.).

1–2 message framework	*Concerning me giving my oldest son instruction. I give him instruction such as this.*
3 HORT. THESIS	*My bringing you to school, it's for this: to go to gain knowledge, you are not to be lazy and are always to go.*
4 supportive	*The reason is this: I your father will no longer be alive [one day] and because of that I send you.*
5 consequence	*Then you also will become big and live later and [then] no longer be alive.*
6 HORT. THESIS	*That being the case, you should always be one who goes without being lazy, listens to whatever the teacher teaches you (plural), learns and follows it.*

The **Dungra Bhil** text is similar. The opening exhortation (1) is followed by supportive material (2–18), with no further exhortations until 19. However, 36–38 repeat earlier exhortations, including 1, so form *inclusios* with them:

1 HORT. THESIS	*Oh, my children, you shouldn't be drinking liquor.*
2–18 supportive	*After all, liquor is like a poison.*
19–22 reported	*As for you, in contrast, someone may tell you that you should work and eat the food you like,*
HORT. THESIS	*and all live happily with love; don't be fighting with one another.*
36–38 HORT. THESES	*Rather, we need to work. We should not drink liquor and we should not fight with one another.*
	We need to live happily and lovingly with all people.

We shall return to the mismatch between how VO and OV languages handle instructions in 2.6.

Note that Kompaoré's "volitive weight" category also includes **APPEALS**: the exhorter, who does not have authority over the exhortee, "appeals to the volition" of the exhortee (Kompaoré 2004:27). An example is David's appeal to God in Psalm 54:1–3 (cited in 2.3). However, I suspect that it is the **urgency** of the appeal that leads David to use deductive reasoning in this Psalm, as hortatory discourses such as *Help me! I'm stuck* also use deductive reasoning.

A noteworthy example of the difference between instruction and persuasion was provided by a text in Rana Tharu [thr] (SV/OV). The speaker was a mother who first instructed her younger daughter-in-law, who was not a Tharu, how to behave to visiting male relatives. She used a series of *inclusios* in this speech. She then turned to her older daughter-in-law, who was a Tharu, and used inductive reasoning to persuade her to set a good example to the younger wife.

Application to the hortatory text in Kalinga (VS/VO)

This text has deductive style. What type of text does this suggest it to be?[21]

Application to the hortatory text in Bariai (SV/VO)

The dominant style in this text is inductive. What type of text does this suggest it to be?[22]

Application to the hortatory text to Philemon in Koine Greek (VS/VO)

The first half of this text (Philemon 4–18) has inductive style. What type of text does this suggest it to be?[23]

---

[21] **Suggested answer** for the Kalinga text: The use of deductive style suggests that the text is instruction. Although the text is entitled "Advice to Students", it consists of instructions on how to behave.

[22] **Suggested answer** for the Bariai text: The use of inductive style suggests that the text is persuasion. This is consistent with the text being an attempt to persuade the exhortees not to drink banana beer and consume marijuana.

[23] **Suggested answer** for the letter to Philemon: The use of inductive style in Philemon 4–18 suggests that Paul is seeking to persuade Philemon to do as he asks. The shift into deductive style in 19–22, however, suggests a move from persuasion to instruction (note the word *obedience* in 21a).

2.5 Types of supportive information

Breeze (1992:317) distinguishes four types of supportive information in Ephesians: situational, motivational, credential and enabling. The following are her definitions of the four types.

- **Situational** information "explains the situation or circumstances out of which the discourse arises and why the exhortation is necessary" (p. 316). It includes the schematic category that Longacre (1983:3) labels "problem". Breeze cites Ephesians 2:1–3 as an example.

- **Motivational** information "encourages the hearer to heed the exhortations in the following ways: by giving the reasons for obeying them; by pointing out certain consequences that might occur if a command is or is not heeded; by drawing attention to the ethical, moral, or religious values of the hearer's society that provide the motivation to conform; and by appealing to one's sense of responsibility" (Breeze 1992:315). Most supportive information is motivational.

- **Credential** information "supports the speaker's or author's right to give the commands with the expectation that they be heeded" (p. 315). Exodus 20:2 provides a particularly clear example: *I am the LORD your God, who rescued you from slavery in Egypt.*

  Chris Vaz (p.c.) cites a speaker of Hill Maria [mrr] (Dravidian, India) who, while giving advice to his children, supports his exhortations by saying, *I'm the one telling you.*

- **Enabling** information "informs or reminds readers of what has already been done to help them keep the commands" (p. 317). Breeze cites the prayer of Ephesians 3:14–21 as an example.

Application of Breeze's classification to other hortatory discourses (especially in OV languages) has led to the following modifications:

- It is useful to distinguish **consequences** from **other motivational** information. Even when a passage generally follows the inductive style (2.3) in which other supportive information leads up to an exhortation, consequences still tend to follow it.

  This is seen when David charges Solomon to build a house for the LORD (1 Chronicles 22:7–16). He begins by describing the situation and giving motivational information that builds up to the exhortations of 11–12. These are followed by the consequences of obeying them (13a), before David concludes the first part of his speech with further exhortations (13b):

7–10 situational/motivational

> *My son, I had it in my heart to build a house for the Name of the LORD my God. But this word of the LORD came to me: "You have shed much blood and have fought many wars. You are not to build a house for my Name, because you have shed much blood on the earth in my sight. But you will have a son who will be a man of peace and rest, and I will give him rest from all his enemies on every side. His name will be Solomon, and I will grant Israel peace and quiet during his reign. He is the one who will build a house for my Name. He will be my son, and I will be his father. And I will establish the throne of his kingdom over Israel forever."*

11–12 HORT. THESES

> *Now, my son, the LORD be with you, and may you have success and build the house of the LORD your God, as he said you would. May the LORD give you discretion and understanding when he puts you in command over Israel, so that you may keep the law of the LORD your God.*

13a consequences

> *Then you will have success if you are careful to observe the decrees and laws that the LORD gave Moses for Israel.*

13b HORT. THESES (supportive)

> *Be strong and courageous. Do not be afraid or discouraged.*

- The **situational** information category needs to be extended to include **topic introducers**. The main body of a hortatory text often begins with such a sentence, stating the theme to be addressed. An example from Amharic [amh] is *Although it is not necessary to teach you that good behaviour comes from upbringing, I would like to point out some things* (about the theme of good behaviour). 1 Corinthians 7:25 is similar, although it does contain some credential information (*Now concerning virgins, I have no command from the Lord, but I give my opinion as one who by the Lord's mercy is trustworthy*).
- It is often difficult – and frequently unnecessary – to distinguish between **situational** information and "other motivational information" (as defined above) that precedes and leads up to an exhortation. See 1 Chronicles 22:7–10 above.
- In addition, it is often difficult – and unnecessary – to distinguish between **enabling** information and "other motivational information" (as defined above) that precedes and leads up to an exhortation. A reviewer of Levinsohn 2006a commented: "Thus a 'reminder' may function as a 'motivation' in a particular epistle of Paul".

The above comments lead to a four-way subclassification of supportive information, as:

- situational (including situational-motivational)
- credential
- consequences
- other: a catch-all category for enabling and other motivational material.

One further distinction is useful, though: between information that supports a THESIS and information that supports supportive information.

Application to the letter to Philemon in Koine Greek (VS/VO)

Section 2.2.4 identified the supportive information in the body of this letter as Philemon 4–16, 19–21 and 22b–c. In addition, the exhortations of 20 reinforced the hortatory THESES of 17–18. We now subclassify the remaining verses.

Credential information. 9b–c appear to fall into this category: *such a one being Paul, an old man, and now also a prisoner of Christ Jesus.*[24] (However, these propositions are part of a larger sentence [8–9] in Greek.)

Consequences. If the exhortation of 18 were obeyed (*charge that to my account*), 19b would be a consequence (*I will repay it*).

21d is an expected consequence of 17–18: (*knowing that*) *you will do even more than I say.*

Other information that supports THESES. 8–14 describe a situation and motivate the hortatory THESES of 17–18 (οὖν 'then' is used in 17).

22b–c supports the hortatory THESIS of 22a (γάρ 'for' is used in 22b).

Other information that supports supportive information. 4–7 in the first instance motivate the supportive material of 8–14 (Διό 'therefore' is used in 8).

7 supports 4–6 (γάρ 'for' is used in 7).

15–16 support 10–14 (γάρ 'for' is used in 15).

Application to the hortatory text in Kalinga (VS/VO)

Credential information: none noted.

Consequences. Between sentences, consequences of heeding or not heeding an exhortation are introduced with *kad* 'then' in 12, 14a and 20 (relating back to 18b). (Consequences of an exhortation are introduced **within** a sentence with *ta* '*PUR*' in 2a–b, 6e and 17d.)

---

[24] In addition, "vv. 1–2 establish the credentials or authority of the text producer" (Russell 1998:8).

Other information that supports THESES. Both within and between sentences, reasons and explanations for preceding exhortations are introduced with *te* 'for': 3, 5c, 7c–e, 9, 13c, 14b, 18c, 19, 19c, 21.[25]

Other information that supports supportive information. In 14b, the material introduced with *te* 'for' supports a consequence of not heeding the exhortation of 13. In 4 and 15, *kad* 'then' introduces a consequence of supportive material introduced with *te* 'for'.

Application to the hortatory text in Bariai (SV/VO)

Credential information: none noted.

Consequences of not obeying exhortations: introduced in 16 with *ngan kado* 'otherwise'.

The expository THESIS *Banana [beer] and marijuana, this is a bad thing* (1, 9) implies that the hearers should avoid these vices. Consequences of not heeding this implied exhortation are found in 3 and 10–14. They are introduced with conditional clauses and *eine ga* (glossed 'this IRR').

Other information that supports THESES. Reasons for the above expository THESIS are introduced **within** sentences in 2 and 4 with *ngansa* 'because'.

Other information that supports supportive information. Sentences 5–7 support the supportive material of 4 (see 6b). They also support the implied exhortation to *get knowledge about God's book's talk* (8a), which leads to the consequences described in 8b–e.

Application to the hortatory text in Dungra Bhil (SV/OV)

Credential information: none noted.

Consequences of obeying or not obeying exhortations: 22, 25–26, 32–33.

Other information that supports THESES. Sentences 2–18 (see further below) explain why *you shouldn't be drinking liquor* (1). Sentence 39 is similar. The reported speech of 19–20 may be judged to be situational, leading to the exhortation of 21.

Other information that supports supportive information. Sentence 2 (*liquor is like a poison*) is the THESIS of an expository section that extends to at least 18. Sentences 3–18 support this THESIS by giving evidence for it (3–6) and by describing the consequences of becoming addicted to liquor (7–18).

Application to the language you are analysing

1. Subclassify the **supportive** information as situational, credential, consequences or other (the catch-all category for enabling and other motivational material).
2. If supportive information is itself supported by other information (sentences 2–18 of the Dungra Bhil text provide an example), identify the THESIS of the supportive unit and how the THESIS is supported.

2.6 Distribution of different types of supportive information in VO and OV languages

This section compares the typical distribution of the most common types of supportive information in VO and OV languages.[26] The following table provides a comparison for the two types.

---

[25] In the case of 19, the relation to the context of the material introduced with *te* is particularly vague (compare the use of Greek γάρ in many contexts). Some of the reasons are actually **possible consequences** of not heeding the exhortation and are characterised by the presence of the potential marker *maka-* (3, 5c, 9, 13c).

[26] It is not unusual for credential information to follow exhortations in natural texts in OV languages, which suggests that such information may occur in the same place in both language types.

Table 1. Supportive information in VO and OV languages

Type of information	Language type	
	VO	OV
Situational/Topic introducers	precede exhortations	precede exhortations
Consequences	follow exhortations	follow exhortations
Other motivational:		
in PERSUASION	precede exhortations	precede exhortations
in INSTRUCTION/urgent appeals	follow exhortations	in the middle of *inclusios* (2.4)

The above table suggests that, when translating from a VO to an OV language, problems in the order in which the information is presented are most likely to arise in **instructional** texts when "other motivational" material such as explanations for exhortations and reasons for obeying them occur. Similar problems arise with explanations for **expository** THESES and reasons for accepting their validity. Such supportive information typically follows THESES in VO languages – an ordering that can be problematic in OV languages.

The following are possible ways of handling such potential mismatches between the two language types when two or more sentences are involved.

Strategy 1. Preserve the deductive style in the receptor language, but introduce the supportive material without a connective.[27] Consider Exodus 20:5–7, for instance, in which THESES (5a, 7a) are followed by supportive material introduced in Hebrew by *kî* 'for':

5a HORT. THESIS	*You shall not bow down to them.*
5b–6 supportive	***For** (kî) I, the* LORD *your God, am a jealous God, punishing the children for the sin of the fathers to the third and fourth generation of those who hate me, but showing love to a thousand generations of those who love me and keep my commandments.*
7a HORT. THESIS	*You shall not misuse the name of the* LORD *your God.*
7b supportive	***For** (kî) the* LORD *will not hold anyone guiltless who misuses his name.*

In an OV language, this passage might be rendered:

5a HORT. THESIS	*You shall not bow down to them.*
5b–6 supportive	*Ø I, the* LORD *your God, am a jealous God, punishing the children for the sin of the fathers to the third and fourth generation of those who hate me, but showing love to a thousand generations of those who love me and keep my commandments.*
7a HORT. THESIS	*You shall not misuse the name of the* LORD *your God,*
7b supportive	*Ø The* LORD *will not hold anyone guiltless who misuses his name.*

However, such juxtaposition has its dangers, as it is very common in SV/OV languages for strengthening material to **precede** the hortatory THESIS to which it relates. In other words, Exodus 20:5b–6 may be understood as supporting verse 7a, rather than 5a:[28]

---

[27] In Inga (an OV language), whenever my cotranslator was drafting a verse in which an exhortation was followed by supportive material introduced with *for*, his first inclination was to preserve the order of propositions and begin the supportive material without any conjunction.

[28] I mentioned this danger during a workshop in India. After the lecture, a translator who was a native speaker of Tamil (Dravidian) came up to me and told me that he had always taken Exodus 20:5b–6 as interpreting 7a, rather than 5a!

2.6 Distribution of different types of supportive information in VO and OV languages

5a HORT. THESIS	*You shall not bow down to them.*	
5b–6 supportive	*Ø I, the LORD your God, am a jealous God, punishing the children for the sin of the fathers to the third and fourth generation of those who hate me, but showing love to a thousand generations of those who love me and keep my commandments.*	
7a HORT. THESIS	[implied *So*] *You shall not misuse the name of the LORD your God,*	

The association of strengthening material with the wrong hortatory thesis may even be made explicit, as has happened in at least one passage in two versions of the Korean Bible. The exhortations of Philippians 2:12 and 2:14 are separated by material that supports 12:

12 HORT. THESIS	*Therefore, my beloved, just as you have always obeyed me, not only in my presence, but much more now in my absence, work out your own salvation with fear and trembling.*
13 supportive	*for* [γάρ] *it is God who is at work in you, enabling you both to will and to work for his good pleasure.*
14 HORT. THESIS	*Do all things without murmuring and arguing.*

In the Korean versions, though, 13 supports 14:

12 HORT. THESIS	*Work out your own salvation with fear and trembling.*
13 supportive	*Ø It is God who is at work in you, enabling you both to will and to work for his good pleasure*-connective[29]
14 HORT. THESIS	*do all things without murmuring and arguing.*

Strategy 2. Preserve the deductive style in the receptor language, but introduce the supportive material with a logical connective such as *because*, *This is because* or *The reason (is that)*, even though such connectives are rarely found in natural texts. Unfortunately, the typical effect of doing this in an OV language is to give more prominence to the reason than to the command that it supports (Levinsohn 1999):

5a HORT. THESIS	*You shall not bow down to them.*
5b SUPPORTIVE	**The reason:** *I, the LORD your God, am a jealous God, punishing the children for the sin of the fathers to the third and fourth generation of those who hate me,* ⁶*but showing love to a thousand generations of those who love me and keep my commandments.*
7a HORT. THESIS	*You shall not misuse the name of the LORD your God.*
7b SUPPORTIVE	**The reason:** *the LORD will not hold anyone guiltless who misuses his name.*

Strategy 3. Change the order of the THESIS and supportive material (thus changing from deductive to inductive style):

7b supportive	*The LORD your God will not hold anyone guiltless who misuses his name.*
7a HORT. THESIS	[*So*] *You shall not misuse his name.*

This is usually acceptable socio-linguistically if the change of order occurs within a verse or involves the reordering of just two verses. The danger of this option is that changing to inductive style may also change the nature of the exhortation from instruction to persuasion (see 2.4).

---

[29] The Korean connective is –니.

Strategy 4. Some reasons or explanations may be changed to a **consequence** of obeying the preceding exhortation (this is a very natural option in many OV languages):

7a HORT. THESIS	*You shall not misuse the name of the LORD your God.*
7b consequence	***If anyone misuses his name,***[30] *the LORD will not hold that person guiltless.*

Strategy 5. Use an *inclusio* by repeating part or all of the THESIS after the supportive material (see the extract from Menya, cited in 2.4).

7a HORT. THESIS	*You shall not misuse the name of the LORD your God,*
7b supportive	*The LORD your God will not hold anyone guiltless who misuses his name.*
7a′ HORT. THESIS	***So you shall not misuse his name.***

Passages in which two or more exhortations precede the supportive material lend themselves to conversion into an *inclusio*. All that is needed is for the final exhortation to be placed after the strengthening material. For example, Exodus 20:4–5 contains two exhortations (*You shall not make for yourself an idol in the form of anything in heaven above or on the earth beneath or in the waters below. You shall not bow down to them*). Placing the second exhortation (5a) after the supportive material of 5b–6 produces a very satisfactory *inclusio*:

4 HORT. THESIS	*You shall not make for yourself an idol in the form of anything in heaven above or on the earth beneath or in the waters below.*
5b–6 supportive	*I, the LORD your God, am a jealous God, punishing the children for the sin of the fathers to the third and fourth generation of those who hate me, but showing love to a thousand generations of those who love me and keep my commandments.*
5a HORT. THESIS	*So you shall not bow down to them.*

Application to the language you are analysing

1. When a hortatory or other THESIS is supported by motivational material other than consequences, is the style typically inductive (with the supportive material preceding the THESIS), deductive (with the supportive material following the THESIS) or a combination of the two (e.g. an *inclusio* with a THESIS both preceding and following the supportive material)?
2. Classify the text as instruction or persuasion (see 2.4).
3. Analyse other hortatory texts to check and expand on your conclusions.

---

[30] The repetition of *misuses his name* in the conditional Point of Departure may well give prominence to the consequence (Taeho Jang p.c.). It might be better to introduce the consequence with the shortest acceptable form of the conditional clause, which in English would be *If anyone does so.*

3

Connectives, Counterpoints and Propositional Order

This chapter concerns ways that relations between propositions and groups of propositions are signalled in hortatory and expository texts. It begins by noting that the default way of coordinating sentences in narrative and non-narrative may differ (3.1). It then looks at countering relations that are expressed in different ways in the source and receptor languages (3.2). This leads to the concept of a "counterpoint": a "contrasting ... idea, used to set off the main element" (*OED*) (3.3). The order of propositions may affect the **connective** used,[1] so 3.4 discusses this. Section 3.5 considers logical relations that may be expressed in different ways in the source and receptor languages. The theme of the final section is the resumption of the theme line of a non-narrative discourse.

Materials which will be needed while studying this chapter include charted hortatory texts in Kalinga (VS/VO), Bariai (SV/VO), Dungra Bhil (SV/VO), and Koine Greek.

3.1 The default way of intersentential coordination in different genres

Section 6.1 of Levinsohn 2015 noted that the default way of coordinating sentences or groups of sentences varies with the language. The two norms for **narrative** (and probably **procedures**) were:

- **juxtaposition** (i.e. without any connective);
- with a **conjunction**.

The default way of coordinating sentences or groups of sentences may also vary with the **genre**. For example, whereas the default way of coordinating in Ancient Hebrew **narratives** is with the conjunction *waw* (symbolized by '&'), in **exhortations** and **expositions**, it is juxtaposition.[2]

Exercise

Look up Exodus 20:2–17 (a hortatory discourse) in Hebrew. Contrast the infrequent use of the conjunction *waw* with its frequent use in a narrative such as Exodus 19.

---

[1] A **conjunction** is "a word used to connect clauses or sentences or words in the same clause" (*OED*). The term connective ("something that connects" – *OED*) is more generic, and includes referential expressions such as *Because of this*, as well as switch reference markers in many OV languages.

[2] In other languages, juxtaposition is the default way of coordinating sentences in both narrative and non-narrative (see 3.1.1 for examples).

3.1.1 The default way of intersentential coordination in non-narrative texts

We now look at the default way of coordination in the four languages we have been examining.

Koine Greek. The default way of coordinating sentences in Greek **narratives** is with the conjunction καί 'and'. In the letter to Philemon, καί never coordinates sentences.

The following chart indicates which of the sentences of the letter to Philemon begin with juxtaposition and which begin with a conjunction.

Table 2. Intersentential connectives in the letter to Philemon

Connective	Verses	Totals
juxtaposition	4, 10, 19, 20b, 21, 23, 25	7
δέ	14, 18, 22	3
γάρ	7, 15	2
διό	8	1
οὖν	17	1
ναί	20a	1
total sentences (16, minus the first sentence)		15

Conclusion: Juxtaposition is the most frequent form of coordination in this letter.

Application to the hortatory text in Kalinga (VS/VO)

In one narrative text in Kalinga, *kad* 'then, when' was used in half of the sentences that presented theme-line events. Which is the most frequent form of coordination in this hortatory text?[3]

Application to the hortatory text in Bariai (SV/VO)

The default way of coordinating sentences in Bariai narratives is by juxtaposition (23 out of 47, in one text). Which is the most frequent form of coordination in this hortatory text?[4]

Application to the hortatory text in Dungra Bhil (SV/OV)

The default way of coordinating sentences in Dungra Bhil narratives is by juxtaposition (51 out of 65, in one text). Which is the most frequent form of coordination in this hortatory text?[5]

Conclusion

In each of the languages we have been examined, the default way of coordinating sentences in **hortatory** texts appears to be juxtaposition. In fact, it may well be the case that, in any text that is not arranged chronologically, juxtaposition is the default form of intersentential coordination.[6]

---

[3] **Suggested answer** for the Kalinga hortatory text: The most frequent form of coordination is juxtaposition (13 out of 22 sentences).

[4] **Suggested answer** for the Bariai hortatory text: The most frequent form of coordination is juxtaposition (12 out of 15 sentences). This suggests that juxtaposition is the default way of coordinating sentences in Bariai in both narrative and non-narrative.

[5] **Suggested answer** for the Dungra Bhil hortatory text: The most frequent form of coordination is juxtaposition (21 out of 38 sentences). This suggests that juxtaposition is the default way of coordinating sentences in Dungra Bhil in both narrative and non-narrative.

[6] Juxtaposition is likely to be the default connective in texts that are not arranged chronologically because it is the 'unspecific' category, whereas the overt connectives typically impose **specific** constraints on interpretation.

3.1.2 The function in non-narrative texts of the default form of coordination in narrative

If the default form of coordination differs between narrative and non-narrative texts, then the function in non-narratives of the default form for narrative needs to be determined. This section considers Koine Greek, Ancient Hebrew and Kalinga.

Koine Greek. We noted in 3.1.1 that καί is the default coordinating conjunction in Greek narratives. In exhortations and expositions, in contrast, it "constrains the material it introduces to be processed as being added to and associated with previous material" (Levinsohn 2000:124).[7]

Thus, when an expository or hortatory THESIS is supported by more than one sentence, καί is used to show that it is these sentences **together** that strengthen the THESIS. In 1 Timothy 2:13–14, for example, καί conjoins the two sentences that are introduced by γάρ 'for'. It is these sentences together that strengthen the THESIS of 12:

12 THESIS[8]		*I do not allow a woman to teach or to have authority over a man, but to keep silent.*
13 support		*For (γάρ) Adam was formed first, then Eve;*
14		*& (καί) Adam was not deceived, but the woman was deceived and became a transgressor.*

Ancient Hebrew. Like καί in Greek, *waw* is used in Hebrew non-narratives to associate propositions together. Psalm 54:3 illustrates this. No conjunction links the parallel exhortations of 2 which constitute the THESES. In contrast, *waw* links the parallel propositions of 3 which are introduced by *kî* 'for' to show that they support the THESES:

2 THESES	*God, hear my.prayer // listen to.the.words-of.my.mouth.*
3 support	*For (kî) strangers arise against.me // & (wə).ruthless.ones seek my.life.*[9]

Application to the hortatory text in Kalinga (VS/VO)

We noted in 3.1.1 that, in one Kalinga narrative, *kad* 'then, when' was used in half of the sentences that presented theme-line events. What is its function as a connective in the hortatory text? (It is a connective in 4, 12, 14, 15 and 20. Its function in 19 is less clear, as *te* provides the primary form of connection.)[10]

Review questions

1. Is the default way of coordinating sentences in narrative always the default way of coordinating sentences in hortatory texts?
2. In Psalm 130:7–8 (below), why is the Hebrew conjunction *waw* '&' used?

   [7]*O Israel, put your hope in the LORD // for (kî) with the LORD is unfailing love*
   *& (waw) with Him is full redemption // *[8]*& (waw) He Himself will redeem Israel from all their sins.*[11]

---

[7] Καί is also used as an ADDITIVE (discussed in Levinsohn 2015, 6.3). In the letter to Philemon, it is an additive in Philemon 9c, 11b, 16d, 21d and 22a.

[8] Throughout this chapter, the label in caps is the HEAD or NUCLEUS relation; the other label is the support relation.

[9] In Exodus 20:5, *waw* associates together two commands that prohibit two aspects of the same thing (*You shall not bow down to them & you shall not worship them*). Commands that prohibit different things are juxtaposed. Further research is needed on when *waw* is used in hortatory texts in Hebrew.

[10] **Suggested answer** for the Kalinga text: *kad* introduces consequences. It is not used to introduce hortatory THESES.

[11] **Suggested answers**:
1. No!
2. In Psalm 130:7–8, the Hebrew conjunction *waw* '&' links the three propositions introduced by *kî* 'for' that together make up the supportive material.

Application to the language you are analysing

1. What is the default form of intersentential linkage in hortatory and expository material: juxtaposition or a connective? If the latter, which connective is the default one?
2. If the default form of intersentential linkage for narrative is different, what is its function in hortatory and expository material?

3.1.3 Leaving a coordinative relation implicit in non-narrative

Even in a language in which juxtaposition is the default means of coordinating sentences in non-narrative, there may be occasions when one would have expected a connective to be used, yet none is present. For example, the UBS text of the Greek of 2 Timothy 4:17–18 has no connective between 17d and 18, even though 18 appears to be "a conclusion drawn from the preceding verse" (Minor 1992: 148 – *NLT* inserts "Yes, and"):

17d καί *I was delivered from the lion's mouth.*
18   Ø   *The Lord will rescue me from every evil attack.*

The following are some factors that may lead to leaving a coordinative relation implicit when one might have expected a connective to be used.

- A coordinative relation may be left unmarked in **theme-line** material, but be obligatorily marked in **supportive** material (see Psalm 54:2–3 – sec. 3.1.2).
- A coordinative relation may be left unmarked because the message is **emotional** (Callow 1992:192). Galatians 3:1–4 is an instance of this.
- A coordinative relation may be left unmarked because the material is **disconnected**. At the end of an epistle, for instance, "the sequence of thought ... is not formal and deliberate" (White 1970:136). 2 Timothy 4:17d–18 (above) is an example of this.

3.2 Encoding countering relations

If two propositions are in a countering relation, many languages do not mark the relation between them by means of a connective unless other conditions are fulfilled.[12] Consequently, a common error in translation is to insert a countering connective (at times, borrowed from the *lingua franca* of the area) when the natural way to encode the relation in the receptor language is different. For specific examples in different contexts, see Levinsohn 2015, 6.4.1.

Section 3.2.1 repeats 6.4.2 of Levinsohn 2015 and lists some factors that may determine when a countering relation is marked or left implicit in a particular language. Further sections discuss the marking of countering relations in the four languages we have been examining.

3.2.1 Factors that may determine when a countering relation is marked or left implicit

The following are some factors that may determine when a countering relation is marked or is left implicit.

- The **default** way of expressing the relation may be to leave it implicit, so that the countering relation is conveyed only by the content of the propositions concerned. The **relation** is marked only when it would otherwise be **unclear** or to **draw attention** to it.

    Under such circumstances, care must be taken not to make a relation explicit when to do so would produce the wrong effect. An early draft of Luke 2:19 in a language of Burkina Faso began with a countering connective (***But** Mary treasured up all these things and pondered them in her heart – NIV*). The effect was to draw an explicit contrast with the events of the previous verse (*all who heard it were amazed at what the shepherds said to them*). This implied that Mary was NOT amazed at what the shepherds said! The translation was changed!

---

[12] The "newly presented proposition ... may lead to the abandoning of an existing assumption" (Blakemore 1987:53).

- In some languages, certain relations are only made explicit when the **proposition** being introduced is **more important** than the preceding one. See 3.2.2 for a Greek example.
- When one proposition of a contrastive pair is POSITIVE and the other one is negative, the **order** of the propositions may well affect the connective used. Roberts (1997:29) found the following correlation between the order of the verb (V) and the object (O), on the one hand, and the order of the POSITIVE and negative propositions, on the other:

Table 3. Constituent order and propositional order correlations

Constituent order	Preferred propositional order
VO	POSITIVE-negative
OV	negative-POSITIVE

Although the above correlations reflect the preferred order of propositions, most languages also allow them to be put in the opposite order. Often, however, the preferred or default order uses the default means of conjoining, whereas the marked order needs a marked connective:

Table 4. Propositional order and means of conjoining correlations

Propositional order	Means of conjoining
default/preferred	default
marked	marked connective

This is illustrated with the POSITIVE-negative correlation in Koine Greek and English (VO). When the propositions occur in their preferred order, the default connective (καί 'and') is used. When they occur in the opposite order, a marked connective (ἀλλά 'but') is required:

default order: *Allow the children to come to me* καί/**and** *do not prevent them!* (Luke 18:16)

marked order: *Lead us not into temptation* ἀλλά/**but** *deliver us from evil!* (Matthew 6:13).

The converse is found in Konso [kxc] (OV). When the default negative-POSITIVE order occurs, the default connective **ka** is used. When the marked POSITIVE-negative order occurs, the marked connective **umma** is used. (In fact, POSITIVE-connective-negative is the preferred order in a number of Ethiopian OV languages, including Amharic.)

3.2.2 Application to Koine Greek

A number of connectives are used to link propositions in a countering relationship. The following factors enable the most common ones (ἀλλά, καί and δέ) to be distinguished.

- To **associate** propositions when the first is **negative** and the second **positive**, ἀλλά is used, as in 1 Thessalonians 5:6:

  So then, let us not be like others, who are asleep, ἀλλά *let us be alert and self-controlled.*

- Otherwise, when propositions in a countering relationship are associated because they are more or less of **equal importance or relevance**, καί occurs, as in Luke 1:52:

  He has brought down rulers from their thrones καί *has lifted up the humble.*

  This includes occasions when the first proposition is POSITIVE and the second negative, as in Luke 18:16: *Allow the children to come to me* καί *do not prevent them!*

- To MARK the second proposition in a countering relationship as **more important or relevant** than the first, the development marker δέ is used (see Levinsohn 2015, 6.5.3), as in 1 Timothy 4:8:
  For physical training is of some value, the δέ *godliness has value for all things.*

  See also 1 Thessalonians 5:20–21, in which the first exhortation is negative and the second, positive:
  Do not treat prophecies with contempt; test δέ *everything.*

Application to the letter to Philemon

1   Propositions are linked with ἀλλά in Philemon 14, 16. Is this to be expected?

2. Propositions or groups of propositions in a countering relation are linked with δέ in 11a–b, 13–14, 16c–d and possibly 17–18.[13] What does this signal?[14]

3.2.3 Countering in the hortatory text in Kalinga (VS/VO)

Although Kalinga has a countering connective (*yakon* 'but'), it is not used in the hortatory text.

(In narratives, *yakon* is used only when the countering proposition is important or relevant to what follows. For example, the sentence *Then they went and built houses, but* (yakon) *there was no name yet for the district* is followed immediately by a description of how the district acquired its name.)

3.2.4 Countering in the hortatory text in Bariai (SV/VO)

The only overt countering connective used in this text is the combination of the general preposition *Ngan* and the verb *kado* 'you do' (16a), which has been translated 'Otherwise'. This combination introduces a consequence of **not** obeying the exhortations of 15.

When propositions are in a countering relation but relate to the same situation, then Bariai uses the **additive** *be*. This is illustrated in sentence 3, where *be* links negative and positive propositions *if anyone doesn't listen to my voice* **be**[15] *consumes bad tobacco and drinks banana [beer]*.

3.2.5 Countering in the hortatory text in Dungra Bhil (SV/OV)

The following means of signalling countering relations are found in this text:

- *pe?e* 'but, rather'. In related Indo-Aryan languages, a related connective introduces countering propositions that are **important**, so such is presumably the case also in Dungra Bhil. See, for example, *We should not roam about without working like other people who roam about without working. **Rather** (pe?e), we need to work.* (35–36)

- *ga?ʈhehe* 'in contrast, on the contrary'. This conjunction may be used following negative propositions (e.g. *he will not get peace*). Placing the conjunction after the subject signals a switch of attention from a corresponding subject (see Levinsohn 2015, 3.1, for conjunctions used as spacers).[16]

---

[13] The combination of δέ and the additive καί (9c, 22) does not usually link propositions or larger units in a countering relation.

[14] **Suggested answers:**
1. Yes, ἀλλά is the expected conjunction in 14 and 16, since the first proposition is negative and the second, positive.
2. Δέ in these contexts marks the second proposition as more important or relevant than the first, as far as Paul's purpose in writing the letter is concerned.

In 11 (*one formerly useless to you, but* [δέ] *now indeed useful both to you and to me*), Onesimus' current state is more relevant than his previous one.

In 13–14 (*whom I was wanting to keep with me, so that he might be of service to me in your place during my imprisonment for the gospel; but* [δέ] *I preferred to do nothing without your consent.*), Philemon's consent is more relevant than what Paul was wanting.

In 16c–d (*especially to me but* [δέ] *how much more to you*), Philemon's attitude to Onesimus is more relevant than Paul's attitude.

Finally, whether or not the exhortations of 17 and 18 are in a countering relation, the way Philemon responds to Onesimus for wronging him is more relevant than the way he responds because he is a partner with Paul in the faith.

[15] Translations of this sentence into English use "but" since a negative proposition precedes a positive one (3.2.1). This does NOT mean that *be* in Bariai is a countering connective. Whereas English *but* constrains the reader to counter something in the context, Bariai *be* constrains the reader to add what follows to something in the context. It is the **content** of the added proposition that leads to the perception of countering, not the presence of *be*.

[16] "Spacers … may have a default grammatical position in the sentence … but alternatively can be placed between constituents with distinct discourse-pragmatic roles" (Dooley and Levinsohn 2001:73).

Both *pe?e* and *ga?ṭhehe* are used in 19. *Ga?ṭhehe* follows the second person pronoun *tumi* to signal a switch of attention from the *liquor-drinking person: Till he dies, all these things will happen like this, but he will not get peace. As for you, **in contrast** (pe?e tumi ga?ṭhehe), someone may tell you ...*

- *to*. In this and related Indo-Aryan languages, this 'contrastive emphasis' marker (Schmidt 1999:210) signals that the **first** of a pair of countering propositions is a **counterpoint** to set off the following THESIS (see 3.3).

Review question

What three factors may determine when a countering relation is marked or left implicit?[17]

Application to the language you are analysing

1. Look for instances of countering relations in your texts, including examples where the relation is left implicit.
2. If more than one countering connective is used, then distinguish their functions.
3. Under what circumstances is the countering relation normally left implicit?
4. If you are working in an **OV** language and encounter a pair of propositions whose order in Greek is POSITIVE-negative, the most natural way of translating them may be to reverse the order. In Inga (OV), for example: *I am telling the truth, I am not lying* (1 Timothy 2:7) became *I, just not lying, tell you what is true.*

If you are working in a **VO** language and encounter a pair of propositions whose order in Greek is negative ἀλλά POSITIVE, the most natural way of translating them may be to reverse the order. For example, the *NRSV* translation of ἵνα μὴ ὡς κατὰ ἀνάγκην τὸ ἀγαθόν σου ᾖ ἀλλὰ κατὰ ἑκούσιον 'that your goodness might not be according to necessity' ἀλλά 'according to willingness' (Philemon 14b–c) is "in order that your good deed might be voluntary and not something forced".

3.3 Counterpoints

The *OED* defines a counterpoint as a "contrasting ... idea, used to set off the main element". Counterpoints are a frequently used rhetorical device in some languages (e.g. Koine Greek and Indo-Aryan), but are rarely found in natural texts in others. Typically, the counterpoint and main point share a common feature (e.g. the verb or complement).

Koine Greek. Greek epistles commonly begin an exposition or exhortation with a point of minor significance that forms the counterpoint for a following THESIS. Typically, the THESIS is introduced with the development marker δέ. This is seen in James 1:9–10; v. 9 provides the counterpoint for the THESIS statement of 10.[18]

9 (counterpoint)	Καυχάσθω	δὲ	ὁ	ἀδελφὸς	ὁ	ταπεινὸς	ἐν τῷ	ὕψει αὐτοῦ,
	let.boast	DM	the	brother	the	humble	in the	height his

'The brother in humble circumstances ought to take pride in his high position.'

10 (THESIS)	ὁ	δὲ	πλούσιος	ἐν τῇ	ταπεινώσει	αὐτοῦ,
	the	DM	rich	in the	humiliation	his

'The rich, in contrast, should take pride in his low position.'

---

[17] **Suggested answer**: The following factors may determine when a countering relation is marked or left implicit:
- The default way of expressing the relation is to leave it implicit. The relation is marked only when it would otherwise be unclear or to draw attention to it.
- The relation is only made explicit when the proposition being introduced is more important than what precedes.
- When a countering relation exists between a POSITIVE and a negative proposition, the relation may be marked only when their relative order is not the default or preferred one.

[18] Since attention switches from *the brother in humble circumstances* to the rich, ὁ πλούσιος 'the rich' is placed first in 10 (see 4.2). The Greek connective μέν often introduces the counterpoint for a following THESIS which is introduced with δέ (Levinsohn 2000, 10.1).

Application to the letter to Philemon

In your opinion, which propositions might be viewed as counterpoints for a following THESIS?[19]

Indo-Aryan. Section 3.2.5 noted that a particle like *to* in Dungra Bhil may be used to mark the first of a pair of countering propositions as a counterpoint for a following THESIS. In the following passage from another Indo-Aryan language, the contrastive emphasis marker (CON) is *tə*.

1 (counterpoint)	tu-stə	wəʒɛw	pror	**tə**	gwo	
	2s-from	axe	wound	CON	went	
2 (THESIS)	tu-stə	wiri	pror	nə-gwəstə	as-ɛi	
	2s-from	speech	wound	not-gone	is-also	

'Although your axe wound has gone, the wound from your words has not gone.'

Question

Why would it be appropriate to call 1 Timothy 4:8a (below) a counterpoint for 8b?[20]

7b *Train yourself in godliness.*

8a	ἡ	γὰρ	σωματικὴ	γυμνασία	πρὸς	ὀλίγον	ἐστὶν	ὠφέλιμος,
	the	for	bodily	training	for	little	is	profitable

'For physical training is of some value.'

8b	ἡ	δὲ	εὐσέβεια	πρὸς	πάντα	ὠφέλιμός	ἐστιν
	the	DM	godliness	for	all	profitable	3s.is

'But godliness has value for all things.'

Application to translation

As noted above, it is common in Koine Greek to begin an exposition or exhortation with a point of minor significance that forms the counterpoint for a following THESIS. The problem is that such a rhetorical strategy is not common to all languages. For example, the uninitiated English reader does not recognise James 1:9 (above) as a counterpoint for the THESIS about the rich.

Ways to counteract this problem include:

- The use of a backgrounding device (see 7.6). For example, *NRSV* translates the counterpoint of 1 Timothy 4:8a with a prenuclear subordinate clause: **while** *physical training is of some value*. To achieve a similar effect, other languages link 8a and 8b with a spacer.
- A development marker or similar connective.
- The selection of an appropriate title. The *GNB* title "Poverty and Riches" at James 1:9 is misleading!

Note: **Cataphoric orienters** such as *This is what I want to tell you* are similar to counterpoints in that they allow an author to begin with a point of minor significance, rather than the THESIS.

3.4 Constituent order and the order of propositions

In 3.2.1, I noted a correlation between the order of the verb (V) and the object (O), on the one hand, and the relative order of POSITIVE and negative propositions, on the other. This correlation is an

---

[19] **Suggested answer:** The use of a prenuclear participial clause in 8, together with μᾶλλον 'rather' in 9, makes 8 a possible counterpoint for a following THESIS in 9. I judge 11a to be a counterpoint for 11b. 14b and 16a are potential counterpoints, but the presence of ἀλλά implies that Paul did not in fact intend them to be so interpreted.

[20] **Suggested answer:** It would be appropriate to call 1 Timothy 4:8a a counterpoint for 8b because 8b (*Godliness is valuable*) is the "main element" (*OED*) that supports the hortatory THESIS of 7b (*Train yourself in godliness*), and 8a is a contrasting idea, used to set 8b off.

3.4 Constituent order and the order of propositions

instance of a more general principle, that VO languages prefer HEAD-dependent ordering, while OV languages favour dependent-HEAD ordering (Greenberg 1963; Dryer 1997). Thus, pairs of propositions that involve **unequal prominence,** NUCLEUS-support relations are typically presented in the same order as other HEAD-dependent pairs in the language (Roberts 1997; Diessel 2001).

3.4.1 Verb-object order and the ordering of unequal prominence relations

The following table displays some HEAD-dependent ordering correlations (see Roberts 1997:16–18).

Table 5. HEAD-dependent ordering correlations

HEAD-dependent ordering	dependent-HEAD ordering
verb-object (VO)	**object-verb (OV)**
PREPOSITION-NP	NP-POSTPOSITION
AUXILIARY-main verb	main verb-AUXILIARY
SUBORDINATOR-clause	clause-SUBORDINATOR
NUCLEUS-support proposition	**support proposition-NUCLEUS**

The following chart (based on Roberts, p. 32) summarises the expected correlations between VERB-object order and the ordering of unequal prominence, NUCLEUS-support propositions.

Table 6. Verb-object order and NUCLEUS-support propositions correlations

VO	OV
POSITIVE-negative	negative-POSITIVE
OBJECT OF COMPARISON-standard of comparison	standard of comparison-OBJECT OF COMPARISON
NUCLEUS-manner	manner-NUCLEUS
COMMAND-assertion	assertion-COMMAND
RESULT-reason	reason-RESULT
RESULT-means	means-RESULT
MEANS-purpose	purpose-MEANS

This ordering of propositions is not only found within sentences; it also occurs **intersententially.**

The above relations (with the exception of POSITIVE-negative – 3.2.1) are now exemplified for English and Greek (VO) and for the Papuan language Amele [aey] (OV) (see Roberts, pp. 21–25, 28–31).

Table 7. Examples of ordering of propositions

VO		OV	
OBJECT OF COMPARISON-standard of comparison: Revelation 1:14			
OBJECT	*His head and hair were white*	standard	*[aey]*
standard	*as snow (is white).*	OBJECT	*so his head and hair were white.*
NUCLEUS-manner: Acts 1:11			
NUCLEUS	*This Jesus ... will come*	manner	*In the same way as you saw Jesus go into heaven,*
manner	*in the same way as you saw him go into heaven.*	NUCLEUS	*like that he ... will come.*

Table 7, continued

VO		OV	

COMMAND-assertion: Matthew 26:26

	(deductive style)		(inductive style)[21]
COMMAND	Take and eat.	assertion	This is my body.
assertion	This is my body.	COMMAND	Take and eat.

RESULT-reason: Acts 2:6

When they heard this sound, a large group of men gathered.

| RESULT | They were confounded | reason | Each one heard them speaking in his own language, |
| reason | because each one heard them speaking in his own language | RESULT | so they were confounded. |

POSITIVE-negative and RESULT-reason: Luke 18:16

POSITIVE	Allow the children to come to me	reason	The kingdom of God belongs to such children.
negative	and do not prevent them.	negative	So do not prevent them;
reason	For the kingdom of God belongs to such.	POSITIVE	let them come to me.

or (using an *inclusio* – see below):

POSITIVE	Allow the children to come to me	negative	Do not prevent the children coming to me.
negative	and do not prevent them.	reason	The kingdom of God belongs to such.
reason	For the kingdom of God belongs to such.	POSITIVE	So let them come.

The RESULT-reason order of propositions in the Greek is particularly problematic for many OV languages, as it occurs so often in the Epistles. See 3.5.3 for the connectives used in the letter to Philemon to introduce reasons and other strengthening information.

RESULT-means: Luke 24:35

| RESULT | He was known to them | means | The Lord broke the bread for them. |
| means | by the breaking of the bread. | RESULT | By this means they knew him. |

MEANS-purpose: Acts 16:30

| MEANS | What must I do | purpose | To be saved |
| purpose | to be saved? | MEANS | what must I do? |

However, the MEANS-purpose order is common even in OV languages (see point 2 of 3.4.2 for a possible reason).

---

[21] See 2.4 on other factors that determine the selection of inductive or deductive style.

3.4.2 Observations

1. In OV languages, *inclusio* structures are often used to enable the NUCLEAR proposition to be stated early, then supported, before concluding with a reiteration of the NUCLEUS (2.6). The following example is from a folktale in Kambaata [ktb]:

a	*They tried various tricks,*
b (RESULT)	*but they couldn't make them quarrel.*
c (reason)	*The reason was that the two friends always lived together & shared what people told them*
d (RESULT')	*so they didn't fall for the tricks.*

   See also the second ordering of Luke 18:16 (3.4.1) in OV languages.

2. The following factors may also affect the order of propositions.

- In some languages, a desire to **preserve chronological or logical sequence** may determine the order (e.g. in reason-RESULT, cause-EFFECT and MEANS-purpose pairs).

- When the **focus** falls on the **support** proposition (Levinsohn 1999:55), the order of the propositions may be reversed. In the following reported conversation from an Oromo [orm] (OV) folktale, for example, the normal reason-RESULT order was reversed because the result was established information:

Speaker A:		*Why won't you come near me?*
Speaker B:	result	*I won't go near you.*
	REASON	*Why ... do the footprints of the people who went to see you enter, but I don't see them coming out?*

- **Marked order** may give extra prominence to a focal constituent. In Matthew 6:10b, the Greek places the standard before the OBJECT (contrast 3.4.1). The effect of postposing the focal constituent *also on earth* is to give it extra prominence (see Levinsohn 2000:34–35).

English:	*Your will be done **on earth, as it is in heaven**.*
Greek:	*Your will be done, **as in heaven, also on earth**.*

Review questions

1. When a language has OV constituent order, what is the preferred order of pairs of propositions of unequal prominence?
2. When the preferred order of propositions is not followed, how may this influence the connective used (see 3.2.1)?
3. What three factors have been observed to influence the order of propositions?[22]

---

[22] **Suggested answers:**
1. When a language has OV constituent order, the preferred order of pairs of propositions of unequal prominence is support-NUCLEUS.
2. When the preferred order of propositions is not followed, a marked connective may replace the default means of connection.
3. The following three factors have been observed to influence the order of propositions:
   - a desire to preserve chronological or logical sequence
   - when the focus falls on the support proposition
   - to give extra prominence to a focal constituent.

Application to the language you are analysing

1. What is the preferred/default order for the propositional pairs listed in 3.4.1, especially when they are found intersententially? Does it correspond to VO versus OV order, or does the preservation of chronological or logical sequence in the ordering seem to be more important? Is deductive versus inductive reasoning a factor?
2. Are other orders possible for some propositional pairs (e.g. if a marked connective is used)? If so, what is their function when they occur?
3. Are *inclusio* structures ever used? If so, what is their function?

3.5 Encoding logical relations

Languages tend to use a logical connective to signal a reason or RESULT only in certain specific circumstances.[23] This section begins with a discussion of specific occasions where some languages prefer not to use a logical connective (3.5.1). It then considers factors that may determine when a logical relation is marked or left implicit (3.5.2). Observations are then made about logical connectives in the four languages we have been examining.

3.5.1 Encoding logical relations in specific contexts

This section alludes to four contexts in which a logical relation appears to exist between propositions, yet certain languages prefer not to use a logical connective.

a) When a RESULT is **expected** because it is constrained by the context, some African and Iranian languages use an **additive** (*also*) where English might use *so*. Luke 6:8 (*NIV*) provides a narrative example where *so* would be replaced by *also* in such languages:

8b *and said to the man with the shrivelled hand, "Get up and stand in front of everyone."*

8c ***So/Also** he got up and stood there.*

b) In some languages, the **RESULT-reason** relation is not made explicit when a constituent of the comment of one sentence becomes the topic of the next.[24] Compare the following pairs of sentences in Marba [mpg] (VO):

RESULT *Do not court another man's wife.*

reason **Kayam** *(for) many have died because of a woman.*

In the next pair, *them* becomes the topic of the reason:

RESULT *I don't want you to associate with them.*

reason Ø *They are people who do not respect their parents.*

c) In some languages, a PURPOSE whose subject is not the same as that of the main clause is typically expressed as an independent clause with an imperfective (IMPF) or irrealis (IRR) marker. In such languages, *I sent her to the river to bring water back* might be rendered *I sent her to the river. She **IMPF/IRR** comes with water.*

d) In some languages, a connective is only used for reason-RESULT (support-THESIS) relations when the RESULT is a **conclusion**. No connective is used when the RESULT is not a conclusion. In the following example from Koorete [kqy] (OV), the supportive material leads to some hortatory THESES. However, because the THESES are not the conclusion of the unit, they do not begin with the connective *ha e gisha* 'therefore, because of this':

---

[23] For charts of the communication relations used in Semantic Structure Analyses (SSAs), see Banker 1996:11–12.
[24] Material arranged in this way is said to be organised **sequentially** (see 4.1).

support		*Also, when you look at it, very many are about to be destroyed.*
HORT. THESES		*Ø I, my brother, am really asking you. I am asking you, 'Get up from this place, from this land! After you get up from here, build in a fitting place!'*

3.5.2 Factors that may determine when a logical relation is marked or left implicit

Sections 3.2.1 and 3.4.2 discussed three factors that sometimes determine when a countering relation is marked or left implicit. The same factors may influence the marking of other relations. The factors discussed were as follows:

- The **default** way of expressing the relation may be to leave it implicit, so that the relation is conveyed only by the content of the propositions concerned. The relation is then marked only when it would otherwise be **unclear** or to **draw attention** to it.[25]
- In some languages, certain relations are only made explicit when the following proposition is at least as **important** as the preceding one.
- The relation may be marked only when the **order** of propositions is not the default or preferred one (see below for examples from French [fra]).

A related factor that may determine when a relation is marked or left implicit relates to whether the style of the paragraph or larger unit is **deductive** or **inductive** (2.4).

- In some languages, certain relations between the THESIS and supportive material are normally left implicit when the style is **deductive**. The following examples reflect the *Bible en français courant* translation into French (SV/VO):

Deductive style (default propositional order): Luke 7:7–8

THESIS		*Just give the order, and my servant will get well.*
support	Ø	*I, too, am a man placed under the authority of superior officers.*

Inductive style (marked propositional order): Matthew 9:37–38

support		*The harvest is plentiful, but the labourers are few;*
THESIS	*therefore*	*ask the Lord of the harvest to send out labourers into his harvest.*

- In other languages, certain relations between the THESIS and supportive material are normally left implicit when the style is **inductive**. The following example from Chadian Arabic [shu] uses inductive style, so the conjunction meaning 'so, therefore' is not used:

support	&	*how will your daughter learn all that? Only with your help, mother.*
THESIS	Ø	*Get this into your head, mother: "If I don't set my daughter an example, she will not turn out as I want."*

3.5.3 Logical relations in the letter to Philemon in Koine Greek

The norm in Koine Greek is to mark intersentential logical relations with a connective. The logical connectives of Greek may be divided into two types:

- **inferential** (inductive or introducing consequences): those that introduce a THESIS, CONCLUSION or RESULT which is inferred from the context.
- **strengthening** (deductive): those that support a THESIS by introducing a reason, ground or explanation.

  Connectives of both types are found in the letter to Philemon. I briefly discuss them in turn.

---

[25] In *Screwtape Letters* (London: HarperCollins), C. S. Lewis seldom uses conjunctions to mark logical relations. Often, when he uses 'For' or 'Hence', the following material relates to **two or more** THESES.

Inferential connectives

In Philemon 8, διό[26] 'therefore it is for that reason that' occurs. This connective typically introduces an expository or hortatory THESIS that is inferred from what has already been said. In this instance, Paul indicates that he is about to make an exhortation (παρακαλῶ 'I appeal'), but does not actually give it till 17![27]

The connective οὖν 'then' (as in v. 17) usually marks the **resumption** and further development of the **same theme** line (3.6). As noted in the last paragraph, 8–9 introduce the exhortation that Paul is about to make. Verse 17 returns to this hortatory theme after the supportive material of the intervening verses.

Strengthening connectives

The connective γάρ 'for, after all' is the **default** strengthening connective, which does NOT indicate a specific logical relation. It is used in Philemon 7, 15 and 22b.

The connective ὅτι 'because, that' is generally NOT used intersententially (but see 2 John 7). However, I include it here for completeness. It is an **interpretive use** marker, showing that what follows relates back to something that has already been said or implied (Levinsohn 2003a; Levinsohn 2015, 7.10). When used as a logical connective, it introduces a reason or evidence for the last assertion (THESIS). In Philemon 7b, for example, it interprets the assertion that *I received much joy and encouragement from your love* by specifying the aspect of *your love* that produced *much joy and encouragement*: *because the hearts of the saints have been refreshed through you*.

3.5.4 Logical relations in the hortatory text in Kalinga (VS/VO)

The norm in Koine Greek is to mark intersentential logical relations with a connective (3.5.3). Does the Kalinga text suggest that the language is similar to or differs from Greek in this respect?[28]

3.5.5 Logical relations in the hortatory text in Bariai (SV/VO)

The norm in Koine Greek is to mark intersentential logical relations with a connective. Does the Bariai text suggest that the language is similar to or differs from Greek in this respect?[29]

3.5.6 Logical relations in the hortatory text in Dungra Bhil (SV/OV)

The norm in Koine Greek is to mark intersentential logical relations with a connective. In what respects does the Dungra Bhil text suggest that the language (a) is similar to (b) differs from Greek?[30]

---

[26] Derived from διὰ ὅ – often associated with sequential progression—see 4.1.

[27] διό is non-developmental. This is illustrated in Acts 27:25, where it introduces a command διὸ εὐθυμεῖτε, ἄνδρες 'be cheerful', which is a reiteration of the command in v. 22 (καὶ τὰ νῦν παραινῶ ὑμᾶς εὐθυμεῖν· 'and now I advise you to be courageous').

[28] **Suggested answer**: Kalinga is **similar** to Koine Greek in that it is the norm in the text to mark logical relations with a connective. *Kad* 'then' as a second-place connective is **inferential** (12, 14 and possibly 19). *Te* (glossed 'for, after all') is the **default** way of introducing **strengthening** material (3, 9, 21; compare Greek γάρ). (Some languages related to Kalinga have a more specific strengthening connective [e.g. *pomon to* 'from, because, due to the fact that' – Obo Manobo] to introduce a reason which is a known fact and which directly leads to the RESULT.)

[29] **Suggested answer**: Bariai **differs** from Koine Greek in that no intersentential connective is used in the text to signal a logical relation. In particular, NO inferential connective introduces the concluding hortatory THESIS of the text. (*Ngansa* 'because' is a strengthening connective that supports a THESIS by introducing a **reason**. However, it is only found within sentences: 2c, 4c, 6b.)

[30] **Suggested answers**:
(a) Dungra Bhil is similar to Koine Greek in that it marks intersentential **inferential** relations with a connective (*tahā* 'then' – 24). However, in Kangri [xnr] (a related Indo-Aryan language), an inferential connective was only used when the consequence was to be given prominence (Robert Eaton p.c.).

Application to the language you are analysing

1. Look for instances of logical relations in your texts, including ones in which the relation is left implicit. Identify how they are encoded. Describe when each is used.
2. In paragraphs with **deductive** style, how is supportive material introduced: with a connective or by juxtaposition? If there is a choice, what factors are involved?
3. Do the same for paragraphs in your texts with **inductive** style.

3.6 Resuming an argument line

When a theme-line THESIS is followed by supportive material or an aside, languages have devices for indicating when the theme line is being resumed. One such device is the use of a development marker or similar connective (see Levinsohn 2015, 6.6). In expository and hortatory material, the connective used is likely to be an inferential, logical one, such as *then* in English when placed in a non-initial position (e.g. *I desire, then, that ...* – see 1 Timothy 2:8 below).

In **Greek**, the inferential connective οὖν is frequently used as a resumptive, following supportive material or an aside. So, if a Greek sentence is introduced with οὖν, you should check whether the immediately preceding material has been introduced with a strengthening connective such as γάρ 'for' or ὅτι 'because'. If it has, then οὖν is almost certainly being used to mark the resumption of the theme line (see Levinsohn 2000:128–129).[31]

This is illustrated in 1 Timothy 2:1–8. Verses 1–2 present a hortatory THESIS, which is followed, in 3–7, by supportive information. When the hortatory THESES are resumed in 8, οὖν is used:

THESIS ¹*First of all, **then** (οὖν), I urge that supplications, prayers, intercessions, and thanksgivings be made for everyone, ²for kings and all who are in high positions, so that we may lead a quiet and peaceable life in all godliness and dignity.*

support ³*This is right and is acceptable in the sight of God our Saviour, ⁴who desires everyone to be saved and to come to the knowledge of the truth. ⁵For (γάρ) there is one God; there is also one mediator between God and humankind, Christ Jesus, himself human, ⁶who gave himself a ransom for all – this was attested at the right time. ⁷For this I was appointed a herald and an apostle (I am telling the truth, I am not lying), a teacher of the Gentiles in faith and truth.*

THESIS ⁸*I desire, **then** (οὖν), that in every place the men should pray.*

See 3.5.3 on οὖν in Philemon 17.

Application to the Kalinga text

Where is the inferential connective *kad* used to mark the resumption of the hortatory theme line?[32]

Application to the language you are analysing

Look for instances in your texts where the theme line is being **resumed** after the presentation of supportive material. Identify the mechanism(s) that are used to indicate the resumption of the theme line.

(b) Dunga Bhil differs from Koine Greek in that a **strengthening** connective such as *kihĩke* 'because' is *never* used intersententially in the text to introduce motivational information that supports a THESIS. (In RESULT-reason pairs, the particle *to* follows the subject when the reason is based on the opposite of the RESULT – see sent. 2.)

Kangri is similar. When the REASON is more prominent than the result, then the REASON precedes the result (see 3.4.2 (2)), and an emphatic connective translated 'having done **this**' introduces the result.

[31] In 1 Timothy 3:2a, οὖν is NOT resumptive; see Levinsohn 2000:126–127. For further discussion of οὖν as a resumptive, see pp. 127–131.

[32] **Suggested answer** for Kalinga: The inferential connective *kad* is used to mark the resumption of the hortatory theme line at 20, following the supportive material of 19.

4

Intersentential Progression within a Paragraph; Variations in Constituent Order

This chapter begins with some observations by Connor (1996) concerning the different ways that paragraphs are organised (4.1). It then gives an overview of factors that underlie variations in constituent order (4.2), before discussing two of these factors: the role of topicalised constituents (here referred to as "points of departure" – 4.3) in non-narrative texts and conformity to Comrie's (1989:127–128) "Principle of Natural Information Flow" (4.4).

4.1 Intersentential and interclausal progression within a paragraph

Connor (1996:84–85 – following Lautamatti 1987) distinguishes three types of intersentential progression, with the following characteristics:[1]

- **Parallel** progression: topics (or points of departure) of successive sentences are the **same**.
- **Sequential** progression: topics of successive sentences are different, as a constituent of the comment of one sentence becomes **topical** in the next. "Topical" means that this constituent becomes either the new topic or (part of) the point of departure for the next sentence.
- *Inclusio*: a passage is **bracketed** by a statement made at its beginning, an approximation of which is repeated at its conclusion (see Guthrie 1998:14).

I exemplify these three types of intersentential and interclausal progression in turn.

Examples of parallel progression[2]

1. English (rededication service of a church)
   You have blessed this church.
   Here the Gospel of Jesus Christ is proclaimed.
   Here the sacraments are celebrated.
   Here the seeker finds faith.

---

[1] I have modified Connor's definitions (for *inclusio*, she uses the term "extended parallel progression").
[2] Throughout this chapter, underlining indicates that the constituent precedes the verb (where present) and is a point of departure (4.3) or preverbal subject (see 4.3.2). Relative pronouns have also been underlined where they establish the topic of the next clause (e.g. in [2] and [4]).

2. Greek (Philemon 10–13)

   (10a *I am appealing to you for my child*)

10b	<u>ὃν</u>	ἐγέννησα	ἐν	τοῖς	δεσμοῖς	Ὀνήσιμον			
	whom	I.gave.birth	in	the	bonds	Onesimus			
11	τόν	ποτέ	σοι	ἄχρηστον	νυνὶ	δὲ	[καὶ] σοὶ	καὶ	ἐμοὶ εὔχρηστον,
	the.one	once	to.you	useless	now	DM	ADD to.you	and	to.me useful
12a	<u>ὃν</u>	ἀνέπεμψά	σοι,						
	whom	I.sent.back	to.you						
12b	<u>αὐτόν</u>,	τοῦτ'	ἔστιν	τὰ	ἐμὰ	σπλάγχνα			
	him	this	is	the	my	inward.parts			
13ab	<u>ὃν</u>	ἐγὼ	ἐβουλόμην	/	πρὸς	ἐμαυτὸν	κατέχειν,		
	whom	I	I.was.desiring		with	myself	to.keep		

   'to whom I became a father during my imprisonment, Onesimus;
   the one formerly useless to you, but now indeed useful both to you and to me;
   whom I am sending back to you –
   him, that is, my own heart;
   whom I was wanting to keep with me.'

Examples of sequential progression

3. Greek (Romans 8:29–30)

   29   *For <u>those whom he foreknew</u> he also predestined to be conformed to the image of his Son …*

30a	<u>οὓς</u>	δὲ	<u>προώρισεν</u>,	τούτους	καὶ	ἐκάλεσεν
	whom	DM	he.predestined	these	also	he.called

   'And those whom he predestined he also called;

30b	καὶ	<u>οὓς</u>	<u>ἐκάλεσεν</u>,	τούτους	καὶ	ἐδικαίωσεν
	and	whom	he.called	these	also	he.justified

   and those whom he called he also justified

30c	<u>οὓς</u>	δὲ	<u>ἐδικαίωσεν</u>,	τούτους	καὶ	ἐδόξασεν.
	whom	DM	he.justified	these	also	he.glorified

   and those whom he justified he also glorified.'

4. Greek (1 Peter 3:18–22)

   18   *For <u>Christ</u> died for sins once for all, the righteous for the unrighteous, to bring you to God, being put to death in the body but made alive by the Spirit,*

   19   *<u>through whom</u> (ἐν ᾧ) also he went and preached to the spirits in prison (20a) who disobeyed long ago in the days of Noah while the ark was being built;*

   20b   *<u>in which</u> (εἰς ἣν) only a few people, eight in all, were saved through water;*

   21   *<u>which</u> (ὃ) symbolises baptism that now saves you also – not the removal of dirt from the body but the pledge of a good conscience towards God, by the resurrection of Jesus Christ,*

   22   *<u>who</u> (ὅς) has gone into heaven and is at God's right hand.*

Examples of *inclusio*

5. English (Connor p. 85): the topics of 1 and 4 are the same.

    1   Body language varies from culture to culture.
    2   *To say yes,* Americans nod their heads up and down.
    3   Japanese and Italians use the same nod to say no.
    4   Body language is an important skill for international managers.

6. Greek (Matthew 7:16–20): the THESIS statement of 16a is reiterated in 20.

    16a By their fruit you will recognise them.
    16b Do people pick grapes from thorn-bushes, or figs from thistles?
    17   Likewise *every good tree* bears good fruit, but *a bad tree* bears bad fruit.
    18   A good tree cannot bear bad fruit, and a bad tree cannot bear good fruit.
    19   *Every tree that does not bear good fruit* is cut down and thrown into the fire.
    20   Thus by their fruit you will certainly recognise them.

A language may be expected to use all three types of intersentential progression. It is likely, though, that it will favour a particular type (e.g. sequential progression in Greek, parallel progression in Hebrew).[3] NOTE, however, that many paragraphs may show little or no evidence of any of the types of intersentential progression described in this section. In other words, the intersentential progression within many paragraphs may be very informal.

Review questions

1. What are the three types of intersentential progression? How do they differ from each other?
2. Which type of interclausal progression is found in Philemon 5–6? Explain!

    5   because I hear of your love for all the saints and your faith toward the Lord Jesus.
    6   ὅπως   ἡ   κοινωνία   τῆς   πίστεώς   σου   ἐνεργὴς   γένηται
         so.that the   sharing   of.the   faith   your   effective may.become

         ἐν   ἐπιγνώσει   παντὸς   ἀγαθοῦ   τοῦ   ἐν   ἡμῖν   εἰς   Χριστόν.
         in   acknowledgment of.every   good.thing   of.the   in   us   for   Christ

    '(I pray) that the sharing of your faith may become effective when you perceive all the good that we may do for Christ.'[4]

---

[3] Connor (1996:34–35, reporting 1972 research by Kaplan) claims that "[Standard] Arabic [arb] develops paragraphs through a series of parallel constructions, both positive and negative. ... Hebrew ... like Arabic, is a Semitic language whose coordinating structure favors rhetorical parallelism". In Exodus 20:2–17, for instance, parallel structures such as *You shall not ...* are used to present the Ten Commandments.

[4] **Suggested answers**:
1. The three types of intersentential progression are parallel, sequential and *inclusio*.
   - In parallel progression, the topics of successive sentences are the same.
   - In sequential progression, the topics of successive sentences are different, as a constituent of the comment of one sentence becomes either the new topic or (part of) the point of departure for the next sentence.
   - In an *inclusio*, a passage is bracketed by a statement made at its beginning, an approximation of which is repeated at its conclusion.
2. **Sequential** progression is found in Philemon 5–6. The topic in 4–5 is *I*, and *your faith* is a constituent of the comment in 5. In 6, *the sharing of your faith* becomes the topic.

Application to the hortatory text in Kalinga (VS/VO)

Which type of intersentential progression is associated with the use of *sadi* 'that' in 4 and 9? (See also 5c.)[5]

Application to the hortatory text in Bariai (SV/VO)

Which type of intersentential progression is found in 13–14? (See also 1–4.)[6]

Application to the hortatory text in Dungra Bhil (SO/OV)

1. Which type of intersentential progression is found in 1–2?
2. Which type of intersentential progression is found in 10–12? (See also 27–29.)
3. What type of intersentential progression does the text as a whole have?[7]

Application to the language you are analysing

Which type of intersentential progression does the language favour? How common are the other types? (REMINDER: Many paragraphs show little or no evidence of any of the types of intersentential progression described in this section.)

4.2 Variations in constituent order: An overview

When there is **parallel** progression between sentences, they each begin in the same way, and the repeated constituent may not be the subject. In passage (1) (repeated from above), for instance, each sentence begins with *here*:

1. English (rededication service of a church)

   You have blessed this church.

   <u>Here</u> *the Gospel of Jesus Christ is proclaimed.*

   <u>Here</u> *the sacraments are celebrated.*

   <u>Here</u> *the seeker finds faith.*

Although *here* begins the above sentences in parallel progression, it is more commonly found following the verb (e.g. *We were sitting* **here** *this morning when …)*

When there is **sequential** progression between sentences, the constituent from the previous comment that becomes topical begins the sentence. This constituent is usually the subject, but does not have to be.[8] In passage (3) (repeated from above), for instance, each of the actions introduced in the previous sentence that becomes topical in the next is the object of its verb (see also τοῦτο 'this' in Philemon 18b):

---

[5] **Suggested answer** for the Kalinga text: The use of *sadi* 'that' in 4, 5c and 9 is associated with **sequential** progression. The referent of *sadi* is the action described in the previous clause or sentence. This action becomes the topic in the next clause or sentence. (Compare Philemon 18, in which τοῦτο 'this' is used in the same way.)

[6] **Suggested answer** for the Bariai text. **Parallel** progression is found in 13–14. Both sentences have *Oatai ngan earum-nga le-m … eta mao* 'You won't experience the planting of any …' (11 is similar).

[7] **Suggested answers** for the Dungra Bhil text:
1. **Sequential** progression is found in 1–2. *Liquor* is introduced in the comment of 1, and becomes the topic of 2.
2. **Parallel** progression is found in 10–12. Each sentence begins with *horu pi-t pohõʔõ* 'after drinking liquor'.
3. The text as a whole forms an ***inclusio***: it is bracketed by a statement made at its beginning (*You should not be drinking liquor* – 1), an approximation of which is repeated near the end of the text (37a). (see 8.5 for other *inclusios* in this text.)

[8] In N.W. Austronesian languages such as Kalinga, the topical constituent does have to be the subject.

3. Greek (Romans 8:29–30)

29 *For <u>those whom he foreknew</u> he also predestined to be conformed to the image of his Son ...*

30a <u>οὓς</u> δὲ <u>προώρισεν,</u> τούτους καὶ ἐκάλεσεν
    whom DM he.predestined these also he.called
    'And those whom he predestined he also called;

30b καὶ <u>οὓς</u> <u>ἐκάλεσεν,</u> τούτους καὶ ἐδικαίωσεν
    and whom he.called these also he.justified
    and those whom he called he also justified

30c <u>οὓς</u> δὲ <u>ἐδικαίωσεν,</u> τούτους καὶ ἐδόξασεν.
    whom DM he.justified these also he.glorified
    and those whom he justified he also glorified.'

Although the object begins each of the above sentences, objects frequently follow the verb in Greek (e.g. Παράγγελλε ταῦτα 'Command these things' – 1 Timothy 4:11a).

The above passages remind us that, in natural texts in all languages, constituents sometimes occur in one position in the sentence and sometimes in another. Many of these variations in constituent order can be explained with reference to three factors that were discussed in chapters 3 and 4 of Levinsohn 2015:

- the provision of an explicit starting point or "point of departure" for the communication;
- the "Principle of Natural Information Flow" (Comrie 1989:127–128);
- prominence ("emphasis", in layman's terms).

The remainder of this chapter concerns points of departure and variations in constituent order that conform to the Principle of Natural Information Flow. The next chapter discusses devices (including the violation of the Principle of Natural Information Flow) that give prominence to constituents.

4.3 Points of departure in non-narrative

In the passages cited in the above sections, certain constituents that began a clause or sentence were underlined to show that they function as "points of departure". This term designates a constituent that is placed at the beginning of a clause or sentence with a dual function (Levinsohn 2015, 3.1):[9]

- It provides a starting point for the communication; and
- It cohesively anchors the subsequent clause(s) to something that is already in the context (i.e. to something accessible in the hearer's mental representation).

For instance, the placement of *νυνί* 'now' at the beginning of Philemon 11b (below) provides a starting point for the assertion *indeed useful both to you and to me*. In addition, it cohesively anchors 11b to the context by signalling a switch from *ποτέ* 'now' in 11a.

11a τόν ποτέ σοι ἄχρηστον
    the.one once to.you useless

11b <u>νυνὶ</u> δὲ [καὶ] σοὶ καὶ ἐμοὶ εὔχρηστον,
    now DM ADD to.you and to.me useful
    'the one formerly useless to you, but now indeed useful both to you and to me;'

The examples of section 4.2 show that points of departure play a significant role in marking intersentential progression. When there is **parallel** progression between sentences, the second sentence is often anchored to the context by a point of departure involving **renewal**. In passage (1), for

---
[9] Connectives (ch. 3) are generally *not* points of departure.

instance, sentence-initial *here* is a point of departure that renews the situation applicable to the previous sentence.

With **sequential** progression between sentences, the second sentence is also anchored to the context by a point of departure involving **renewal**, in the sense that a constituent of the comment of the first sentence becomes topical in the second. For example, Romans 8:30b is anchored to 30a by the repetition of ἐκάλεσεν 'he called'.

At the same time, when sequential progression extends over a series of sentences, each point of departure also signals a **switch** from the previous point of departure. Again in Romans 8:30b, οὓς ἐκάλεσεν 'whom he called' both renews ἐκάλεσεν 'he called' from Romans 8:30a and signals a switch from οὓς προώρισεν 'whom he predestined' in 30a.

In fact, all points of departure anchor what follows to the context either by renewal or by a switch from a corresponding constituent of the context (implying a discontinuity in that dimension). Both types are found in the four languages we have been examining.

4.3.1 Points of departure in Koine Greek

Points of departure in Greek anchor what follows to the context either by switch or by renewal.[10] Such anchoring may be situational or referential (a cover term for references to participants and themes – see the final paragraph of Levinsohn 2015, 2.4). Note that discussion of preverbal subjects in Greek is delayed until the next section, because of the special problems they pose.

Switches of situation

Switches of situation include switches of time (e.g. from ποτέ 'once' in Philemon 11a to νυνί 'now' in 11b – illustrated above), place, condition, reason, purpose and comparison (see Levinsohn 2015, 3.1, for examples and discussion). Most switches of situation in non-narrative texts, though, are signalled with conditional points of departure.

Thus, Philemon 18 begins with a conditional clause (εἰ τι ἠδίκησέν σε ἢ ὀφείλει 'if he has wronged you in any way or owes you anything') that signals a switch of situation from that of 17 (Εἰ με ἔχεις κοινωνόν 'if you consider me your partner').

Switches of reference

1 Thessalonians 4:9a provides an example in which a point of departure signals a switch of theme. The sentence begins with the prepositional phrase Περὶ τῆς φιλαδελφίας 'Concerning [the] brotherly love'. This point of departure signals a **switch of theme** from sexual matters (3–8) to brotherly love (9–12).

Renewal of situation

We have already illustrated the use of points of departure involving renewal in connection with parallel and sequential progression. Philemon 22 provides an additional example; it begins with the temporal point of departure ἅμα 'at the same time, together', which signals "the coincidence of two actions in time" or "in place" (Arndt and Gingrich 1957:41).

In narrative, "[o]ne reason for using a situational point of departure involving renewal is to introduce **different episodes** that occur in the same general setting" (Levinsohn 2015, 3.2.2).[11] Situational points of departure involving renewal function in a similar way in non-narrative texts, in that they may introduce different THESES applicable to the same general setting. Such is the case in Philemon 22; the request to *prepare a guest room for me* is quite different from the exhortations to *welcome him [Onesimus] as you would welcome me* (17).[12]

---

[10] For a detailed discussion of points of departure in Greek non-narrative texts, see Levinsohn 2000:22–26.

[11] Points of departure by renewal are also used to slow down the discourse in order to highlight what follows; see 7.7.

[12] Section 5.2.1 discusses the preposed constituent διὰ τῶν προσευχῶν ὑμῶν 'through your prayers' in 22c.

Renewal of reference

A possible example is found in Philemon 9b–c, which begins with τοιοῦτος 'such a one'. After indicating that he is appealing to Philemon on the basis of love (9a), Paul presents some credential information (2.5). Since Paul was already the subject in 8–9a, I take τοιοῦτος to be a preverbal subject or "referential point of departure".[13] Such points of departure commonly "introduce background information" (Levinsohn 2015, 3.2.1).

Potential points of departure that do not in fact begin a clause or sentence

If a potential point of departure would NOT indicate the primary basis for relating the clause or sentence to the context, then it is NOT placed in an initial position. If this is an unfamiliar concept to you, then please read section 3.3 of Levinsohn 2015.

Potential points of departure include **conditional** clauses that do not begin a sentence. Second Corinthians 13:5 (below) provides an example. The conditional clause εἰ ἐστὲ ἐν τῇ πίστει 'if you are in the faith' follows the main clause because it does not provide a starting point for the communication. Instead, it is part of the communication itself (it is focal – 5.1):

5a Ἑαυτοὺς   πειράζετε εἰ   ἐστὲ   ἐν   τῇ   πίστει,
    selves   test   if   you.are in   the faith
    'Examine yourselves (to see) whether you are in the faith.'

Other potential points of departure are **temporal** expressions that do not begin a clause or sentence. Acts 1:5b provides an example. The temporal expression οὐ μετὰ πολλὰς ταύτας ἡμέρας 'not many days from now' follows the main clause because it is not the primary basis for relating 5b to 5a. Rather, 5b relates to 5a on the basis of a switch of attention from *John* to *you* (see 4.3.2):

4   *He ordered them not to leave Jerusalem, but to wait there for the promise of the Father …*
5a ὅτι   Ἰωάννης μὲν   ἐβάπτισεν ὕδατι,
    because John   on.one.hand baptised   with.water
    'for John, on the one hand, baptised with water;
5b ὑμεῖς δὲ ἐν πνεύματι βαπτισθήσεσθε   ἁγίῳ **οὐ** **μετὰ** **πολλὰς** **ταύτας** **ἡμέρας**
    you   DM in Spirit   will.be.baptised Holy not   after   many   these   days.
    You, on the other hand, will be baptised with the Holy Spirit not many days from now.'

I close this section with a reminder that constituents may be preposed in Greek for **other** reasons than to establish points of departure (Levinsohn 2015, 4.2). We will discuss this further in 5.2.

4.3.2 Preverbal subjects in Koine Greek

In Levinsohn 2000:22ff., I treat preverbal subjects in non-narrative material in Greek as referential points of departure, since they anchor what follows to the context by switch or by renewal. Other linguists find difficulties with this analysis, since most overt subjects in non-narratives precede the verb (Terry 1995:147; Porter 1992:295). Indeed, only one overt subject in the letter to Philemon follows the verb (Philemon 23–24) and this can be explained by reference to the Principle of Natural Information Flow (see 4.4).

Simon Dik's approach to constituent order can explain why subjects often follow the verb in Greek narrative but more often precede it in non-narrative material. He proposed a template that is particularly applicable to Koine Greek, Ancient Hebrew and any other language that, like Kalinga, allows the subject and object to follow the verb fairly often. Dik's template (1989:363) is:

---

[13] See Banker (1999) for discussion of other interpretations of the function of τοιοῦτος in this verse.

P1 P2 V X, where
V is the verb;
X denotes the constituents that follow the verb;
position P1 can be occupied by one or more TOPIC constituents, and
position P2 can be occupied by a FOCUS constituent.[14]

Dik's template does NOT imply that the language to which it is applied has VS/VO as its default order. The template allows, for example, that it be the **norm** for P1 to be occupied by a topical subject (as is the case in Bantu languages). Rather, we find that some constituents in 'X' nearly always precede V and occupy the P1 position (e.g. temporal and conditional expressions in all languages and subjects in much Koine Greek non-narrative material). Other constituents occupy the P1 position only occasionally (e.g. expressions of reason and purpose). When they do so, though, it is for the same basic reason.[15]

I noted above that overt subjects in the letter to Philemon nearly always precede the verb. In Philemon 13a, for instance, the pronoun ἐγώ 'I' precedes the verb (see also Philemon 19a [cited below], where the preverbal subject is ἐγὼ Παῦλος 'I Paul'):

13ab ὃν   ἐγὼ   ἐβουλόμην   /   πρὸς   ἐμαυτὸν   κατέχειν
     whom   I   I.was.desiring   with   myself   to.keep
     'whom I was wanting to keep with me'

However, subject pronouns may also follow the verb, as in Colossians 1:23:

23 οὗ   ἐγενόμην   ἐγὼ Παῦλος διάκονος.
    of.which I.became   I   Paul   minister.
    'of which I, Paul, became a minister.'

Most **preverbal subjects** in Greek non-narrative signal a switch of attention to the new subject-topic. Many of these switches of attention are **from the current centre of attention**. Because hortatory texts deal "with how people ... should behave" (Longacre 1996:9), the default centre of attention in a letter is its recipient(s). Consequently, many Greek subjects are preverbal in hortatory material to signal a switch of attention from *you* to another referent.

In Philemon 6a, for example, attention switches from *you* to ἡ κοινωνία τῆς πίστεώς σου 'the sharing of your faith'. In 19a, the switch is from *you* to ἐγὼ Παῦλος 'I Paul'. In 7b, whose subject is τὰ σπλάγχνα τῶν ἁγίων 'the hearts of the saints', the switch is probably from *you*, too, even though the immediately preceding subject is *I*.[16]

In Philemon 10–13 (passage [2] of 4.1), the repeated relative pronouns establish Onesimus as the centre of attention. This probably explains why Paul places ἐγώ 'I' before the verb in 13a (above); it is to mark the switch of attention to himself.

Even when an overt subject precedes the verb when there is **no** change of subject, it may be present to maintain attention on other than the default centre of attention. This is seen in Philemon 19b (below). Philemon is the default centre of attention in this passage (see 18), but there is a switch of attention to Paul in 19a, which continues into 19b.[17]

---

[14] Dik's template has **P0** instead of **P2**. The concept of focus is discussed in Levinsohn 2015, ch. 4, and in 5.1 of this volume.

[15] Levinsohn (2000:23) discusses why subjects more frequently precede the verb in non-narrative material than in narrative.

[16] The subject also precedes the verb in 14b (see 5.2.1, footnote 8).

[17] When the subject remains the same and precedes the verb, then the proposition makes a **distinct assertion** about the same referent; see 4.3.1 and Levinsohn 2015, 3.2.

A further example with ἐγώ 'I' (20a) can be analysed as involving a switch of subject from that of the immediately preceding clause (19d) or keeping the same subject as the last **comparable** clause (19b).

When a topical subject is seemingly 'redundant', it may highlight the comment about it (8.8).

18 *And if he has wronged you in any way or owes you anything, this charge to my account.*

19a ἐγὼ   Παῦλος   ἔγραψα   τῇ   ἐμῇ   χειρί,
    I   Paul   wrote   with.the my   hand

19b ἐγὼ   ἀποτίσω
    I   I.will.repay

'I, Paul, am writing this with my own hand: I will repay it.'

Now for **subjects that follow the verb**. When a subject follows the verb in a **topic-comment** sentence in Ubunit, attention does **not** switch to that subject. This happens for a couple of related reasons:[18]

- because the centre of attention is **other** than the new subject
- because there is **topic continuity.**

The centre of attention is other than the new subject. This is illustrated below in 1 Thessalonians 4:7. Although there is a change of subject in 7 to *God* (ὁ θεός), attention remains on *us*, including the recipients of the letter (in 8, they are warned of the dangers of rejecting the instruction in 6).

6 *and that in this matter no one should wrong his brother or take advantage of him, since the Lord will punish men for all such sins, as we have already told you and warned you.*

7 οὐ   γὰρ   ἐκάλεσεν   ἡμᾶς   ὁ   θεὸς   ἐπὶ   ἀκαθαρσίᾳ   ἀλλ'   ἐν   ἁγιασμῷ.
   not   for   called   us   the   God   to   impurity   but   in   sanctification

'For God did not call us to be impure, but to live a holy life.'

8 *Therefore, he who rejects this instruction does not reject man but God, who gives you his Holy Spirit.*[19]

Topic continuity. This is illustrated below in 1 Thessalonians 4:3b–4, where *you*, the recipients of the letter, are already the centre of attention. Consequently, the pronominal references to *you* as the subject of 3b and 4 follow the verb:

3a *For this is God's will for you—your sanctification:*

3b ἀπέχεσθαι   ὑμᾶς   ἀπὸ   τῆς   πορνείας,
   to abstain   you   from   the   fornication

4 εἰδέναι   ἕκαστον   ὑμῶν   τὸ   ἑαυτοῦ   σκεῦος   κτᾶσθαι   ἐν   ἁγιασμῷ   καὶ τιμῇ,
   to.know   each one   of you   the   own   vessel   to control   in   sanctification   and honour

'that you should avoid sexual immorality; that each of you should learn to control his own body in a way that is holy and honorable'[20]

The placement of a subject after the verb in Koine Greek in order to maintain continuity of topic is part of a more general pattern that relates to any point of departure. One function of points of departure is to indicate discontinuities of situation, referent or topic. Conversely, the absence of any point

---

[18] The subject may also follow the verb in Greek when it is **not** the topic about which a comment is made (see also 4.4). Such is the case in 1 Corinthians 1:27–28 (e.g. ἀλλὰ τὰ μωρὰ τοῦ κόσμου ἐξελέξατο ὁ θεός 'But it is what is foolish in the world that God chose …'). Verse 26 states that, among those called by God, there are not many wise, powerful or well-born people; vv. 27–28 then contrast such people with those that God has called: the foolish, weak and low-born. These sentences have identificational articulation (2.1), with *God has chosen 'X'* as their presupposition and who 'X' is as their focus.

[19] Colossians 1:23 (cited above) is similar. The preposing of the object pronoun ὑμᾶς 'you' in 21 established the recipients of the letter as the centre of attention. Failure to prepose the reference to Paul in 23 ensures that they remain the centre of attention.

Levinsohn 2000:23–25 discusses postverbal subjects in James 1:9 and 1:11 and Titus 1:12a and 1:15c.

[20] The subject in James 1:7 is also postverbal because of topic continuity (see Levinsohn 2000:23).

of departure often implies continuity of topic, etc. (see Levinsohn 2015, 3.3).[21] I return to this subject at the end of the chapter.

4.3.3 Points of departure in the Kalinga (VS/VO) text

This text uses points of departure to signal switches of theme and of situation. In fact, an exhortation can be preceded by **two** points of departure: one signalling a switch of theme and the other signalling a switch of situation.[22] Sentence 8 (below) illustrates this. The nominalised clause *Sa mi-baga bos* 'What I'm also saying' signals a change of theme, while the conditional clause *nu inggaw-kayu si adayu* 'if you stay far (away)' provides the situation for the following exhortation:

8 <u>Sa</u>   <u>mi-baga</u>   <u>bos</u>   <u>nu</u>   <u>inggaw-kayu</u>   <u>si</u>   <u>adayu</u>,
    what   PASS-tell   also   if   stay-2p.ABS   LOC   far

    adi-kayu   ang-gakagakay   kan   pat   si   barkada.
    NEG-2p.ABS   AG.IMPF-DUR.roam   and   fond.of   OBL   peers

'What I'm also saying is, if you stay far (away), don't be fond of (going out with) your peers.'

Questions

1. What other sentences begin with an NP or nominalised clause to signal a switch of theme?[23]
2. Which are the other sentences in which a conditional clause precedes the main clause to signal a switch of situation?
3. How does the first conditional clause of 20 (*nu awad i-gangput-yu* 'If/When you've finished') anchor what follows to the context?
4. Why does the second conditional clause of 20 (*nu ang-das-kayu 'k kewaal-yu* 'if/provided you find work') follow the main clause?

I now turn to **temporal** expressions in the text. Expressions such as *sillalabi-na* 'sometimes' (7e, 12) and *sinsana* 'nowadays' (14) usually begin a clause or sentence to establish a starting point for what follows. However, the temporal clauses of 3c–d follow the main clause (3b), as they do not provide a starting point for the communication, but rather are part of the communication itself:

---

[21] "If *no* potential point of departure begins a sentence, then the pragmatic effect is often to convey *continuity* with the context" (Levinsohn 2000:14).

[22] Romans 11:30 (discussed at the end of Levinsohn 2015, 3.1) provides a comparable example in Greek.

[23] **Suggested answers**:
1. The other sentences that begin with an NP or nominalised clause to signal a switch of theme are 2 (*Sa um-una* 'The first thing' signals a **switch** from the generic exhortation *you need to do this when you go to school in a far place* (1) to the first specific exhortation *think hard*); 5, 6, 13, 16 and 18.
2. The other sentences in which a conditional clause precedes the main clause to signal a switch of situation are 6 and 16 (following a nominalised clause), 17 (following *Dikayu bos abeng* 'Also, you children'), 21 and possibly 20 (see question 3).
3. The first conditional clause of 20 anchors what follows to the context by **renewing** the situation that is urged on the children in 18 (*the need for you to finish your studies*). This point of departure by renewal is an instance of **resumptive** tail-head linkage (Levinsohn 2015, 3.2.3).
4. The second conditional clause of 20 follows the main clause because it does not provide a starting point for the communication. Rather, it is part of the communication, as it encodes an indirect exhortation.

3b	ka-adu-wan'	e	maka-taktak	si	an-uswila,			
	REC-many-REC	LK	POT-delay	OBL	AG-study			
3c		adi-na	pun	kad	pion	awa	illus-na	iy-enrol
		NEG-3s	NEG	when	want	EXIS	TH.start-3s	TH-enrol
3d		i-kasin-na	bos	ang-ala	'k	osa	'k	courso.
		TH-repeat-3s	also	AG-take	OBL	one	OBL	course

'There are many who are delayed in their studies when they don't like what it is they enrolled in and so take another course.'

4.3.4 Points of departure in the Bariai (SV/VO) text

Subject-initial languages typically use a **spacer** ... or **left-dislocation** to separate the subject from the rest of the sentence and indicate that it is a point of departure.

Left-dislocated points of departure are separated from the rest of the sentence by a **pause** (or a comma, in written material). Typically, a pronominal **trace** of the left-dislocated constituent occurs in its usual position in the clause. (Levinsohn 2015, 3.1)

The Bariai text uses **left-dislocation** to indicate when a subject is also a point of departure. In 1 (below), for instance, *Iaba ga mariuana* 'Banana [beer] and marijuana' is left-dislocated, with the resumptive pronoun *ein* 'this' in its usual position in the clause. In providing a starting point for the communication, this left-dislocated constituent establishes the theme for the text:

1	Iaba	ga	mariuana,	ein	danga	paeamao.	
	banana.sp	&	marijuana	this	thing	bad	('banana.sp' means 'species of banana')

'Banana [beer] and marijuana, this is a bad thing.'

Questions

1. Which other sentences contain left-dislocated constituents? What do they signal?
2. What is the function of the conditional clause that begins 8?
3. What is the function of the conditional clauses that begin 3?
4. What is the function of the conditional clause in 4c?[24]

4.3.5 Points of departure in the Dungra Bhil (SV/OV) text

As noted in 4.3.4, subject-initial languages "typically use a **spacer** ... or **left-dislocation** to separate the subject from the rest of the sentence and indicate that it is a point of departure" (Levinsohn 2015, 3.1). The Dungra Bhil text uses **spacers** to indicate when a subject is also a point of departure.

In 19, for instance, the connective *ga?ʈhehe* 'in contrast' acts as a spacer by separating the subject pronoun *tumi* 'you (plural)' from what follows. The effect is to signal a switch of attention from *a liquor-drinking person* (17) to *you*.

---

[24] **Suggested answers:**
1. The other sentences that contain left-dislocated constituents are 2, 4 and 9 (each of which renews the expository THESIS of 1, to introduce supportive material).
2. The conditional clause that begins 8 signals a switch of situation from that of 7.
3. The conditional clauses that begin 3 mostly renew the point of departure from 2b, to introduce a consequence of not obeying the implied exhortation to *listen to my voice*.
4. The conditional clause in 4c, which renews the situation described in 4b, provides a starting point for what follows (4c). We shall see in 7.7.1 that such repetition highlights 4d.

17 Similarly, <u>in the house of a liquor-drinking person</u> there will never be any peace.
18 Till he dies, all these things will happen like this, but he will not get peace.
19 pe?e   tumi   ga?ʈhehe   ekhũhũ   mahũ?ũ   tuma-ha   ko[j]
    but   2p   in.contrast   someone   person   2p.OBL-ACC   say
    'But <u>as for you</u>, in contrast, someone may tell you …'

Questions

1. In sentence 2 of the Dungra Bhil text (see Appendix D), what device indicates that the subject is also a point of departure? What does the point of departure signal?
2. We noted in 4.1 that parallel progression is found in 10–12. Each sentence begins with the adverbial clause of time *horu pi-t pohõ?õ* 'after drinking liquor'. What type of point of departure is this?[25]

Dungra Bhil does NOT use subordinate clauses of **condition** to provide situational starting points for the following assertions. Instead, imperatives or independent clauses in the future are immediately followed by the assertion. For example (sentences 5 and 13 are similar):

21a ehnoho   to?o   tuma-ho   ko-je
     like.this   that   2p.OBL-ACC   say-FUT
21b tahã   tumi   tijaa   guʈhi   manu-hũ   dʒuve.
     then   2p   3ms.POS   speech   accept-INF   OBLIGATION
     '(If) this is what that person says to you, then you should accept his counsel.'

This section has not discussed a number of occasions in the Dungra Bhil text when a constituent precedes the subject. This is because there is another factor that results in constituents being placed before the subject, especially in SV/OV languages: the Principle of Natural Information Flow. We turn to consideration of this principle in 4.4.

Application to translation

Most languages handle most points of departure in a very similar way (the one major exception being subjects that are also points of departure – see 5.4). This means that a first option in translation is to **render a point of departure as a point of departure**.

Points of departure that do not relate to intersentential progression typically signal a discontinuity in the relevant dimension (see Levinsohn 2015, 3.1). A common error in translation is to **introduce a discontinuity** into the text by means of a point of departure when there was no discontinuity in the source language.

In one OV language, for example, a draft of 1 Thessalonians 4:15a (*For this we say to you by a word of the Lord*) began the clause with "According to Lord's own word". The effect was to introduce a discontinuity with the previous verse. A translation that avoids this pitfall and conforms to the Principle of Natural Information Flow is, "We / to you / according to Lord's own word / this / tell".

Another common error in translations is to **change the primary basis** for relating what follows to the context by starting with the wrong point of departure. For example, *NIV* changes the basis for relating Acts 1:5b to 5a (discussed in 4.3.1) by translating 5b, "but <u>in a few days</u> you will be baptised with the Holy Spirit".

---

[25] **Suggested answers**:
1. In sentence 2 of the Dungra Bhil text, the particle *to* indicates that the subject is also a point of departure. This point of departure signals a switch from the exhortation not to be drinking liquor to the theme of liquor itself.
2. When there is parallel progression between sentences, the second sentence is often anchored to the context by a point of departure involving **renewal** (4.3). Such is the case in 10–12.

Finally, I offer a few comments on what to do with **preverbal subjects** in Koine Greek or Ancient Hebrew when translating into SV languages (those in which the subject almost always precedes the verb). Consider 1 Corinthians 1:12c, where Ἐγὼ μέν εἰμι Παύλου **is literally, 'I on.the.one.hand I.am of.Paul'.**

- In **pro-drop** languages (whether SV/VO or SV/OV), the equivalent of a preverbal subject in the source language is likely to be an independent pronoun (e.g. Spanish **Yo soy de Pablo** 'I I.am of Paul').
- In many **SV/OV** languages, the equivalent of a preverbal subject in the source language is often the combination of a subject and some sort of topic marker (e.g. 'I-TOP Paul.of I.am'). Such is the case in Inga, even though it is a pro-drop language.
- In **SV/VO** languages that are **not pro-drop**, the situation is more complex. The choice facing the translator is often between ignoring the fact that the subject is preverbal in the source language and employing some type of topicalisation.

Thus, English translations of 1 Corinthians 1:12c include "I belong to Paul" (*NRSV*) and "**As for me**, I belong to Paul" (Miller and Martens 1998). How about "I, **for my part**, belong to Paul"? Translations into French, in contrast, typically begin such a sentence with **Moi je** 'Me I'. In yet other languages, "I here" expresses the same idea.

4.4 Constituent order changes and the Principle of Natural Information Flow

The "Principle of Natural Information Flow" (Comrie 1989:127–128) was introduced in 4.2.1 of Levinsohn 2015. When this principle is adhered to, then, to the extent that the syntax of the language permits, the established information in the utterance will precede the nonestablished information. A number of changes from the default order of constituents conform to this principle.

When the Principle of Natural Information Flow is adhered to in an SV/OV language like Dungra Bhil, constituents **other than the verb** that convey established information are presented before those that convey nonestablished information. Clause 9a (below) is an example. The object *tija-ha* 'to him', which conveys established information, is presented before *koɖa* 'no one' and *pojsa* 'money', which convey nonestablished information. As for the relative order of these last two constituents, the subject *koɖa* precedes the object *pojsa*: because the default order is SV/OV:

9a	ESTABLISHED		NONESTABLISHED			
	ono	*tija-ha*	*koɖa*	*pojsa*	*naj*	*ap-e*
	&	3ms.OBL-ACC	no_one	money	NEG	give-FUT

'And no one will give him money'

Thetic sentences present or introduce a new entity or event (2.1). Such sentences often conform to the Principle of Natural Information Flow, with the reference to the new entity or event after any reference to the location.

In sentence 17 of the Dungra Bhil text, for instance, *in the house of a liquor-drinking person*, which conveys established information, occurs before *never any peace*, which presents nonestablished information:

17	ESTABLISHED- - - - - - - - - - - - - - - ->			NONESTABLISHED			
	ihĩkojite	*horu*	*pi-nara-a*	*koʔ-me*	*kedihi*	*sāti*	*naj*	*uve.*
	likewise	liquor	drink-AG-POS	house-in	never	peace	NEG	become

'Similarly, in the house of a liquor-drinking person there will never be any peace.'

James 2:2 provides a Greek example of the same ordering. (If the subject had been the topic of the proposition, it would have preceded the adjunct *into your assembly*):

```
2       ESTABLISHED                              NONESTABLISHED- - - - - - - - - - - - - - - - - - - - - - ->
        ἐὰν γὰρ εἰσέλθῃ εἰς συναγωγὴν ὑμῶν  ἀνὴρ χρυσοδακτύλιος  ἐν  ἐσθῆτι  λαμπρᾷ,
        if  for  enters  into  assembly  your  man  gold-ringed.finger  in  clothing  splendid
```
'For suppose a person with gold rings and in fine clothes enters into your assembly.' OR
'For suppose there enters into your assembly a person with gold rings and in fine clothes.'

As I noted in 4.3.2, the only postverbal subject in the letter to Philemon is found in 23–24. This subject lists the people who join Paul in sending greetings to Philemon, so also conveys nonestablished information:

```
23–24          ESTABLISHED  NONESTABLISHED- - - - - - - - - - - - - - - - - - - - - - - - - - - - - - - - ->
               Ἀσπάζεταί σε    Ἐπαφρᾶς  ὁ  συναιχμάλωτός  μου  ἐν  Χριστῷ  Ἰησοῦ,
               greets  you     Epaphras  the  fellow.prisoner  my  in  Christ  Jesus
```
'Epaphras, my fellow prisoner in Christ Jesus, sends greetings to you.' OR
'Greetings are sent to you by Epaphras, my fellow prisoner in Christ Jesus.'

Application to the language you are analysing

1. Classify the points of departure used in your texts as situational or referential (relating to themes), and as involving a switch of attention or renewal. Then state why each was used.

   Reminder. Connectives (ch. 3) are generally NOT points of departure.

2. Look for clauses and sentences in your texts in which the constituents are in other than what you consider to be default order (including potential points of departure that do not in fact begin a clause or sentence). Mark those that conform to the Principle of Natural Information Flow. (Those that violate the Principle of Natural Information Flow will be considered in the next chapter.)

Application to translation

The Principle of Natural Information Flow operates in many languages, but translators often fail to obey it. In this connection, consider 1 Thessalonians 4:6a in Greek. The norm in Greek is for adjuncts to follow objects. In this clause, however, the adjunct ἐν τῷ πράγματι, which refers to previously established information, precedes the object τὸν ἀδελφὸν αὐτοῦ, which conveys nonestablished information. The clause therefore conforms to the Principle of Natural Information Flow.

```
6a                              ESTABLISHED           NONESTABLISHED
     τὸ μὴ ὑπερβαίνειν καὶ πλεονεκτεῖν ἐν τῷ πράγματι  τὸν ἀδελφὸν αὐτοῦ,
     the not to overstep and to wrong  in the matter   the brother his
```
'and that no one should wrong his brother or take advantage of him in this matter.'

Natural texts in both OV and VO receptor languages represented in recent workshops typically deviated from default constituent order in similar ways to Greek in order to place nonestablished information after established information. Nevertheless, translators of this verse had invariably placed the object before the adjunct in the draft they brought to the workshop. However, as soon as a consultant prompted them to change the order, they agreed that it sounded better that way!

5

Focal and Emphatic Prominence

This chapter applies the principles presented in chapter 4 of Levinsohn 2015 to the hortatory texts that we have been analysing. I begin by reminding the reader how I use the technical terms "focus" and "prominence" (5.1). Section 5.2 concerns violations of the Principle of Natural Information Flow. The Principle may be violated not only in identificational sentences, but also for contrastive or emphatic prominence (as defined below), and through the preposing of a foil (a constituent that serves to set off a later constituent to advantage by contrast). Other devices that give prominence to a focal constituent include the postposing or isolation of the dominant focal element (DFE – Heimerdinger 1999:167; Levinsohn 2015, 4.2.4) and the use of prominence markers (5.3–5.4). Section 5.5 concerns devices that give prominence to only part of a constituent. Section 5.6 briefly looks at markers of emphasis in the texts we have been using.

5.1 Two technical terms: focus and prominence

The chapter is particularly concerned with **focus**, where the focus of an utterance is defined as "that part which indicates what the speaker intends as the most important ... change to be made in the hearer's [reader's] mental representation" (DFE – Heimerdinger 1999:167; Dooley and Levinsohn 2001:62). Such a change is usually brought about by the presentation in the utterance of **nonestablished** information.

Every utterance has a focus, whatever its articulation. I illustrate this from the examples I cited to illustrate sentence articulations in 2.1.

- In an utterance with **topic-comment** articulation, the focus is usually all the information in the comment that has not already been established in the hearer's mental representation. Consider clause 3b of the Dungra Bhil text, together with its context (3a):

3a *Look at the eyes of a liquor-drinking person;*

3b TOPIC - - - - - - - >   COMMENT - - - - - - - - - - - - - >

    tijaa   *ḍua* / *ekdom*   *rata rata*   *dekh-a.*

    3ms.POS   eye.OBL   complete   red red   see-PASS

    'his eyes   appear completely red.'

In 3a, no reference is made to the eyes of a liquor-drinking person appearing completely red, so the comment about the topic *his eyes* only contains nonestablished information. This means that the focus of 3b is all the information in the comment: *appear completely red*.

- In an utterance with **identificational** articulation, the focus is the element of nonestablished information that is being sought or supplied. 1 Corinthians 1:13b has a presupposition that, except for one element, is assumed to be known ([someone] *was crucified for you*). The focus is the element that was lacking in the presupposed proposition (who the someone was – or wasn't, in this case).[1]

13b		FOCUS	PRESUPPOSITION--------->		
	μὴ	Παῦλος	ἐσταυρώθη	ὑπὲρ	ὑμῶν,
	[surely].not	Paul	was.crucified	for	you.PL

'Was **Paul** crucified for you?' (expected answer: No!)

- In an utterance with **thetic** articulation, the focus is the entity or event that is being presented. In sentence 17 of the Dungra Bhil text, the proposition presents or introduces a new event (the absence of *peace*) into the text:

17					FOCUS ----->			
ihĭkojite	*horu*	*pi-nara-a*	*koʔ-me*	*kedihi*	*sāti*	*naj*	*uve.*
likewise	liquor	drink-AG-POS	house-in	never	peace	NEG	become

'Similarly, in the house of a liquor-drinking person, there will never be any peace.'

Remember: focus is NOT the same as (propositional) topic.
- A propositional topic CANNOT be focal.
- A point of departure CANNOT be focal.

This is because points of departure and propositional topics provide STARTING POINTS for the utterance and relate to what has already been **established** in the hearer's mental representation. In contrast, focus concerns information that has **not** previously been established or that needs to be **re**-established.

Topic	correlates with	established
Focus	correlates with	not established

Another technical term introduced in chapter 4 of Levinsohn 2015 was **prominence**. This is a general term for "any device whatever which gives certain events, participants, or objects more significance than others in the same context" (Callow 1974:50).

I follow Callow in distinguishing focal and thematic prominence:[2]
- **focal** prominence (some device is used to give prominence to a focal constituent – 4.3)
- **thematic** prominence (prominence is given to "what I'm talking about" – 4.6).[3]

For example, a **focal** constituent can be given prominence. Compare the following utterances (based on 1 Thessalonians 5:7b). In both, *at night* is focal. However, prominence is given to *at night* in the English of (b) by the employment of a "cleft" construction:[4]

(a) *Drunkards get drunk at night.*

(b) *It is **at night** that drunkards get drunk.*

---

[1] Bolding is used in the examples to indicate that a focal constituent has been given extra prominence (see below).
[2] For Callow, **emphatic** prominence (to express strong feelings about an item or to indicate that what follows is unexpected) is a separate category from focal or thematic prominence. Since both focal and thematic constituents may be emphasised, though, I prefer to think of emphasis proper as a reason for giving prominence to a constituent.
[3] Thematic prominence is discussed in chapter 6.
[4] Crystal (1997:63) defines a cleft sentence as "a CONSTRUCTION where a single CLAUSE has been divided into two separate sections, each with its own VERB".

Similarly, in both of the following Greek utterances, νυκτὸς 'by night' is focal. However, prominence is given to νυκτὸς in the Greek of (d) by preposing it:

(c) οἱ   μεθυσκόμενοι   μεθύουσιν   νυκτὸς
the   ones being drunk   are drunk   by night

(d) οἱ   μεθυσκόμενοι   **νυκτὸς**   μεθύουσιν
the   ones being drunk   by night   are drunk

If you are not familiar with the concepts of topic, focus and prominence, then please read sections 4.1–4.5 of Levinsohn 2015 before continuing with this chapter.

5.2 Violating the Principle of Natural Information Flow

In 4.4, we noted the tendency in some languages for the order of constituents in a topic-comment utterance to conform to the Principle of Natural Information Flow by placing the established information in the utterance before the nonestablished focal information. However, most, if not all, languages violate the Principle under certain circumstances by presenting the less established information before the more established information.

Many languages (including English) violate the Principle as a matter of course in **identificational** sentences (Kiss 1998:271). 1 Corinthians 1:13b (cited in 5.1) provides a Greek example.

Other languages violate the Principle to give focal prominence to the preposed element in additional circumstances.[5] Most commonly, such violations are for **contrastive** or **emphatic** prominence (Levinsohn 2015, 4.2.3). However, the Principle is also violated by **foils** for later contrasting constituents and by the preposing of **cataphoric demonstratives**. In 5.1, versions (b) and (d) of 1 Thessalonians 5:7b illustrate this effect (νυκτὸς 'by night' is a foil for ἡμέρας 'of day' – 5:8).

The following sections discuss reasons for violating the Principle of Natural Information Flow in three of the languages we have been considering.[6]

5.2.1 Violations of the Principle of Natural Information Flow in the Greek of Philemon

Focal constituents may be preposed in Greek, thus violating the Principle of Natural Information Flow, for contrastive or emphatic prominence or, through the preposing of a foil or cataphoric demonstrative, to give prominence to a later constituent. I illustrate each of these in turn.

Contrastive prominence

A clear example of the preposing of a focal constituent for **contrastive** prominence is found in Philemon 15b, where αἰώνιον 'eternally' contrasts with πρὸς ὥραν 'for an hour' (15a):

15a   *Perhaps this is the reason he was separated from you for a while,*

15b   ἵνα   **αἰώνιον**   αὐτὸν   ἀπέχῃς,
       that   eternally   him   you.might.have
       'so that you might have him back forever,'

See also Philemon 9a (διὰ τὴν ἀγάπην 'on the basis of love' probably contrasts with πολλὴν ἐν Χριστῷ παρρησίαν 'much boldness in Christ' – 8a; see below), 13b (πρὸς ἐμαυτόν 'with myself' contrasts with σοι 'to you' – 12a), 13c (ὑπὲρ σοῦ 'in your place' partially contrasts with πρὸς ἐμαυτόν 'with myself' – 13b) and 19d (καὶ σεαυτόν 'even your own self' contrasts with the τι 'anything' that Onesimus owes Philemon – 18a).

---

[5] I originally read this claim in Werth (1984), but have not been able to locate his book in recent years.
[6] Although the Principle of Natural Information Flow may be violated in Bariai in order to give prominence to focal constituents, no example occurs in the text we have been using.

Emphatic prominence

Emphasis proper involves expressing strong feelings about an item or indicating that what follows is unexpected (Callow 1974:52). A clear example of the preposing of a focal constituent for emphatic prominence is found in Philemon 21d, as the use of *even* in the translation into English indicates. Paul is confident that Philemon will do as he asks, yet he knows that, contrary to expectation, Philemon will do even more than that:

21a–b   *Confident of your obedience, I am writing to you,*
21c–d   εἰδὼς   ὅτι   **καὶ**   **ὑπὲρ**   ἃ   λέγω   ποιήσεις.
          knowing   that   ADD   above   what   I.say   you.will.do

'knowing that you will do even more than I say.'

The following appear also to be instances of preposing for emphatic prominence:

- ἐνεργής 'effective, active' (Philemon 6b), following the preverbal subject *the fellowship/sharing of your faith*. Following one interpretation of this verse, Paul wants Philemon to demonstrate *the fellowship of the faith* in an effective way by welcoming Onesimus as he would welcome Paul (17).
- χαρὰν πολλήν 'much joy' (Philemon 7b). Paul emphasises the extent of his joy.[7]
- χωρὶς τῆς σῆς γνώμης 'without your consent' (Philemon 14a). As the rest of 14 shows, it is important to Paul that he have Philemon's consent.
- ἐμοί 'to me' (Philemon 18b). One would not expect Onesimus' debt to Philemon to be charged to Paul.

Foils

The concept of a **counterpoint** was discussed in 3.3: an idea or *proposition* that serves to set off the THESIS proposition by contrast. It is common for the order of constituents within a counterpoint to be marked, so that one of its constituents is prominent. Such a constituent is often a **foil** for a later constituent.

"The *OED* defines a foil as 'anything that serves to set off another thing distinctly or to advantage by contrast'. The concept of a foil is useful for explaining some unusual intonation patterns and otherwise unexplained instances of prominence" (Levinsohn 2015, 4.8).

In Philemon 14b, for instance, the focal constituent ὡς κατὰ ἀνάγκην 'as according to necessity' is preposed in order to set off κατὰ ἑκούσιον 'according to willingness' to advantage by contrast (14a had already emphasised the importance of Philemon giving his consent – see above):[8]

14a   *but I preferred to do nothing without your consent,*
14b   ἵνα   μὴ   **ὡς**   **κατὰ**   **ἀνάγκην**   τὸ   ἀγαθόν   σου   ᾖ
        that   not   as   according.to   necessity   the   goodness   your   might be
14c   ἀλλὰ   κατὰ   ἑκούσιον.
              but   according.to   willingness

'in order that your good deed might not be something forced but voluntary.'

See also Philemon 8a (πολλὴν ἐν Χριστῷ παρρησίαν 'much boldness/confidence in Christ'). Giving prominence to the "ample authority" that Paul has "in Christ to command Philemon to do what should be done" (Banker 1999) sets off διὰ τὴν ἀγάπην 'on the basis of love' (9a) to advantage by contrast.

---

[7] When a coordinative constituent is given focal prominence, it is normal for the first part to precede the verb and the second part to follow it (Levinsohn 2000:57–58). In 7b, χαρὰν πολλήν 'much joy' precedes the verb, whereas καὶ παράκλησιν 'and encouragement' follows it.

[8] When a focal constituent is preposed in Koine Greek, it is quite common for a constituent conveying established information to precede the verb, as well (in this case, τὸ ἀγαθόν 'your goodness'). This ordering seems to make the violation of the Principle of Natural Information Flow more explicit and thus increases the prominence given to the focal constituent (Levinsohn 2015, 4.5).

Remember:
- A **foil** is a *constituent* that serves to set off a later *constituent* to advantage by contrast.
- A **counterpoint** is an idea or *proposition* that serves to set off the THESIS *proposition* by contrast.

Cataphoric demonstratives

Cataphoric demonstratives are similar to foils in that they are not important in themselves, but point forward to their referent. When preposed, they give prominence to the material to which they refer.

In Philemon 15a, for instance, "The use of διὰ τοῦτο 'because of this, for this purpose' and its forefronting before the verb show that it is marking the ἵνα purpose clause (15b) as prominent" (Banker 1999).

15a	τάχα	γὰρ	διὰ	τοῦτο	ἐχωρίσθη	πρὸς	ὥραν,
	perhaps	for	because.of	this	he.was.separated	for	hour
15b	ἵνα	αἰώνιον	αὐτὸν	ἀπέχῃς,			
	that	eternally	him	you.might.have			

'Perhaps this is the reason he was separated from you for a while, so that you might have him back forever,'

Residue

Section 4.5 of Levinsohn 2015 points out that, when a language has the option of preposing focal constituents, this means that both focal constituents and points of departure can occur at the beginning of the sentence. Please review that section, as it suggests how to distinguish them.

Philemon 22c begins with the preposed constituent διὰ τῶν προσευχῶν ὑμῶν 'through your prayers' Because no previous reference has been made in the letter to *your prayers*, this constituent could be judged to be nonestablished information and, therefore, focal. The sense would then be, *I am hoping to be restored to you **through your prayers***. However, 22b–c support the exhortation to *prepare a guest room for me* (22a), so the focus of 22b is more likely to be on *to be restored to you*. Paul may well have assumed that Philemon would be praying for him, in which case *through your prayers* could be a point of departure for the rest of 22c; hence, the translation *I am hoping <u>through your prayers</u> to be restored to you.*

5.2.2 Violations of the Principle of Natural Information Flow in Kalinga (VS/VO)

Kalinga is like Koine Greek in that focal constituents may be preposed for contrastive or focal prominence. In addition, a foil may be preposed in order to give prominence to a later contrasting constituent. Unfortunately, there are no clear examples of such preposing in the text we are using.

The following is part of a hortatory text in Sama Bangingih, which is also a N.W. Austronesian language of the Philippines. The bolded constituent in part a is the **foil** for the bolded constituent in part b:[9]

a	*pimpom,*	*in*	*pagpangadjih*	*atawa*	*anuntut*	*ilmuh,*	
	Pimpom	TM	education	or	seek	knowledge	
	dumain	***sadja***	*da*	*allaw*	*atawa*	***dambulan***	*ya*	*ni-itung;*
	not-so	only	one	day	or	one-month	DEM	PASS-count
b	*malaingkan*	***tahun***					*ya*	*ni-itung*
	rather	year					DEM	PASS-count

'Pimpom, when getting an education or seeking knowledge, it will not be just one **day or one month** that is counted. Rather, (it is) **years** that will be counted.'

---

[9] This text was given to JoAnn Gault (p.c.) by Mr. Binsalih Barhama. TM is the thematic prominence marker (see 6.2).

Question

In sentence 1 of the Kalinga text, what is the effect of placing *annaya* 'this' before the verb?[10]

5.2.3 Violations of the Principle of Natural Information Flow in Dungra Bhil (SV/OV)

Many OV languages can choose to arrange the constituents of a clause or sentence other than the verb either to conform to the Principle of Natural Information Flow or to violate it. Section 4.4 cited instances from the Dungra Bhil text which conformed to the Principle. The text also contains instances in which the Principle was violated.

For example, the constituents that follow the subject in 5a violate the Principle of Natural Information Flow because nonestablished information precedes established information:[11]

5a		NONESTABLISHED		ESTABLISHED	
	tuʔu	*ek*	*vaʔa*	*horu*	*pit-neje,*
	3ms	one	time	liquor	drink-COMP

'(if) he liquor-drinks all at one go'

Question

In 5a (above), **why** does the author violate the Principle of Natural Information Flow?[12]

Clause 3a (below) also violates the Principle of Natural Information Flow. Although the author has introduced the theme of drinking liquor, he has not previously referred to the eyes of a liquor-drinker, so the initial constituent *horu pi-nara mahõ-õ ḍua* 'the eyes of a liquor-drinker' contains nonestablished information. This constituent precedes the subject *tumi* 'you', which is established information (clause 4 is similar):

3a			NONESTABLISHED		ESTABLISHED	
	horu	*pi-nara*	*mahõ-õ*	*ḍua*	*tumi*	*pala,*
	liquor	drink-AG	man-POS	eye.OBL	2p	see.IMP

'Look at the eyes of a liquor-drinking person; (3b) his eyes look completely red.'

Question

In 3a (above), **why** does the author violate the Principle of Natural Information Flow?[13]

When Dungra Bhil wishes to gives prominence to a **complex** focal constituent, the constituent is **left-dislocated** (4.3.4–5). Typically, it is followed immediately by a proximal demonstrative adverb with the same referent.[14]

Sentence 9 provides an example. The left-dislocated reported speech *tuʔu daruṛju hoje* 'he's a drunkard' conveys nonestablished information (the hearer did not previously know what people would

---

[10] **Suggested answer** for the Kalinga text: *Annaya* 'this' is a cataphoric demonstrative placed before the verb in order to give prominence to the exhortations that follow.

[11] The combination *horu pit-* may be an instance of **noun incorporation**, which is why I translate it 'liquor-drinking'. Noun incorporation typically involves the incorporation into the verb or VP of an **indefinite** object, in order to designate an "institutionalized activity" (Mithun 1984:848).

[12] **Suggested answer** for the Dungra Bhil text: The author violates the Principle of Natural Information Flow in 5a to **emphasise** *ek vaʔa* [one time] 'all at one go'.

[13] **Suggested answer** for the Dungra Bhil text: The author probably violates the Principle of Natural Information Flow in 3a to direct the hearers' attention **specifically** to *ḍua* 'eyes'. *His eyes* becomes the topic of 3b (an instance of sequential progression – 4.1).

[14] Hindi [hin] is among other Indo-Aryan languages that also left-dislocate complex focal constituents. Section 6.4 discusses the functions of the different demonstratives in Dungra Bhil.

say) and is followed by *ehnoho* 'like these'. The effect is to give focal prominence to the reported speech (19–21 is the same):

9a *And no one will give him money*

9b–c *kihĩke [tuʔu daruṛju hoje]:* **ehnoho** *maʔhe tija-ha ko-je.*
because 3ms drunkard be like.this people 3ms.OBL-ACC say-FUT

'because "You're a drunkard": **that's** what people will say to him.'

Question

In 9b (above), **why** does the author violate the Principle of Natural Information Flow?[15]

See also 12 (the left-dislocated thought *ekhahũ maʔi ṭak-unoʔo naj tahã suri koʔ-unoʔo* 'killing someone or stealing something') is followed (though not immediately) by *ehnana* 'like these'.

Application to the language you are analysing

1   Look for examples in your texts in which the Principle of Natural Information Flow has been violated. For each example, suggest why the constituent concerned has been preposed (e.g. for identificational focus, contrastive prominence, emphatic prominence, to set up a foil for a later contrasting constituent).

2. If the language has the option of preposing focal constituents and you are uncertain whether certain prenuclear constituents in your texts are points of departure or focal, use the pointers of Levinsohn 2015, 4.5 to determine the function of each.

5.3 Postposing or isolating the DFE

As section 4.3 of Levinsohn 2015 indicates, preposing is not the only way that a focal constituent can be given prominence. The postposing of certain constituents or, especially in Bantu languages, the isolation at the end of the sentence of the dominant focal element (DFE – Levinsohn 2015, 4.2.4) is another way of giving prominence to a focal constituent.

Consider the **verb** in Koine Greek, for example. Because the verb often begins a clause or sentence, Greek postposes it to give it prominence (even though the resulting order conforms to the Principle of Natural Information Flow). In 1 Thessalonians 4:11d, for instance, the verb παρηγγείλαμεν 'we charged' is focal and has been postposed to give it prominence:[16]

11d καθὼς ὑμῖν **παρηγγείλαμεν**,
even as you we charged

'just as we **told** you,'

Suri [suq] (SV/VO) (Nilo-Saharan, Ethiopia) is similar. Although the verb normally precedes the object, it is postposed for focal prominence:

ŋa-lɔk-tonu tamaratɔ wo.
DEM-situation-that 2p.refuse EMP

'**Reject** that situation!'

---

[15] **Suggested answer** for the Dungra Bhil text: The author violates the Principle of Natural Information Flow in 9b to **emphasise** (express strong feelings) about what people will say.

[16] If a Greek clause consists of only two constituents and the verb is at the end, this can be for two reasons:
- the verb has been postposed to give it focal prominence, *or*
- the other constituent has been preposed, either to provide a point of departure or for focal prominence.

See Levinsohn 2000:40ff. for discussion of this problem.

Now consider the following sentence in Makonde [mde] (SV/VO).[17] The author's father and two other family members have died. The elders met to decide what to do and concluded:

mkubidi	*matanga*	*tundatenda*	*mwaka*	*wowo*	*au.*
it.is.necessary	ceremonies	we.will.do	year	same	this

'We must perform the final funeral ceremonies **before the end of this year**.'

The default position of the object *matanga* 'ceremonies' is after the verb. To give extra prominence to 'before the end of this year', the object is preposed, leaving *mwaka wowo au*, the DFE, isolated at the end of the sentence.

Application to the language you are analysing

1. Look for examples in your texts in which a constituent has been postposed from its normal position. For each example, suggest why the constituent has been postposed.
2. Look for instances in your texts in which a constituent of the comment has been preposed from its normal position in order to leave the DFE isolated at the end of the sentence.

5.4 Other devices used to give prominence to a focal constituent

Sections 5.2 and 5.3 have described the use of marked constituent orders to give prominence to a focal constituent. Other devices that give prominence to a focal constituent include "**spacers** which separate the focal constituent from the rest of the proposition", often resulting in cleft sentences, and dedicated **prominence markers** (a "characteristic **affixation** or a **particle** associated with either the focal constituent or the verb") (Levinsohn 2015, 4.3, 4.9).

Spacers and cleft sentences

Section 5.2.4 of Levinsohn 2015 points out that the same spacer may be used not only to separate the subject from the rest of the sentence and indicate that it is a point of departure (4.3.4), but also to separate the focal constituent from the rest of the proposition. To illustrate this, consider sentences 2 and 32a of the Dungra Bhil text:

1   *Oh, my children, you should not drink liquor.*

2   ESTABLISHED   NONESTABLISHED - - - - - >

horu	*to*	*ek*	*dʒer*	*hudu*	*hoje.*
liquor	SPACER	one	poison	like	be

'Liquor is like a poison.'

31   *If you don't do any work in the fields in these days for working, what will there be for us to eat?*

32a   FOCUS   PRESUPPOSITION - - - - - - - - - - - - - >

	apũ	*to-me*		*phuko*	*moj*	*dʒa-hũ*
	1in	SPACER-?		hunger.OBL	die	go-be.1p.FUT
32b	*ono*	*apũ-ũ*	*pujre*	*bi*	*phuko*	*moj*	*dʒa-je.*
	&	1in-POS	children	also	hunger.OBL	die	go-FUT

'Not only will **we** die from hunger, but **our children also** will die from hunger.'

In 2, *to* separates the subject from the rest of the proposition and indicates that it is a point of departure. It is preceded by established information and followed by nonestablished information.

---
[17] This sentence is part of an account given to Benjie and Rhoda Leach by Pius Aldeia Ntushi in November 2003.

5.4 Other devices used to give prominence to a focal constituent

In contrast, all the information in 32a was established in 31, and *to* separates the focal constituent (the foil for 'our children' in 32b) from the rest of the proposition.

In the following extract from a Bhatri [bgw] text (an Indo-Aryan SV/OV language related to Dungra Bhil), the focal material, separated from the rest of the sentence by same spacer *ţo,* is a subordinate clause:

1–3 *I hear that you have been caught. I had told you to remember my words. Why did you not obey my words?*

4	mor	goţ	ke	na	sunlis	gunuk	ţo	ţoke	dʌri	nelaj.
	my	words	ACC	not	you.listen	because	SPACER	you.ACC	catch	took.3p

'It is **because you did not listen to my words** that they caught you.'

Section 4.9 of Levinsohn 2015 discussed types of "*it*-cleft" structures in English (the translation into English of Bhatri sentence 4 is an *it*-cleft). In English cleft sentences, a relative pronoun (*that, who*) acts as a spacer to separate the focal material from the rest of the sentence.

You should now reread section 4.9 of Levinsohn 2015, as it shows that focal material may either precede or follow the relative pronoun (spacer).

Some languages move the **vocative** from its default position and use it as a spacer to give prominence to what follows. In Koine Greek, the noninitial position of a vocative such as ἀδελφοί 'brothers' may identify what follows as "an important new idea" (Ellingworth and Nida 1976:19, commenting on 1 Thessalonians 2:1).[18]

The following example is from Kambaata (SV/OV). The author has warned his children, *be really careful, since there are lots of ways in this world that lead people astray.* He then tells them:

Every holy day go to church and pray,

luus-a	woqq-eechchi	ɱagan-o	baraar-inne.	
mistake-GEN	way-ABL*	God-Oh	survive-us	(*ABL = ablative)

'From going astray, O God, **deliver** us'

Dedicated prominence markers

In many languages, the association of certain particles or affixes with a constituent always gives prominence to that constituent.[19] One such marker in Dungra Bhil and Bhatri is the exclusive suffix *-dʒ(e)/-tʃi* (sometimes translated 'only, just'). This marker is used to give prominence to focal constituents, whether or not they have been preposed.

In sentence 18 of the Dungra Bhil text, for example, *-dʒ* is attached to a focal constituent in a topic-comment sentence that conforms to the Principle of Natural Information Flow:

18	moj	dʒaj	taʔhũ	dʒãʔa	iʔi	akho	ehnoho-**dʒ**	uve
	die	go.FUT	then	till	these	all	like.this-EXC	become

'Till he dies, all these things will happen **just like this**,'

In the following extract from the same Bhatri text, in contrast, *-tʃi* is attached to a focal constituent that has been preposed for contrastive prominence:

---

[18] See also 1 Thessalonians 2:14a (cited in 5.5 and 7.7). Vocatives are also used to mark the beginning of a new unit (8.9).

[19] König (1991) talks of "focus particles". However, many such particles give prominence not only to focal constituents, but also to thematic material such as points of departure and connectives (see Levinsohn 2015, 4.6).

12 ṭor-tʃi   lagi   ʌsʌb   hojla.
    your-EXC   reason   like.this   became
    'It is because of **you** that this happened.'

Other constructions

Reduplication is one of the ways that contrastive prominence is given to a focal constituent in Yemba [ybb] (SV/VO). In the following sentences, *work together* contrasts with *by himself*. This contrast is given prominence by the habitual *be* verb *gó* and the reduplication of the verb for *work together*:

a   *No one creates a village by himself.*
b   Mɛ́   gɔ   **mbō**   **epo**   nkwɛ́tɛ́   alá'
    one   be   SS.work.together   work.together   SS.attach   village
    'It is **by working together** that one creates a village.'

Before the following Yemba sentences with **identificational** articulation, the speaker has been insisting that it is not the ancestors who will drink the wine that is being offered. The presupposition is that someone will drink it; the focus is on who (we). This focal constituent is followed by *mé*.

Sentence 1 is the default way of marking a focal subject in an utterance with identificational articulation (Harro and Haynes 2002:22):

1   Ḿpɛ   mé   nnú'
    1in   FOC   drink
    'It is **we** who will drink it.'

Sentence 2 illustrates a marked way of presenting the same information. In this structure, the presupposition is presented as the goal of the verb *gʉɔ* 'go'. This construction does not imply that we will be going anywhere to drink the wine. Rather, it is a stronger way of implying that we, rather than the ancestors, will be the ones drinking it (Gnintedem Jean-Claude p.c.):[20]

2   Ḿpɛ   meà   **gʉɔ**   gʉɔ   nnú'
    1in   FOC   go   to   drink
    'It is **we** who will be the ones drinking it.'

Application to the language you are analysing

1. Look in your texts for any instances in which a spacer separates a focal constituent from the rest of the proposition. Check whether the focal constituent always occurs before the spacer, or whether it can also follow the spacer.
2. Look for any particles or affixes that always give prominence to the constituent with which they are associated. If there is more than one such marker, then distinguish their functions.

5.5 Giving prominence to part of a constituent

I am aware of four devices that languages use to give prominence to part of a constituent:
• using an apparently 'redundant' relative clause
• using a prominence marker

---

[20] Other ways of giving contrastive prominence to a focal constituent in Yemba include tone perturbation and the placement of a focal auxiliary to give prominence to the immediately following verb.

- splitting the constituent
- topicalising the nonfocal part of the constituent.

I discuss these devices in turn.

Using a relative clause or similar construction

When a language has the option of modifying a noun directly or by means of a relative clause, then one of the reasons for using the relative clause is in order to give prominence to the modifier, rather than the phrase as a whole.

To say *your jerrycan* in Me'en [mym] (SV/VO), for example, the possessive may be placed directly after the noun: *jarikani denu* 'jerrycan of.you'. To give contrastive prominence to *your* (**your** *jerrycan* as distinct from mine), a relative clause is used: *jarikani de denuo* 'jerrycan REL of.you-SUBORDINATOR' (where *de* is a relative clause marker and *-o* is a subordinator).[21]

Application to the Kalinga text

In sentence 17, the vocative has the form *ðikayu abeng* 'you children'.
In 13 and 21, in contrast, it has the form *ðikayu e bubai* 'you girls' (where *e* is a linker). Why is the linker used in 13 and 21, but not in 17?[22]

Using a prominence marker

Another way of giving prominence to part of a constituent is to associate a prominence marker with the part of the constituent that is prominent. In English, for example, the emphatic particle **even** can precede a modifying adjective to give it prominence, as in "**Even** some **older** people attended the school children's demonstration". See also "**Only three** demonstrators were arrested".

Application to the Kalinga text

In sentence 13, what two devices are used to give prominence to *importante* 'important' in the constituent *ʃa importante pagay e mibaga* [the important really LINKER TH-tell] 'The really important thing I'm saying'?[23]

Splitting a constituent

"A phrase is considered to be discontinuous [split] … when it consists of more than one word but the words are *not contiguous* because another constituent occurs between them" (Levinsohn 2000:57).

The following is an example from Sangil [snl], a N.W. Austronesian language of the Philippines related to Kalinga. The limiter *méntì* 'only' usually precedes the verb (e.g. *tataw kapang méntì ni-tallimà* 'three groups only were received'). To give contrastive prominence to *tataw* 'three', *méntì* separates the number from the head noun:[24]

There were 73 groups of people who were very religious and worshipped God;

gaydé	**tataw**	**méntì**	**kapang**	nitaŕimà	u	Mavu	nkasù	su	soŕogà.
however	three	only	group	be.received	by	God	enter	into	paradise

'however, **only three of the groups** were received by God, enabling them to enter Paradise.'

---

[21] I am grateful to Achim Diehl (p.c.) for providing me with this example.

[22] **Suggested answer** for the Kalinga text: The linker *e* is used in 13 and 21 to give prominence to *bubai* 'girls'. In 17, in contrast, no special prominence is to be given to one part of the vocative rather than another, so no linker is used.

[23] **Suggested answer** for the Kalinga text: The two devices used to give prominence to *importante* 'important' are the linker *e* and the prominence marker *pagay* 'really'.

[24] I am grateful to Don and Brenda Scheller (p.c.) for providing me with this example. Verb affixes are not indicated.

It is common in **Koine Greek** for a constituent to be split in order to give prominence to just part of it.²⁵ Constituents "may be discontinuous [split] because only the *first* or preposed part is in focus, whereas the remainder is supportive" and/or "because only the second part relates to what follows" (Levinsohn 2000:57).

1 Timothy 4:6b includes a split constituent in which "only the *first* or preposed part is in focus". Timothy is already a *servant of Christ Jesus*. Separating the adjective καλός 'good' from the rest of the constituent gives prominence to good, rather than the whole constituent:

6a *If you put these things before the brothers*

6b **καλὸς** ἔσῃ   διάκονος Χριστοῦ   Ἰησοῦ,
    good   you will be servant   of Christ Jesus

'you will be a **good** servant of Christ Jesus'

1 Thessalonians 2:14a includes a split constituent of which "only the second part relates to what follows". *You became imitators* has already been stated in 1:6. In contrast, the second part of the constituent activates *the churches of God in Judea*, which leads to the condemnation of the Jews in 15–16:²⁶

14a ὑμεῖς γὰρ **μιμηταὶ** ἐγενήθητε, ἀδελφοί, **τῶν** **ἐκκλησιῶν** **τοῦ** **θεοῦ** **τῶν**
     you   for imitators   became   brothers of the   churches   of the   God   of the

     οὐσῶν   ἐν   τῇ   Ἰουδαίᾳ
     being   in   the   Judea

'For you became **imitators**, brothers, **of God's churches in Judea**'

14b *in that* (ὅτι) *you suffered from your own countrymen the same things those churches suffered from the Jews,*

Topicalising the nonfocal part of the constituent

In a hunting text in Awara [awx] (SV/OV), the hunters were looking for wallabies. To give prominence to the number that were caught, the author topicalised *wallaby* by adding the marker *–u*. This allowed the focus to be on *five*, rather than *five wallabies*:²⁷

P-ä-ke   ku-na   meläm-u   homu-tä   paipela yä-ha-kut.
po-take-SS.PF   go-1p.SR wallaby-TOP   dog-by   five   3po-bit-3s.PAST

'We took them (the dogs) and went, and a dog killed **five** wallabies.'

Application to the language you are analysing

Look in your texts for devices that are used to give prominence to only part of a constituent.

Application to translation

The above sections have noted that, because Koine Greek is a VS/VO language, the preposing of part or all of a constituent is a particularly common device for giving focal prominence to part or all of that constituent. The language you are analysing also has devices for giving contrastive or emphatic prominence to part or all of a constituent. However, unless you are also analysing a VS/VO language, it

---

²⁵ Focal constituents may also be split in Greek when they are coordinative (see 5.2.1 for discussion of Philemon 7b).

²⁶ The position of the vocative ἀδελφοί 'brothers' before this second part also identifies what follows as "an important new idea" (Ellingworth and Nida 1976:19) (see 5.4).

²⁷ I am grateful to Susan Quigley (p.c.) for providing me with this example (SR: switch-reference marker; SS: same subject marker).

is unlikely that simple preposing will be as frequent as in Greek. Note, for instance, the frequency with which left-dislocation occurred in the Dungra Bhil text, rather than simple preposing. Furthermore, simple preposing may not even have the same effect in the language you are analysing as in Greek.

So, your challenge is to identify the devices that the language you are analysing uses naturally to give prominence to part or all of a constituent, and then to use the one that will have the same **effect** as the device used in the Greek text.

5.6 Markers of emphasis

First, a reminder that the term **emphasis** is not used in this course as a synonym for prominence (see the introduction to this chapter). Rather, emphatic prominence "normally involves the speaker-hearer relationship in some way" (Callow 1974:52); the speaker feels strongly about something or considers that an event is unexpected. Emphatic prominence may be given to a constituent of a sentence or to a whole sentence.

You should now reread section 4.7 of Levinsohn 2015, which gives examples of markers of emphasis from a number of languages.

We have already seen that one way of conveying emphatic prominence in both Koine Greek and Dungra Bhil is by violating the Principle of Natural Information Flow (5.2.1, 5.2.3). We now note some other markers of emphasis in the texts we have been using.

Application to the Kalinga text

Does glossing *ay* EMP: marker of emphasis (1, 13a, 13b, 14b, 21b) describe its function correctly?[28]

Application to the Bariai text

Which adverb is used to emphasise a following assertion?[29]

Application to the Dungra Bhil text

Look for three devices mentioned in 4.7 of Levinsohn 2015 that are used in the first few sentences of this text for emphasis (other than changes of constituent order).[30]

Application to the language you are analysing

List the devices used in your texts for **emphatic** prominence. Which ones emphasise a focal constituent? A nonfocal constituent? A hortatory or expository THESIS?

---

[28] **Suggested answer** for the Kalinga text: *ay* does seem to be used in this text to indicate that "the speaker feels strongly about something". In 1, its attachment to the cataphoric demonstrative *annaya* 'this' suggests that the speaker feels strongly about the following exhortations (see also its use in 13a). In 13b and 21b, it emphasises the relevance of the utterances to the female addressees. In 14b, it shows how the speaker feels about the assertion *you children do whatever you want* (hence the use of *just*). It does, therefore, seem to be a marker of emphasis.

[29] **Suggested answer** for the Bariai text: The adverb *tautaunga* 'truly' is used in 2a and 4a to emphasise the following assertion.

[30] **Suggested answer** for the Dungra Bhil text: The following devices mentioned in 4.7 of Levinsohn 2015 are used in the first few sentences of this text for emphasis: the inclusive adverb *ekdom* 'complete(ly)' (3b), repetition (*rata rata* 'red red' – 3b) and a rhetorical question (7). The interjection *o* 'oh' (1) is probably a marker of emphasis, too.

6

Determiners and Thematic Prominence

Thematic prominence involves devices that draw attention to "what I'm talking about" (Callow 1974:50). This chapter is concerned particularly with devices used to draw attention to a referent because it "will have a significant role to play in the subsequent discourse" (Levinsohn 2015, 4.6.1). Such devices include so-called 'emphatic' **pronouns** (see Lowe 1998:36), one or more of the sets of **demonstratives** found in the language (Levinsohn 2015, 9.2) and, especially in Ancient Hebrew and many African languages, those **relative clauses** that "contain information which is not really needed to establish the identity of the referent" (10.3.7). In addition, "Some of the devices used to give prominence to a focal constituent … may also be employed to give prominence to a point of departure or connective", thereby highlighting the material that follows (4.6.2).

You should now reread sections 4.6, 9.2 and 10.3.6–7 of Levinsohn 2015, as they give examples of markers of thematic prominence in a number of languages.

The following four sections discuss determiners and thematic prominence in the languages we have been using for illustration. The final section deals with relative clauses in non-narrative material.

6.1 Determiners and thematic prominence in Koine Greek

We observed in 4.3.2 that many preverbal subjects in Greek non-narrative texts signal a switch of attention from the default centre of attention (typically, the addressees) to another referent that temporarily becomes the centre of attention. This partially explained the frequent use of the first person **pronoun** ἐγώ 'I' in the letter to Philemon.[1]

The following subsections consider the function in non-narrative texts of the following Greek determiners: the distal demonstrative ἐκεῖνος 'that', the proximal demonstrative οὗτος 'this', and the article. First, though, you should reread Appendix 1 to chapter 9 of Levinsohn 2015 on the functions of ἐκεῖνος and οὗτος in narrative.

6.1.1 The distal demonstrative ἐκεῖνος 'that'

> The core meaning of the demonstratives in Greek is NOT thematic or athematic. The core meaning of *ekeinos* is 'distal' (not at the deictic centre) and the core meaning of *houtos* is 'proximal' (close to the deictic centre). Nevertheless, in certain contexts, a pragmatic effect of using *ekeinos* is to identify the referent as athematic. Conversely,

---
[1] When a topical subject is seemingly 'redundant', it may highlight the comment about it (see 8.8).

a pragmatic effect of using *houtos* in certain contexts is to identify the referent as thematic. (Levinsohn 2015, ch. 9, app. 1)[2]

Because referents of ἐκεῖνος are not at the deictic centre, such referents are usually **athematic**; i.e., not the current centre of attention. This is illustrated by the following examples from Hebrews. In each case, ἐκεῖνος is used to refer to potential themes that are not in fact the centre of attention:[3]

- Hebrews 4:2 (*For we have indeed the good news preached to us, just as **those ones** [κἀκεῖνοι]*): we are the centre of attention, not those ones.
- Hebrews 8:7 (*For if **that** [ἐκείνη] first covenant had been faultless, there would have been no need to look for a second one*): the theme of the passage is the second covenant, not the first.
- Hebrews 11:15: the centre of attention is *a better country, that is,*[4] *a heavenly one* [16], *not **that one** [ἐκείνης] from which they had left*.

The use of ἐκεῖνος to mark referents as athematic explains why Jesus is referred to with ἐκεῖνος in 1 John 2:6; 3:3, 5, 7; 3:16; 4:17. In each instance, the addressees are thematic, and reference to Jesus is made to reinforce the author's message to them. See, for example, 3:3: *And everyone who has this hope in him purifies himself, just as **he** (ἐκεῖνος) is pure*. Whereas ἐκεῖνος may give some prominence to its referent, its primary function is to indicate that the referent is not the current centre of attention.[5]

6.1.2 The proximal demonstrative οὗτος 'this'

Οὗτος is used in two ways in the letter to Philemon:

- **cataphorically** (i.e. for referents which have yet to be stated), in which case it is **focal**. In Philemon 15, the referent of διὰ τοῦτο 'because of this' is the subordinate clause introduced with ἵνα:

    15 *After all, [it was] perhaps because of this* [διὰ τοῦτο] *[that] he was separated from you for a while, so that* [ἵνα] *you might have him back forever*[6]

- **anaphorically** (i.e. for activated referents), in which case its referent is **thematic**. In Philemon 18b, the referent of τοῦτο 'this' is whatever Onesimus owes Philemon, which remains thematic into the next verses:

    18 *And if he has wronged you in any way or owes you anything, charge this* [τοῦτο] *to my account. (19) I, Paul, am writing this with my own hand: I will repay it.*

For passages in Hebrews where the referent of οὗτος is thematic, see 3:3, 7:27, 8:3, 10:12 (οὗτος refers to Jesus, who is contrasted with Moses and earthly high priests), 7:1, 7:4 (Melchizedek), and 11:12, 11:13, 11:39 (heroes who exercised faith).

6.1.3 The article

Greek uses the article to indicate that the reader is to locate the referent in his or her current mental representation (see Levinsohn 2015, 9.2.4).[7] For example, the concept of godliness is activated in 1 Timothy 4:7b without the article (πρὸς εὐσέβειαν 'for godliness'). When *godliness* is referred to again in 8b, it occurs with the article (ἡ εὐσέβεια '[the] godliness'). This indicates that it is now an activated concept that the reader will be able to locate in his or her current mental representation.

---

[2] For a more detailed discussion of ἐκεῖνος and οὗτος, see Levinsohn 2003b.
[3] Ἐκεῖνος is NOT used in the letter to Philemon.
[4] The referent of οὗτος in the expression τοῦτ' ἔστιν 'this is' (also found in Philemon 12b) is a VERY local theme!
[5] For instances in which Jesus is thematic in 1 John and is referred to with οὗτος, see 1 John 5:6, 5:20. Ἐκεῖνος is also used in 1 John 5:16, which refers to *sin that is mortal* – NOT the sin about which John has been talking.
[6] The majority of instances of οὗτος in 1 John are cataphoric (e.g. ***This** is the message which we have heard from him and proclaim to you: that* [ὅτι] *God is light.* – 1 John 1:5). For an exophoric instance of οὗτος, see Hebrews 9:20 (citing Exodus 24:8): *he sprinkled both the scroll itself and all the people saying, "**This** is the blood of the covenant that God has ordained for you."*
[7] Articles are determiners that do not have a deictic-exophoric usage – Levinsohn 2015, 9.2.4. See Levinsohn and Dubis 2019 on the use and nonuse of the article in 1 Peter.

Question

In Philemon 3, *from God our Father* lacks the article (ἀπὸ Θεοῦ Πατρὸς ἡμῶν). In 4a, *to my God* has the article (τῷ Θεῷ μου). Why is the article used in 4a?[8]

In the letter to Philemon, Paul's first reference to Philemon's love and faith (Philemon 5a) is with the article (σου τὴν ἀγάπην καὶ τὴν πίστιν [lit. of.you **the** love and **the** faith]). This shows that these attributes of Philemon are already active in Paul's mind as he is writing.

Omission of the article

Greek authors sometimes omit the article when referring to a particular activated entity or concept, to give **prominence** to that referent or to a significant action performed by that referent (Levinsohn 2015, 9.2.4). I find no examples of this phenomenon in the letter to Philemon, so illustrate it by the references to *God* (θεός) in 1 Thessalonians.

Once *God* is activated (1 Thessalonians 1:1), the article is used to refer to Him whenever the constituent in which θεός occurs is NOT focal. See, for example, 1:2. When the constituent in which θεός occurs IS focal and prominent, then the article is omitted. See 2:4b, 2:5, 2:13d, 2:15c and 4:1b.[9]

6.2 Determiners in languages of the Philippines, including Kalinga

Appendix 2 of chapter 9 of Levinsohn 2015 gives an overview of the use of demonstratives in languages of the Philippines. Please read that section before applying the observations to the Kalinga text.

Application to the Kalinga text

The demonstratives used in the Kalinga text are **proximal** (ending in *-na*) or **distal** (ending in *-di*). In addition, the absolutive marker *sa* begins noun phrases and clauses whose referent is established or accessible, so acts a bit like an **article** or nominaliser (e.g. *sa um-una* 'the first thing' – 2; *sa osa e mi-baga kan dikayu* 'the one thing I'm telling you ...' – 5).

The 'emphatic' proximal demonstrative *annaya* 'this' is used cataphorically in 1 (see 5.2.2). In 19b, the use of *anna* is probably exophoric (*these* [anna] *difficulties we are having as a family*). The following questions mostly concern distal *sadi* 'that' and proximal *sana* 'this'.

Questions

1. *sadi* 'that' (4, 5c, 9) is the usual way to refer to the event of the previous clause or sentence when there is sequential progression (4.1). In 13c, though, *sana* 'this' is used in the same way. In the light of the above comments about distal and proximal demonstratives in Philippine languages, how might we expect *sadi* and *sana* to be distinguished?

2. *sana* 'this' is also used anaphorically in 22. What prominence, if any, does it seem to give to its referent?

3. How does *sana* 'this' seem to be used in 18c (*si sana* is translated 'at this time')?

---

[8] **Suggested answer** for the Greek of Philemon: The article in Philemon 4a indicates that *God* is now an activated concept that the reader will be able to locate in his or her current mental representation. The reader is thereby led to understand that *my God* refers to the same person as *God our Father* in 3.

[9] The article is also omitted when the referent of θεός is not an activated entity. For example, θέλημα θεοῦ (1 Thessalonians 5:18) can mean 'the divine will' (though the referent is focal, anyhow). The same is true of 1:9 and 4:16.

The only occasion on which the article is used in 1 Thessalonians when θεός is part of a focal constituent is in 1 Thessalonians 4:8 (τὸν θεὸν τὸν [καὶ] διδόντα τὸ πνεῦμα αὐτοῦ τὸ ἅγιον εἰς ὑμᾶς [lit. the God the.one also giving the Spirit the Holy to you]). In this instance, though, the head noun is modified by an adjectival phrase ("the God who gives you his Holy Spirit" – Richard 1995:186) which is there to underline the fact that we are called by God *to a state of holiness* (7) by the same God who gives the **Holy** Spirit to us. In other words, the DFE is *holy*, not *God*, hence the use of the article.

4. In 6.1 we noted the frequent use of the first person pronoun ἐγώ 'I' in the Greek of the letter to Philemon. Why does 19b of the Kalinga text begin with the pronoun *dikani* 'we'?[10]

6.3 Determiners and thematic prominence in the Bariai text

Since Bariai is an Austronesian language, the *-ne* ending of the proximal demonstrative (*ein(e)* 'this', *beda-ne* 'like this') is probably related to Kalinga *-na*. Proximal demonstratives are used frequently in the text. Distal demonstratives are used twice (4d, 15a), in the expression *kado-nga toa beda-oa* 'behaviour that (is) like that'.

Questions

1. The author usually uses the expression *kado-ne toa beda-oa* 'behaviour that (is) like this' (4b, 4c, 6b; 8a is similar). Why does he use *kado-nga toa beda-oa* in 4d and 15a? (You may get a hint from the way distal demonstratives are used in languages of the Philippines.)
2. The first person subject pronoun *gau* is used in 2a and 9a. Why is it omitted in 4a?[11]

6.4 Determiners and thematic prominence in the Dungra Bhil text

The demonstratives used in the Dungra Bhil text are the following:
- The adverbs *ehnono* 'like this' and *ehnana* 'like these' (proximal) and *tetaha* 'that much' (distal).
- The adjectives *ija/iʔi/ĩʔĩ* 'these' (proximal) and *tija* 'that' (distal), which has the same form as the third person masculine singular oblique pronoun.
- The pronoun *tõʔo/toʔo* 'that' (distal).[12]

Proximal demonstratives may be used for cataphoric, exophoric or anaphoric reference. Typically, the referent relates closely to the current theme or centre of attention.

We noted in 5.2.3 that, to give prominence to a complex focal constituent, the constituent is left-dislocated and is followed (usually immediately) by a proximal adverb with the same referent (9, 12, 19–21). A proximal demonstrative may also follow a complex **topic** that has been left-dislocated, provided the referent relates closely to the current theme. For example, the referents of *ĩʔĩ* 'these' in 39 (below) are activities that are mentioned in the left-dislocated constituent that immediately precedes them. These are activities that the speaker has already urged his children not to engage in, so relate closely to his main theme:

---

[10] **Suggested answers** for the Kalinga text:
1. When *sana* 'this' is used in 13c, we might expect it to give thematic **prominence** to its referent. This would imply that the theme of being careful of one's body (13–14) is given more prominence than the themes of enrolling in the right course (3–4), homesickness (5c) and the group one goes around with (8–9), which are referred to with *sadi*.
2. In 22, the use of *sana* 'this' gives **thematic** prominence to *these teachings*, which refers to the theme of the whole letter.
3. In 18, *sana* 'this' appears to be used exophorically, to refer to 'nowadays' as distinct from previous times.
4. 19b begins with the pronoun *dikani* 'we' to signal a temporary switch of attention from the addressees.

[11] **Suggested answers** for the Bariai text:
1. Distal demonstratives do NOT give thematic prominence to their referent, so the author uses *kado-nga toa beda-oa* 'behaviour like that' in 4d and 15a in anticipation of a switch to a description of good behaviour (5–6a, 15b–c).
2. When the first person subject pronoun *gau* is used in 2a and 9a, the author is (re)introducing himself. In the context of 4a, in contrast, he is already an active participant (see *if anyone doesn't listen to my voice* – 3a).

[12] A second set of distal demonstratives is also found in Dungra Bhil. For example, one narrative refers to *that tiger* both as *tõ vag* (for thematic prominence) and as *tõa vag* (in background comments).

6.4 Determiners and thematic prominence in the Dungra Bhil text

39b [*horu pi-noʔo,   viɽa-noʔo,   suri   koʔ-unoʔo*],   **ĩʔĩ**   *akho   kaj   kamo-o   naje.*
    liquor drink-GER fight-GER theft do-GER   these   all   any   work-POS NEG
    'liquor-drinking, fighting and stealing: none of these is of any use.'

When *tija* and the other third person pronouns are used as adjectives, they function like articles and are the default (nonthematic) way of making an anaphoric reference. As in Greek, they precede nouns that refer to a particular entity or concept to tell the reader to locate the referent in his or her current mental representation. They typically occur early in the sentence in line with the Principle of Natural Information Flow, as in 14: *tija mahõ-õ koʔ-mẽ* 'in that man's house'.

Like ἐκεῖνος in Greek, a **distal** demonstrative like *toʔo* 'that' gives some prominence to its referent, but at the same time indicates that the referent is athematic (other than the current theme or centre of attention). In 21, for instance, prominence is given to the referent of *tõʔo* because of the importance of his or her advice. However, the centre of attention is *you*:

21 *ehnoho   tõʔo   tuma-ha ko-je,   tahã   tumi tijaa guʈhi   manu-hũ   dʒuve.*
    like this that   to you   say-FUT   then   you   his   speech   accept-INF OBLIGATION
    '(If) this is what that person says to you, then you should accept his counsel.'

Questions

1. In 18, why are proximal demonstratives (*ĩʔĩ akho* 'all these' and **ehnoho**-*dʒ* 'just like this') appropriate?
2. In 13, why is a distal demonstrative (*toʔo* 'that') appropriate?[13]

A comparison of the determiners in Dungra Bhil and Koine Greek suggests that the proximal and distal demonstratives are used in fairly similar ways. However, the article is much less frequent in Dungra Bhil than in Greek. In the texts examined, it was only attached to points of departure or propositional topics. If this restriction holds for other texts, then the article would only be used in translation into Dungra Bhil when the constituent concerned was a preverbal subject in Greek or had been preposed to establish a point of departure (see 4.3.1–2).

Application to the language you are analysing

In section 9.2 of Levinsohn 2015, the Application reads as follows: "Describe the system of determiners used, together with the deictic-exophoric and text-related functions of each. Which set of determiners or pronouns, if any, is used for thematic references? For athematic references?"

Analyse the determiners used in your non-narrative texts. Then correct or amplify the conclusions you reached after analysing your narrative texts.

Application to translation

Because of the potential mismatches between the use of determiners in Greek and in the receptor languages, it is essential that you determine how the different determiners are used in natural texts in the receptor language, then compare their functions with those of the Greek determiners. This is because, when there is a mismatch between the languages, there is no guarantee that a mother-tongue translator will automatically make the correct substitution.

We saw this clearly when translating into Inga. When the Spanish text had a proximal demonstrative (e.g. *murieron todos éstos* 'these all died' – Hebrews 11:13), our cotranslator invariably used a proximal demonstrative in his draft translation. Yet proximal demonstratives in Inga never refer to

---

[13] **Suggested answers** for the Dungra Bhil text:
1. In 18, proximal demonstratives are appropriate because the referents of *ĩʔĩ akho* 'all these' and *ehnono-dʒ* 'just like this' relate closely to the current theme (the results of becoming addicted to liquor).
2. In 13, a distal demonstrative is appropriate because it gives prominence to the referent of *toʔo* 'that (any food that is in the house)' and because the referent is other than the current theme (the results of becoming addicted to liquor).

an activated participant, so an Inga listener would expect the demonstrative to be **followed** by a list of those who died! Our solution was to replace the proximal demonstrative with a distal one in the Spanish text (e.g. *murieron todos **aquellos*** 'those all died')!

6.5 Relative clauses in non-narrative material in African languages and Hebrew

Section 10.3 of Levinsohn 2015 notes that most relative clauses in African languages are **restrictive**.[14] This means that they restrict and identify the referent of the head noun. For example, in the NP *the ways the disease spreads* (Kambaata [OV] – cited below), the relative clause *the disease spreads* identifies *the ways* the speaker is referring to. In other words, the relative clause restricts the referent of *the ways* to those by which *the disease spreads*.[15]

[***moosu-s   tar-ano***   *woqqaakka-ta*] *da-ggeenanta-ga   amma`n-aammi.*
disease-ANA contaminate-PRE.3sm ways-ACC   know-PRE.2p-like believe-PRE.1
'I believe you know [the ways **the disease spreads**]'

Relative clauses and prominence

The same section also noted that relative clauses in many African languages are typically used for **thematic** prominence and to **intensify** a quantifier such as *all* or *none*. If such is the case for narrative in a particular language, then it will also be the case for other genres.

Thus, in a hortatory text about the ancestors in Yemba (SV/VO), relative clauses often refer to the items that the addressees should or should not be offering to their ancestors, and which therefore are highly thematic. *This wine that we will be drinking* is one such item:

[*Melu'*   *mīi*   ***ḿpɛ***   *é*   *gɔ*   *ēnú*   *lā*]
wine   REL   1in   CLASS2 go   IRR-drink ANA

'[this wine **that we will be drinking** …], will we first take a drop of the wine and throw it to them, for them to then drink?'

When a head noun is modified by *all* or *none*, a relative clause may be used to **intensify** the inclusiveness of the referent. In the following example from Konzime [ozm] (SV/VO), the relative clauses *that are in the forest* and *that are in this world* do not restrict *all the animals* in any way. Instead, they intensify the inclusiveness of *all*:

*Call [all the animals **that are in the forest**]! Call [all the animals **that are in this world**]!*

Relative clauses and nonestablished information

Restrictions on the use of relative clauses vary from language to language. Wiesmann (2000:72) finds that nonestablished information is never given in a restrictive relative clause in Toussian [wib] (SV/OV), and the relative clause is never part of a focal constituent. In contrast, relative clauses in Yemba may convey nonestablished information, and the relative clause may be part of the focal constituent. In sentence 7 of the text about the ancestors, for instance, the head noun (*message*) is established information (see 6), but the relative clause itself contains new information:

---

[14] Research is needed into how relative clauses function in non-African languages.
[15] Some African languages also use nonrestrictive relative clauses (Levinsohn 2015, 10.3.2–4).
   In the examples of this section, the NP that includes the relative clause is enclosed in square brackets. The relative clause itself is bolded.
   In some languages, relative clauses are also used in cleft constructions (see 5.4; e.g. *It's you **who put the milk in***). The comments of this section do not necessarily apply to such relative clauses, as they do not modify the head noun, but rather occur in a different part of the construction.

6.5 *Relative clauses in non-narrative material in African languages and Hebrew*   77

6   *We have just heard that message.*
7   É   gɔ   [ŋke   yīi   Ndém   a   le   kɔ́ŋ   á   yímpɛ   tɛ   ntsékne]
    it   be   message   REL   God   LOC   PAST4   love   LOC   1in   until   finish
    'It is [the message **that God loved us extraordinarily**].'

Mona Perrin (p.c.) points out that, when an NP that contains a relative clause conveys **completely new** information in an African language (in other words, neither the head noun nor the relative clause conveys established information), then the head noun will be very **generic**. Often, the head noun can only be *thing(s), person/people, time* or *place*, with the relative clause identifying which thing, person, time or place is referred to. Such is the case throughout a text that gives advice in Bafut [bfd] (SV/VO), as in:

ò   ŋwà'ànə̀   [tsîʔ   ɨnnù   jìi   mə   ò   zi aà]
2s   write   only   things   REL   that   2s   know
'write [only the things **that you know**]'

Relative clauses in Hebrew

The above comments about the use of relative clauses to convey prominence apply also to many Hebrew clauses that begin with the relative pronoun *'ašer* (see 10.3.7 of Levinsohn 2015).

For instance, in Genesis 3:11 (*From* [*the tree* **'ašer** *I commanded you not to eat*]), *the tree* is highly **thematic**.

Similarly, the three relative clauses of Exodus 20:4 (below) are not there to identify what the referent is like, but to **intensify** the inclusiveness of *kol* 'all, any' and, thence, the prohibition against making graven images:

4   *You shall not make for yourself a graven image* & [*any* (kol) *likeness* **'ašer** [*is*] **in the heavens above** & **'ašer** [*is*] **in the earth beneath** & **'ašer** [*is*] **in the waters under the earth**].

Relative clauses in Greek

Many relative clauses in Greek cannot be translated into African languages with a relative clause because they are *not* restrictive. Nonrestrictive relative clauses may be:

- **descriptive**, serving "merely to give the hearer an added piece of information about an already identified entity, but not to identify that entity" (Comrie 1989:138).
- **continuative**. Such clauses typically describe the next event (in narrative) or point (of an argument) "that involves the referent of the relative pronoun" (Levinsohn 2015, 10.3.4).

Even when a relative clause in Greek is restrictive, it may be presenting nonestablished information, yet NOT have a generic noun as its head.

Furthermore, it may be inappropriate to give prominence to the noun which the relative clause is modifying because it is NOT thematic.

Questions

1. Why should Luke 15:16a (*He longed to fill his stomach with* [*the pods* **that the pigs were eating**]) *not* be translated into most African languages with a relative clause?
2. Why should Acts 1:11 ([*This Jesus,* **who has been taken from you into heaven**], *will come back.*) *not* be translated into most African languages with a relative clause?[16]

---

[16] **Suggested answers:**
1. Luke 15:16a should not be translated into most African languages with a relative clause because *the pods* are a minor prop in the parable, so are not thematic. Also, *the pods* are not a generic noun, even though the whole

Application to the letter to Philemon

Four relative clauses are used in this letter to modify noun heads: 5b, 10b, 12a and 13a.

1. Is the relative clause of 5b restrictive or nonrestrictive? Is its referent thematic or not?

5a	σου	τὴν	ἀγάπην	καὶ	τὴν	πίστιν
	your	the	love	and	the	faith

5b	ἣν	ἔχεις	πρὸς	τὸν	Κύριον	Ἰησοῦν	καὶ	εἰς	πάντας	τοὺς	ἁγίους,
	which	you.have	for	the	Lord	Jesus	and	for	all	the	saints

   'your love that you have for all the saints and your faith toward the Lord Jesus'

2. Is the relative clause of Philemon 10b restrictive or nonrestrictive? Is its referent thematic or not?

10a	περὶ	τοῦ	ἐμοῦ	τέκνου
	concerning	the	my	child

10b	ὃν	ἐγέννησα	ἐν	τοῖς	δεσμοῖς,
	whom	I.gave.birth	in	the	bonds

   'concerning my child to whom I became a father during my imprisonment'

3. Are the relative clauses of Philemon 12a and 13a restrictive or nonrestrictive?[17]

11	τοῦ	ποτέ	σοι	ἄχρηστον	νυνὶ	δὲ	[καὶ]	σοὶ	καὶ	ἐμοὶ	εὔχρηστον,
	the.one	once	to.you	useless	now	DM	ADD	to.you	and	to.me	useful

   'the one formerly useless to you, but now indeed useful both to you and to me'

12a	ὃν	ἀνέπεμψά	σοι,	αὐτόν,	(12b)	τοῦτ᾽	ἔστιν	τὰ	ἐμὰ	σπλάγχνα;
	whom	I.sent.back	to.you	him		this	is	the	my	inward.parts

   'whom I am sending back to you him'   'that is, my own heart'

13a	ὃν	ἐγὼ	ἐβουλόμην	πρὸς	ἐμαυτὸν	κατέχειν,
	whom	I	I.was.desiring	with	myself	to.keep

   'whom I was wanting to keep with me'

NP conveys nonestablished information. To avoid the problem, one could say: "The pigs were eating pods. He longed to fill his stomach with them."

2. Acts 1:11 should not be translated into most African languages with a relative clause because it is nonrestrictive. Although Jesus is thematic in this verse (the two men are talking about him), the relative clause is not used to identify which Jesus they were talking about (how many Jesuses were present?). To avoid the problem, one could say, "Jesus, *the one* who has been taken from you into heaven" (see 6.1.2 on the function of οὗτος 'this'.)

[17] **Suggested answers:**
1. Philemon 5b is probably a restrictive relative clause, as it identifies the objects of *your love* and *your faith*. Its referent is thematic, as Paul's appeal to Philemon is *on the basis of love* (9a).
2. Philemon 10b is a restrictive relative clause, as it identifies the child that Paul is talking about. Its referent is thematic, as the theme of Paul's letter is *my child, Onesimus*.
3. The relative clauses of Philemon 12a and 13a are nonrestrictive. To avoid this problem, one could say, "I am sending him back to you" and "I was wanting to keep him with me".

Application to the language you are analysing

In sections 10.3.4 and 10.3.6 of Levinsohn 2015, the Applications read as follows:

1. Indicate whether relative clauses can be used in a nonrestrictive sense. If they can, describe their function(s) (descriptive or continuative).
2. If the language uses more than one type of restrictive relative clause, distinguish their functions.
3. When relative clauses are used in a restrictive (identifying) sense, describe where they occur and what their function(s) are. (For example, they may usually not be found in clauses that describe theme-line events; they may always relate to thematic prominence.)
4. When relative clauses only recapitulate established information, what is their function? (For example, they may slow down the story and thus highlight the next event to be described.)

Analyse the relative clauses used in your non-narrative texts. Then correct or amplify the conclusions you reached after analysing your narrative texts.

7

Backgrounding and Highlighting Devices, Including the Relative Potency of Different Forms of Exhortation

This chapter begins by considering the relative potency of different forms of exhortation and when each form is appropriate (7.1). The following four sections discuss different forms of exhortation in the languages we have been considering (7.2–5). Section 7.6 reviews and illustrates the backgrounding devices that were presented in chapter 5 of Levinsohn 2015. The final section concerns devices that commonly highlight propositions or groups of propositions in non-narrative material.[1]

7.1 The relative potency of different forms of exhortation

Speakers may express exhortations in a variety of ways. Consider the following ways that Paul might have expressed his first exhortation to Philemon (17b):

1. *Welcome him as you would me.*
2. *I appeal to you to welcome him as you would me.*
3. *I would like you to welcome him as you would me.*
4. *You should welcome him as you would me.*
5. *Please welcome him as you would me.*
6. *You will welcome him as you would me.*
7. *You must welcome him as you would me.*

One way to distinguish different forms of exhortation is on the basis of their relative **potency**. Wendland (2000:58) defines the potency of an exhortation as "its relative directness, urgency, or degree of mitigation". "Mitigate" means "make less severe" (*OED*).

Exercise

Order the above forms of exhortation from the most potent (in your opinion) to the least potent.[2]

---

[1] For an application of the contents of this chapter to medical texts in Persian [pes], see Zeynali Dastuyi 2018.
[2] **Suggested answer**. Twelve native English speakers who are not linguists ordered the first six of these exhortations from most potent to least potent. Most of them considered 6 to be most potent, followed by 1, 2, then 4, 5, then 3. I placed 5 before 4!

7.1.1 What makes an exhortation potent?

The potency of a form of exhortation depends on a number of factors, including the following:

- **mood**. Imperatives (e.g. 1 above) are typically more potent than exhortations expressed with indicatives or other moods (e.g. 4). However, certain mood markers (e.g. English *will*) may be judged to be more potent than the imperative.
- **person**. An exhortation in second person is typically more potent than one in first person, which in turn is typically more potent than one in third person. Compare *You must work* (Dungra Bhil 29), *We must work* (27) and *People must work*.
- **dependence**. Exhortations expressed with independent verbs are typically more potent than those expressed with nominalised verbs or in dependent clauses (with certain exceptions). Compare *Do not smoke!* and *No smoking!*
- **mitigating expressions**. Expressions like *please* (5) make an exhortation less potent. Certain **orienters** (e.g. *I would like you to* – 4) also make an exhortation less potent.

7.1.2 Factors influencing the form of exhortation chosen

I now discuss five factors that influence the form of exhortation chosen: the social relationship between the exhorter and the exhortee(s), the type of discourse in which it appears, its position in the text, the degree of prominence each exhortation is to receive, and its scope (whether or not it is to be acted on just once and/or immediately).

Social relationship

One factor that influences the potency of the forms of exhortation used is the social relationship of the exhorter to the exhortee(s): his or her "power, authority, eldership, knowledge and wisdom superiority" (Kompaoré 2004:24).[3] Consequently, when Dungra Bhil villagers exhort a government officer, they employ terms of respect and mitigation such as *Tahasil officer* and *please* (see 2.3), to reflect the officer's superior status in society. Such terms do not appear in the Dungra Bhil father's exhortation to his children not to drink liquor.

The type of hortatory discourse

The type ("volitive weight" – Kompaoré 2004:40) of hortatory discourse (2.4) also influences the potency of the forms of exhortation selected. In particular,

- **Instruction** tends to be more potent than **persuasion**;
- **Rebukes** tend to be more potent than **counsels**.

One problem for the translator arises when a particular form of exhortation is more potent in one language than in another. For example, Koine Greek instruction uses imperatives not only to counsel, but also to rebuke. In some African languages, however, imperatives tend to be interpreted only as rebukes. Consequently, if imperatives are used in such languages to translate Paul's imperatives in 1 Thessalonians 5:14–22, he will be understood to be rebuking his readers, rather than counselling them!

The position of the exhortation in the text

When more than one form of exhortation is employed in a text that gives **counsel**, the exhorter usually **begins** with **less potent** exhortations and **concludes** with **more potent** ones.

This is seen in the Greek of 1 Thessalonians 4:18–5:27. The first imperative of the letter does not occur till 4:18 and its content is affirming (*Therefore encourage one another with these*

---

[3] Hélène Dallaire (2004) claims that the use of different forms of exhortation in Hebrew "is connected to one of the following contexts: 1. Where one of higher social status addresses one of lower social status. 2. Where one of lower social status addresses one of higher social status."

7.1 The relative potency of different forms of exhortation 83

words – also in 5:11).[4] The next exhortations (5:6, 8) are first person (*So then let us not sleep*). The following ones are introduced with the orienter ἐρωτῶμεν ὑμᾶς 'we ask you' and are expressed in infinitival clauses (5:12–13). Further ones are introduced with a more demanding orienter, παρακαλοῦμεν ὑμᾶς 'we urge/appeal to you' (5:14) and are encoded as imperatives. To cap it all, an even more demanding orienter, Ἐνορκίζω ὑμᾶς τὸν κύριον 'I adjure you by the Lord' introduces the final exhortation of the book: *this letter to be read to all the brothers* (5:27).

When a text is given in order to **rebuke**, in contrast, it may well **begin** with a **potent** exhortation. Such is the case in the Dungra Bhil text. The first sentence (*you shouldn't be drinking* (ma piha) *liquor*) is probably the most potent in the text (20a–b, which are comparable, occur in reported speech). Later exhortations become less potent (see discussion in 7.5).

The first exhortation of 1 Corinthians (1:10) is similar: *Now I appeal to you* (Παρακαλῶ ὑμᾶς), *brothers, by the name of our Lord Jesus Christ, that* (ἵνα) *all of you be in agreement and that there be no divisions among you, but that you be united in the same mind and the same purpose.* Prominence is given to this exhortation to be united by the positive – negative – positive paraphrase and by giving the exhortation by the name of our Lord Jesus Christ.

The relative prominence of different exhortations

When a text contains a number of exhortations, some of them are likely to be more important than others, as far as the exhorter is concerned (see 6.2 on the use of the proximal demonstrative *sana* 'this' to give prominence to one of the themes in the Kalinga text). One way to give more prominence to one exhortation over against another is to increase its potency (see below). Conversely, one way to background one exhortation over against another is to decrease its potency (see 7.2.1 and 7.2.3 for examples in Greek).

The following passage (1 Corinthians 10:6–11) uses a switch from first to second person in order to make the following exhortations **more potent** (see discussion below):

6   *Now these things occurred as examples for us, so that we might not desire evil as they did.*

    7   *Do not become idolaters* (μηδὲ εἰδωλολάτραι γίνεσθε) *as some of them did; as it is written, "The people sat down to eat and drink, and they rose up to play."*

        8   *We must not indulge in sexual immorality* (μηδὲ πορνεύωμεν) *as some of them did, and twenty-three thousand fell in a single day.*

        9   *We must not test* (μηδὲ ἐκπειράζωμεν) *Christ, as some of them did, and were destroyed by serpents.*

    10   *And do not complain* (μηδὲ γογγύζετε) *as some of them did, and were destroyed by the destroyer.*

11   *These things happened to them to serve as an example, and they were written down to instruct us.*

The above passage is arranged chiastically (see 8.6) and the direct exhortations (7–10) are surrounded by an *inclusio* (6, 11) which is directed to *us* (*examples for us ... to instruct us*). One would therefore expect the exhortations to also be in first person. Consequently, when Paul switches from first to second person in 7 (and again in 10), the effect is to make the exhortation more potent than would otherwise be the case.

The motivation for the first of these switches is found in 14: *Therefore, my dear friends, flee from the worship of idols*, which returns to a theme that Paul has been considering since chapter 8 (Fee 1987). (see 7.5 for a similar switch in Dungra Bhil.)

The scope of the exhortation

Exhortations that are to be acted on **just once** and/or **immediately** (e.g. *Welcome him as you would me* – Philemon 17b) are often encoded differently from those that are **more general** (e.g. *Honour widows who are really widows* – 1 Timothy 5:3). Here are some examples.

---

[4] In 1 Thessalonians 2:9, *you remember* (μνημονεύετε), *brothers, our toil and hardship* is taken to be indicative, rather than imperative, as the connective used is γάρ 'for'.

In Inga, imperatives are used only for exhortations that call for an immediate response. Exhortations that are to be acted on later or are of a more general nature are encoded with an indicative verb that lacks a marker of tense.

In the Greek of Philemon and other Pauline letters, forms with perfective aspect ("aorists") are used for exhortations that call for a single, usually immediate response. Forms with imperfective aspect ("presents") are used for those of a more general or indefinite nature.[5]

We now consider different forms of exhortation in the four languages we have been considering.

Review questions

1. Name four factors that influence the potency of an exhortation.
2. Name five factors that influence the selection of one form of exhortation over against another.
3. If a commentator writes that a Greek imperative, subjunctive or infinitive is in the "present", what does this mean?
4. When do we have to be particularly careful when translating Greek imperatives into another language?[6]

7.2 Different forms of exhortation in Koine Greek

All the direct exhortations in the letter to Philemon are imperatives (see 7.2.4), so I have turned to other New Testament letters, especially 1 Timothy, 1 Thessalonians and 1 Corinthians, to illustrate further forms of exhortation.

The following subsections discuss some of the ways that exhortations are encoded in these letters. They are presented in three sets:

- those that are directed to the exhortee(s) themselves (7.2.1), such as *welcome him as you would welcome me* (Philemon 17b)
- those that the exhortee is to pass on to others (7.2.2), such as *If any believing woman has relatives who are really widows, she must assist them* (1 Timothy 5:16)
- participial forms (7.2.3), such as *doing nothing on the basis of partiality* (1 Timothy 5:21), since their potency is often determined by the clause to which they are subordinated.

7.2.1 Exhortations that are directed to the exhortee(s)

We have seen that the potency of an exhortation is influenced by its mood, its person, its encoding in an independent or dependent clause, and the presence or otherwise of a mitigating expression (7.1). The following details apply to Koine Greek:

- **Mood**. Imperatives are more potent than exhortations expressed as subjunctives or indicatives.
- **Person**. Exhortations in second person are more potent than those in first person, which in turn are more potent than those in third person.

---

[5] Greek imperatives are usually described as "present" or "aorist", which may give the impression that they are marked for tense. In fact, the distinction is between imperfective and perfective aspect. This is reflected in the way Wallace (1996:485) explains their function: "With the *aorist*, the force generally is to *command the action as a whole*, without focussing on duration, repetition, etc. With the *present*, the force generally is to *command the action as an ongoing process*." In the Greek of 1 Peter, the distribution of the two aspectual forms is different.

Tense-type labels for Greek infinitives, subjunctives and participles should also be reinterpreted as aspects.

[6] **Suggested answers**:
1. Four factors that influence the potency of an exhortation are its mood, its person, its encoding in an independent or dependent clause, and the presence or otherwise of a mitigating expression.
2. Five factors that influence the selection of one form of exhortation over against another are the social relationship between the exhorter and exhortee(s), the type of hortatory discourse, the position of the exhortation in the text, its relative prominence and its scope.
3. If a commentator writes that a Greek imperative, subjunctive or infinitive is in the "present", this means that it has imperfective aspect.
4. Particular care has to be taken in translation when a Greek imperative has been used to counsel, rather than rebuke.

- **Dependence**. Exhortations expressed in independent clauses are more potent than those expressed in subordinate clauses.
- **Mitigating expressions**. Some of the **orienters** that introduce exhortations act as mitigating expressions. Others provide motivation for obeying the exhortations and may even give them prominence.

I consider these factors in turn.

Mood

Exhortations in Greek may be expressed in independent clauses with imperatives (most potent), subjunctives (less potent) or indicatives (least potent).

Imperatives. The second person imperative is the default way of expressing an instruction-type exhortation in Greek. In 1 Timothy, for example, although the first imperative does not occur until 1 Timothy 4:7, it is then the preferred way of encoding both positive and negative exhortations.[7]

Imperatives encode both theme-line exhortations and supportive ones used as attention getters (2.2.4). Examples of attention getters include Ἀκούετε 'Listen!' (Mark 4:3) and Μηδεὶς ἑαυτὸν ἐξαπατάτω 'No one should deceive himself!' (1 Corinthians 3:18a).

Subjunctives. 1 Timothy 5:1a uses a second person subjunctive instead of a negative imperative. This more mitigated form of expression backgrounds the negative exhortation with respect to the positive one that follows (1b), which is in the imperative:

1a   *You should not rebuke* (μὴ ἐπιπλήξῃς) *an older man;*

1b   *rather, exhort* (παρακάλει) *him as if he were your father.*

1 Corinthians 16:11 is similar, except that the subjunctive is third person: *No one should despise* (μή ... ἐξουθενήσῃ) *him, then; rather, send him on his way* (προπέμψατε) *in peace.*

Although imperatives are the default way of giving instruction in Greek, more mitigated forms of exhortation are used in **persuasion**. In Acts 23:21, for example, the theme-line exhortation of Paul's nephew to the Roman tribune is in the subjunctive:

21   *You, then, should not be persuaded* (μὴ πεισθῇς) *by them.*

Indicatives. Many commentators (e.g. Kelly 1963:137) take the first person future indicative in 1 Timothy 6:8 to be hortatory. This form of exhortation is very mitigated:[8]

8   *but if we have food and clothing, with these we will be content* (ἀρκεσθησόμεθα).

Person

Exhortations in Greek may be in second person (most potent), first person (less potent) or third person (least potent). See 7.1.2 on the gradual build-up of potency in the hortatory material of 1 Thessalonians 5:6–22, with **first** person used in 5:6 and 5:8, and **second** person in 5:14–22.

I stated above that a second person imperative is the default way of expressing an instruction-type exhortation in Greek. However, the context for the exhortations of 1 Corinthians 10:7–10

---

[7] In some languages, the default for a particular type may be different for positive and negative exhortations. In the Hebrew of the Ten Commandments, for instance, the negative exhortations are expressed with an imperfective declarative, whereas the positive ones use an infinitive (but see Levinsohn 2021).

[8] The second person future indicative in 1 Timothy 5:18 is a quotation from Deuteronomy 25:4 (*for the scripture says, "You shall not muzzle* (οὐ φιμώσεις) *an ox while it is treading out the grain"*). This translates the imperfective *yqtl* form of Hebrew, which is used to express exhortations that apply all the time (7.1.2). The equivalent in Greek would be an imperfective imperative.

(cited in 4.1.2) is first person (see vv. 10:6 and 10:11). Consequently, the use of second person imperatives in 10:7 and 10:10 gives prominence to these exhortations.

See 1 Corinthians 16:11 (above) for the use of a **third** person subjunctive to background *No one should despise him* with respect to *send him on his way in peace*.

We have already noted that **persuasion** tends to use more mitigated forms of exhortation than instruction. This explains why the main exhortations of a persuasive text are often in third person. Acts 2:36, for instance, uses a third person imperative:[9]

36 *Let the entire house of Israel know with certainty* (ἀσφαλῶς γινωσκέτω), *then, that God has made him both Lord and Messiah, this Jesus whom you crucified.*

Dependence[10]

Exhortations sometimes occur in infinitival clauses or in final clauses subordinated by ἵνα followed by the subjunctive. Exhortations in subordinate clauses are inherently more indirect and less potent than those in independent clauses.

Infinitival clauses. Romans 12:15 uses infinitival clauses to encode exhortations (*Rejoice* [χαίρειν] *with those who rejoice, weep* [κλαίειν] *with those who weep*). Miller (1992:174–175) suggests that infinitival exhortations "encode *moral duty*". Wendland (2000:61) considers infinitives to be a very mitigated way of expressing exhortations.

Final clauses. The exhortation of 1 Timothy 3:15 occurs in a final clause subordinated by ἵνα, and is introduced with the modal verb δεῖ 'ought', which Wendland considers not to be potent, even when in an independent clause (see 7.2.2). Here, because of the subordination, the exhortation is very indirect indeed:

14 *I am writing these things to you although I hope to come to you soon,* (15) *if I am delayed, so that* (ἵνα) *you may know how one ought* (δεῖ) *to conduct oneself in the household of God.*

Orienters

Orienters often introduce exhortations in Greek. The exhortations themselves are most often expressed in infinitival clauses, though they may be encoded as imperatives (see below) or final clauses[11]. Some orienters act as mitigating expressions. Others provide motivation for obeying the exhortations and may even highlight them.

In 1 Thessalonians 4:13, which begins a new hortatory section, the orienter Οὐ θέλομεν ὑμᾶς 'we do not want you' acts as a mitigating expression for the exhortation that it introduces. The exhortation itself (*not to be ignorant ... that you do not grieve ...*) is expressed in the infinitival clause and the following final clause:

13 *Brothers, we do not want you* (οὐ θέλομεν ὑμᾶς) *to be ignorant about those who fall asleep, so that* (ἵνα) *you do not grieve like the rest of men who have no hope.*

Reporting an exhortation may mitigate it. Acts 17:22–31 is a persuasion-type speech by Paul to philosophers in Athens. Paul mitigates his main exhortation (*to repent*) by presenting it as a report of what God commands (the orienter is παραγγέλλει 'commands'):[12]

---

[9] See also Acts 17:30, cited below.

[10] Exhortations expressed in participial clauses are discussed in 7.2.3.

[11] For examples in which an orienter is followed by exhortations encoded as final clauses, see 1 Corinthians 1:10 (cited in 7.1.2) and 1 Timothy 5:21a (cited in 7.2.3).

[12] See 7.5 for a similar example in Dungra Bhil. Note, however, that if the reported speaker is an authority figure, this will increase the potency of the exhortation (e.g. 'Thus saith the Lord').

30 *Whereas God has overlooked the times of human ignorance, now he commands (παραγγέλλει) all people everywhere to repent.*

Other orienters provide **motivation** for obeying the exhortations. In 1 Timothy 6:13–14, for instance, the exhortation that is introduced with the orienter παραγγέλλω [σοι] 'I charge you' is reinforced by giving it *in the presence of God ... and of Christ Jesus*:

13 *I charge you (παραγγέλλω [σοι]), in the presence of God, who gives life to all things, and of Christ Jesus, who in his testimony before Pontius Pilate made the good confession, (14) to keep the commandment without spot or blame until the manifestation of our Lord Jesus Christ*

Finally, in 1 Thessalonians 5:14, the orienter παρακαλοῦμεν ὑμᾶς 'we urge/appeal to you' introduces exhortations that are encoded as **imperatives** (*warn those who are idle, encourage the timid, help the weak, be patient with everyone*). The presence of the orienter presumably highlights exhortations that are already potent.

When an exhortation is introduced with an orienter, the degree of potency depends on a number of factors, including:[13]

- the orienter(s) chosen. Contrast the potency associated with παρακαλοῦμεν ὑμᾶς 'we urge/appeal to you' (1 Thessalonians 5:14) and Οὐ θέλομεν ὑμᾶς 'we do not want you' (1 Thessalonians 4:13).
- how many orienters are used. The amount of prominence given to what follows probably increases with the number of orienters used (1 Thessalonians 4:1 uses two: ἐρωτῶμεν ὑμᾶς καὶ παρακαλοῦμεν 'we ask and urge/appeal to you').
- whether the exhortation is reinforced (see 1 Timothy 6:13, discussed above).

The way the actual exhortations are encoded (infinitive, subjunctive or imperative) should also affect their potency, with the imperative being most potent.

7.2.2 Exhortations that the exhortee is to pass on to others

The **default** way to express an exhortation that is to be passed on to others is with a third person imperative. See, for example, 1 Timothy 3:12a:

12a *Deacons are to be (διάκονοι ἔστωσαν) the husband of one wife.*

One way to **mitigate** an exhortation that the exhortee is to pass on to others is with the impersonal modal verb δεῖ 'it is necessary' plus an infinitival clause. Wendland (2000:58) considers this form of expressing an exhortation to be of little potency. 1 Timothy 3:2 provides an example:

2 *Now it is necessary (δεῖ) for an overseer to be above reproach*

Exhortations to be passed on to others may also be encoded in a final or infinitival clause, following an **orienter**. The degree of potency associated with the orienter varies considerably, as the following three examples indicate.

In 1 Timothy 5:14, the orienter is βούλομαι 'I want':

14 *So I want (βούλομαι) younger widows to marry, to have children, and to manage their households*

A very indirect form of exhortation is found in 1 Timothy 2:12. By using the orienter οὐκ ἐπιτρέπω 'I do not allow', Paul is indirectly exhorting Timothy to follow his example:

---

[13] Wendland (2000:58) makes a two-fold distinction for 1 Peter between "a direct appeal 'I beseech' (παρακαλῶ) by the author to his addressees" (more potent) and "the performative mention of an order or prohibition followed by indirect speech" (less potent).

12   *I do not allow* (οὐκ ἐπιτρέπω) *a woman to teach or to have authority over a man*

Finally, the imperative form of the orienter ὁρᾶτε 'see' ensures that the exhortation of 1 Thessalonians 5:15 (encoded in a final clause) is very potent:

15   *Make sure* (ὁρᾶτε) *that nobody pays back wrong for wrong*

7.2.3 Exhortations expressed or implied in an anarthrous participial clause

This section concerns participial clauses that are dependent on a nuclear clause that expresses an exhortation.[14] If the participial clause follows the nuclear clause, it usually takes on the potency of the nuclear exhortation. If the participial clause precedes the nuclear clause, it is usually backgrounded with respect to the nuclear exhortation.

Participial clauses that follow an exhortation

Participial clauses that are dependent on and follow a clause that expresses an exhortation usually take on the potency of the preceding exhortation (see below for an exception). Most often, the participial clause has imperfective ("present") aspect.

Thus, a participial clause that depends on and follows a second person **imperative** is as potent as the imperative. This is seen in 1 Timothy 6:20; Timothy is exhorted both to guard what has been entrusted to him and, equally, to turn *away from the profane chatter and contradictions of what is falsely called knowledge* (expressed in a participial clause with imperfective aspect):

20a   *Timothy, guard* (φύλαξον) *what has been entrusted to you,*

20b   *turning away from* (ἐκτρεπόμενος) *the profane chatter and contradictions of what is falsely called knowledge;*

Similarly, in 1 Thessalonians 5:8, the participial clause that depends on and follows the **first person** plural subjunctive is probably as potent as that exhortation. *We* are exhorted both to *be sober* and, equally, to *put on faith and love as a breastplate, and the hope of salvation as a helmet.* Unlike 8b, though, the participle has perfective ("aorist") aspect. "This implies an action antecedent to the action of the main verb" (Martin 2001:166):

8a–b   *We, in contrast, being* (ὄντες) *of the day, let us be sober* (νήφωμεν),

8c   *having put on* (ἐνδυσάμενοι) *faith and love as a breastplate, and the hope of salvation as a helmet.*

A participial clause that depends on and follows an exhortation introduced with an **orienter** is also as potent as its nuclear verb. The combination of the orienter Διαμαρτύρομαι 'I earnestly testify' and the call on God to be a witness ensure that the exhortations of 1 Timothy 5:21 are very potent. Timothy is both *to keep these instructions without prejudice* and, equally, to *do nothing on the basis of partiality* (a participial clause with imperfective aspect):

21a   *I earnestly testify* (Διαμαρτύρομαι) *in the presence of God ... that* (ἵνα) *you keep these instructions without prejudice,*

21b   *doing* (ποιῶν) *nothing on the basis of partiality.*

The participial clauses discussed above have either imperfective or perfective aspect. If a participial clause has **perfective** aspect and follows an exhortation, its status may be different.

For instance, Hebrews 10:22 features two participial clauses with perfective aspect (22b–c) that depend on the nuclear exhortation of 22a. Although they can be interpreted as exhortations, commentators

---

[14] An anarthrous participle in Greek is one that is not preceded by the article.

7.2 *Different forms of exhortation in Koine Greek* 89

tend to view them as expressing "accompanying circumstances" or "a reason" (see Greenlee 1998:392 for a useful summary):

22a   *let us draw near* (προσερχώμεθα) *with a sincere heart in full assurance of faith,*
22b   *our hearts having been sprinkled* (ῥεραντισμένοι) *from a guilty conscience*
22c   *and our bodies having been washed* (λελουσμένοι) *with pure water.*

Anarthrous participial clauses that precede an exhortation

Anarthrous participial clauses that **precede** a nuclear exhortation typically describe a situation or "attendant circumstance" (Wallace 1996:642) that must hold but is less important than the exhortation itself. First Thessalonians 5:8 (above) provides an example. Verse 5 has already indicated that *you* are all *sons of the day*; ἡμέρας ὄντες 'being of the day' is therefore backgrounded to and provides the reason for the following exhortation, *let us be self-controlled.*

In Matthew 28:19, the prenuclear participial clause expresses an attendant circumstance that can also be taken as an exhortation. "The disciples have to go before they can make disciples. At the same time, the act of going is of secondary importance with respect to the act of making disciples" (Levinsohn 2000:183n5):

19   *Having gone* (πορευθέντες), *then, disciple* (μαθητεύσατε) *all nations,*

7.2.4 Application to the letter to Philemon

Section 2.4 noted that the use of inductive style in Philemon 4–18 suggests that Paul is seeking to persuade Philemon to do as he asks. "The shift into deductive style in 19–22, however, suggests a move from persuasion to instruction (note the word *obedience* in 21a)."

This mixture of persuasion and instruction is reflected in the forms of exhortation used. The exhortations are introduced with an orienter παρακαλῶ σε 'I urge/appeal to you' (Philemon 10a, also in 9a), which could perhaps be viewed as a mitigating device, reflecting the persuasive nature of this section. However, the exhortations themselves, which are separated from the orienter by other supportive material, are all encoded as imperatives, reflecting instruction.

Two of the imperatives are perfective (Philemon 17, 20); the other two are imperfective (18, 22). Both of the **perfective** imperatives are exhortations that Philemon is to act on immediately:

17   (*So, if you consider me your partner, welcome him as you would welcome me.*) Paul is calling on Philemon to act as soon as he receives the letter by welcoming Onesimus.

20   (*Yes, brother, let me benefit from you in the Lord. Refresh my heart in Christ.*) The same response is desired: *Refresh my heart in Christ* by welcoming Onesimus *as you would welcome me.*

Both of the **imperfective** imperatives are tentative in nature, and neither encodes an exhortation that Philemon is to act on immediately:

18   (*If he wronged you in any way or owes you anything, charge that to my account.*) 19 (*I say nothing about you owing me even your own self*) suggests that Paul does not in fact expect Philemon to act on this command (Alford 1863:III.434). He is certainly not calling on him to act immediately.

22   (*Prepare a guest room for me, for I am hoping through your prayers to be restored to you.*) Paul does not expect Philemon to prepare the guest room as soon as he receives the letter. Rather, he is to be ready to fulfil the command whenever he hears that Paul has been released from his prison and is on his way.

Review questions

1. What is the default way of expressing exhortations in Greek instruction?
2. Exhortations are mitigated in various ways in persuasion-type material. Name three of the ways.

3. In instruction, do exhortations tend to be more mitigated at the beginning or at the end?
4. Which anarthrous participial clauses in Greek take on the potency of the exhortation on which they depend?[15]

7.3 Different forms of exhortation in the Kalinga text

According to section 2.2, the following sentences contain exhortations: 2, 5–8, 10–11, 13, 16–18, 20, 22, together with 1 (pointing forward to later exhortations). Of these, 1 and 22 are supportive.

Questions

1. Which of these exhortations appear to be imperatives?
2. Which exhortations use the modal verb *ma-sapul'* 'it is necessary'?
3. Which exhortations use *okyan* 'should'?
4. Which exhortations are introduced with an orienter? (*i-baga-k os kan dikayu* 'I'm also telling you' [7] is an example).
5. Which exhortations are given indirectly?[16]

The suggested answers to the above questions indicate that, of the 14 exhortations found in this text, only the two or three imperatives have been encoded in a potent way. The others appear to be more mitigated. This suggests that the exhortations not to *be fond of roaming and (going out) with your peers* (8), to *Be careful (and) watch how you spend your money* (10) and to *be careful of your body* (13) are more important to the exhorter than the other exhortations. (See below on devices used to give prominence to the exhortation of 13.)

The limited use of imperatives, together with the frequent use of orienters, may also reflect the **social relationship** between the exhorter and the exhortees (7.1.2). A Kalinga mother may have little authority over her grown-up children. In contrast, a text entitled "Advice to My Son Dong" in the Sarangani Bilaan [bps] language of the Philippines (McLachlin and Blackburn 1971:67–78) contains a number of imperatives that are not mitigated with orienters (e.g. *Taman, Dong, fala ge fatlagad dmawat i Dwata* 'So, Dong, first you get ready and receive God'). This use of imperatives is consistent with the social relationship of a Sarangani father to his son being more one of authority.

Among the orienters used in the Kalinga text, that of 13 (*sa importante pagay e mi-baga* 'The really important thing I'm saying') gives particular prominence to the exhortation that follows (see 5.5 on the prominence given to *important*). Further prominence is given to the exhortation by the proximal demonstrative *sana* 'this' (6.2).

---

[15] **Suggested answers**:
1. The default way of expressing exhortations in Greek instruction is with second person imperatives.
2. Ways that exhortations are mitigated in persuasion-type material include the use of subjunctives, third person forms and appropriate orienters.
3. In instruction, exhortations tend to be more mitigated at the **beginning** than at the end of it (compare the exhortations of 1 Thess. 4:13 and 4:18).
4. The anarthrous participial clauses in Greek that take on the potency of the exhortation on which they depend **follow** the imperative. They usually have imperfective aspect.

[16] **Suggested answers** for the Kalinga text:
1. The following exhortations appear to be imperatives: 8, 13 and, probably, 10 (though *umma-nya* 'be careful' could be an imperative orienter). In addition, *ila-nyu* 'see' is an imperative orienter in 20, with the exhortation expressed in a final clause subordinated with the purpose marker *ta*.
2. The following exhortations use the modal verb *ma-sapul'* 'it is necessary': 6, 7, 11, 16 and 18, plus 1–2 (*To think hard ...* is the complement of *The first thing* [2], with *you need to do* implied from 1).
3. The following exhortations uses *okyan* 'should': 5, 11, 17, 18 and 22.
4. The following exhortations are introduced with an orienter: 5, 6, 7, 8, 13, 16, 18 and 20 (there may be others).
5. The following exhortation is given indirectly: 22 (*am-balu* 'it's good if ...'). In 20, the postnuclear conditional clause translated *provided you find your work/job* could also be taken as an indirect exhortation (a number of languages of the Philippines use postnuclear conditional clauses to encode indirect exhortations).

Other forms of exhortation found in texts in Philippine languages include:

- The verb for *do/make* used as an auxiliary (e.g. *Let us do/make read ...*, probably meaning "Let us always read", according to Obo Manobo speakers).
- Reduplication of the verb root to intensify the action being called for.
- More potent and less potent forms of negative exhortation. In Kalagan, the prohibitive *ayaw* is used for main exhortations, whereas the negative particle *di* is used for those that complement main exhortations (e.g. *Be at peace with each other and do not* (di) *quarrel!*).
- In a Kalinga text entitled "Advice to a newly married couple", some exhortations were particularly mitigated by being given in third person, perhaps to avoid suggesting that the addressees would ever behave in the way described.

7.4 Different forms of exhortation in Bariai

Only one sentence of the text we have been using is an actual exhortation: *You must* (manta) *leave behaviour like that, and so follow good behaviour as God likes* (15). According to Steve Gallagher (p.c.), second person exhortations with *manta* 'must' are potent and reflect the fact that the exhortation is made **in the light of** previously stated supportive material.

In addition to 15, the expository THESIS *Banana [beer] and marijuana, this is a bad thing* (1) implies an exhortation not to *drink banana [beer] or consume marijuana* (10). This THESIS is highlighted by repeating it in 2. The highlighting is increased by introducing 2 with a vocative (*Elders and young people*) and the orienter *I speak truly to you*:

1. *Banana [beer] and marijuana, this is a bad thing.*
2. *Elders and young people, I speak truly to you, the behaviour with regard to drinking banana [beer] and consuming marijuana tobacco, this is a bad thing, because it destroys our living in the village.*

Exhortations in Bariai may be **mitigated** by orienters such as *gau tinig* 'I don't want' and the polite prohibitive *padam* 'please don't', which contrasts with the default prohibitive *nao* 'don't'. First person forms (e.g. *If we want good lives, we must* (manta) *follow God's Word*) were used to present the main exhortations of a speech by an adult to the rest of his community.

7.5 Different forms of exhortation in the Dungra Bhil text

According to section 2.2, the following sentences contain exhortations: 1, 3a, 4, 21, 23–24, 27–29, 34–38 and, possibly, the rhetorical question of 30 (plus, in reported speeches, 19b–20). Of these, 3a and 4 are attention getters.

Questions

1. Which of these exhortations contain the prohibitive (PRO) marker *-ma*?
2. Which other exhortations are imperative (marked with *-a/ja/va* '-IMP' or *-ha* 'be.PL')?
3. Which exhortations are first or second person future indicatives (marked with *-dʒi*)?
4. Which exhortations are gerunds (marked with *-unoʔo*)?[17]

---

[17] **Suggested answers** for the Dungra Bhil text:
1. The following exhortations contain the prohibitive marker *-ma*: 1, 20a–b.
2. The following additional exhortations are imperative: 19b–d, 23, 24a–c; plus the attention getters 3b, 4.
3. The following exhortations are future indicatives (marked with *-dʒi*): 27–28 (first person inclusive) and 29 (second person).
4. The following exhortations are gerunds (marked with *-unoʔo*): 34–38.

As noted in section 7.1.2, the Dungra Bhil text is a **rebuke** of existing behaviour and begins with a potent exhortation: *you shouldn't be drinking* (ma piha) *liquor* (1). Overall, the exhortations in the second half of the text (21b–39) gradually become **less potent** (see below on the reported exhortations of 19b–20b). The first exhortation has the obligation marker *-dʒuve* (21b – see further in 7.7.1) and is followed by some imperative forms with *-ha* 'be' (23–24 – see below). The next set of exhortations are first and second person future indicatives (27–29), while the final set are first person gerunds (34–38), the negative forms of which take the negative particle *naj(e)*, rather than the potent prohibitive *-ma*.

One exception to the above movement from more to less potent forms of exhortation occurs in 29, where the speaker switches from first to second person. The presence of the vocative *maa pujra* 'my children' may also highlight the following exhortation (see also 8.9):

28 *If not,   then we must* (-dʒi) *buy cattle and make a business in the fields.*

29 *My children, you must* (-dʒi) *work in the fields.*

We noted for Greek that participial clauses that follow an exhortation usually take on its potency. When exhortations with *-ha* 'be' immediately follow an exhortation in Dungra Bhil, a similar effect is achieved.

For example, the presence of *-ha* seems to associate the exhortations of 20 with 19 (23–24 are similar). This is reflected in the following free translation by translating 20 with participles:

19 *and all live* (dʒi-va) *happily with love, not fighting* (viḍa-ha ma) *with one another and not falling* (ma poḍ-ha) *in with other people's evil counsel.*

I suggested above that the **rhetorical question** in 30 (*Why, in these days for working, are you roaming about without working?*) could be viewed as an indirect exhortation. In fact, rhetorical questions of the *why* type appear to be used in the same way in Dungra Bhil and in Greek. Both use such rhetorical questions to rebuke exhortee(s) for inappropriate behaviour. Typically, the question is followed, sooner or later, by an explicit exhortation.

Thus, in Matthew 7:3–5, the rhetorical question, *Why do you look at the speck of sawdust in your brother's eye and pay no attention to the plank in your own eye?* is followed by the exhortation, *You hypocrite, first take the plank out of your own eye.*

Similarly, the rhetorical question of 30 in Dungra Bhil is followed, eventually, by a series of exhortations (e.g. *We need to work hard* – 34).[18]

Application to the language you are analysing

1. List the different forms of exhortation found in your texts.
2. Begin to determine their relative potency by considering their mood, person and dependence, together with the presence of any mitigating expressions and orienters (see 7.1.1).
3. Identify the default form of exhortation for each instruction and persuasion-type text, in the light of the social relationship between the exhorter and exhortee(s) (7.1.2).
4. If any of the texts contain more than one form of exhortation, then determine the factors that may have led the exhorter to use either more or less potent forms (see 7.1.2).

7.6 Devices used to background propositions in non-narrative texts

This section reviews the backgrounding devices that were presented in chapter 5 of Levinsohn 2015 and exemplifies them for non-narrative texts.

Background material in narrative texts consists of all the material that concerns non-events, together with those events that are backgrounded in some way (Levinsohn 2015, 5.2). Background material in <u>hortatory</u> texts is defined in a similar way:

---

[18] Sec. 7.7.4 discusses rhetorical questions that are answered immediately by the person who posed them.

- all the material that does not present exhortations, together with
- any exhortations that are backgrounded in some way.

Review question

Name two mitigated forms that are used in Greek to background one exhortation over against another. (If necessary, review 7.2.1 and 7.2.3.)[19]

The following are among the devices used in languages to background propositions:

1. **subordination**, especially of **prenuclear** clauses. In hortatory material, see 7.2.3 for examples of backgrounding involving a Greek prenuclear participial clause.
2. **specific verb forms**. In hortatory material, such forms make an exhortation less potent. See 7.2.1 for the use of the subjunctive in Greek to background a negative exhortation with respect to the positive one that follows.
3. **connectives** and **spacers**. For example, direct exhortations in Greek are never introduced with γάρ 'for', which is reserved for supportive material. In many Indo-Aryan languages, a spacer is used to mark the counterpoint for the main point (3.3).

I now exemplify the backgrounding of propositions from the Kalinga and Dungra Bhil texts.

7.6.1 Application to the Kalinga text

The following devices background propositions in the Kalinga text.

Subordination

No exhortations are expressed in prenuclear clauses. On numerous occasions, though, a prenuclear clause (often establishing a point of departure) forms the background for the exhortations that follow. The conditional clause of 8b (underlined) provides an example:

8   *What I'm also saying is, if you stay far (away), don't be fond of roaming and (going out) with your peers.*

Contrast 20, in which an exhortation is encoded indirectly in a postnuclear conditional clause (*provided you find your work/job* – discussed in 7.3).

Specific verb forms

A number of the forms of exhortation discussed in 7.3 are mitigated and, therefore, potentially backgrounded with respect to those that are encoded with imperatives.

Clear evidence of backgrounding was found in a hortatory text given by a church elder to fellow elders in another Philippine language, Palanan Agta [apf]. The main exhortations of this text were encoded with first person plural imperatives. However, a more mitigated form, involving *dapat* 'it is necessary that', was used for the introductory and closing exhortations. The effect was to background them with respect to the main exhortations. The same phenomenon has been observed in other Philippine languages.

In other hortatory texts in Philippine languages, switches between second and first person plural (inclusive) forms have been noted. The two forms of exhortation may well differ in importance.[20]

---

[19] **Suggested answer**: Two mitigated forms that are used in Greek to background one exhortation over against another are subjunctives and prenuclear participial clauses.
[20] The switches may be a form of "detachment" (see Levinsohn 2015, 5.2.3, end of point 1).

Connectives and spacers

In the Kalinga text, the connective *te* 'for', which introduces supportive information, never introduces an exhortation.

In Palanan Agta, the linker-spacer *ay*, which follows points of departure when there is continuity in the theme line, occasionally occurs elsewhere in a sentence to separate information of unequal importance. The following sentence illustrates this. Although the first clause is in the form of an exhortation, the presence of *ay* backgrounds it with respect to the consequence:

exhortation	*you still continue in your work*
CONSEQUENCE	*ay that also (is) what your members will do.*

7.6.2 Application to the Dungra Bhil text

Specific verb forms are used to background propositions in the Dungra Bhil text.

Because this text is a rebuke, the exhortations in the second half become less potent (7.5). Such forms are, therefore, potentially backgrounded with respect to those that are encoded with imperatives.

A further way to background propositions in hortatory material in Dungra Bhil may be with **third person subjects**. For example, all the supportive material of 2–19 is in third person.

On one occasion, an independent clause in the **future** is immediately followed by the exhortation (*Like this is what that person says* (ko-je 'say-FUT') *to you, then you should accept his counsel* – 21).[21]

Application to the language you are analysing

Describe the devices used in your non-narrative texts to background propositions or groups of propositions. Distinguish their functions.

7.7 Highlighting propositions in non-narrative texts

This section concerns devices that highlight propositions or groups of propositions in non-narrative texts. We have already mentioned six devices that may highlight the material that immediately follows them:

- imperatives used as **attention getters** (2.2.4); e.g. Ἀκούετε 'Listen' (Mark 4:3); *horu pi-nara mahõ-õ ḍua tumi pala* 'Look at the eyes of a liquor-drinking person' (Dungra Bhil 3a).
- **counterpoints** (3.3); e.g. *For **physical training is of some value*** (COUNTERPOINT), *the* δέ *godliness is of value in every way* (1 Timothy 4:8).
- **cataphoric** expressions (5.2.1); e.g. ***this*** (annaya) *is what you need to do when you go to school in a far place* (Kalinga 1).
- **vocatives**. Some languages move the vocative from its default position and use it as a spacer to give prominence to what follows (5.4). Just using a vocative may also highlight what follows (7.4; e.g. *kapeipei ga kakau* 'Elders and youth' – Bariai 2).
- **switches from less potent to more potent** forms of exhortation, such as the switch from first to second person in 1 Corinthians 10:6–10 (7.1.2) and between sentences 28 and 29 of the Dungra Bhil text (7.5).
- certain **orienters**, such as *sa importante pagay e mi-baga* 'The really important thing I'm saying' (Kalinga 13 – 7.3) and *gau na-keo tautaunga pa-gimi* 'I speak truly to you' (Bariai 2 – 7.7.3). Using more than one orienter, as in 1 Thessalonians 4:1 (7.2.1), probably increases the prominence given to what follows, as does the presence of reinforcing material such as *in the presence of God ... and of Christ Jesus* (1 Timothy 6:13–14 – 7.2.1).

---

[21] This suggests that a future might appropriately translate the Greek prenuclear participial clause in 1 Thessalonians 5:8 into Dungra Bhil.

7.7 Highlighting propositions in non-narrative texts

Other devices that commonly highlight propositions or groups of propositions in non-narrative material include:[22]

- slowing-down devices, such as the presentation of redundant information (including simple repetition) immediately prior to an important THESIS (7.7.1)
- repetitions or paraphrases of important THESES (7.7.2)
- presentative particles (7.7.3)
- rhetorical questions that are answered immediately by the exhorter (7.7.4)
- other marked patterns or structures (7.7.5).

7.7.1 The presentation of established information immediately prior to an important THESIS

A common rhetorical device for highlighting a THESIS is to repeat information that has already been stated before the THESIS is presented. This has the effect of slowing down the discourse and thus drawing the hearer's attention to what follows. For example, in the Hebrew of Genesis 4:13–14, Cain repeats what the LORD has said in 12, as he builds up to his concluding THESIS *whoever finds me will kill me* (see 7.7.3 on *hen* 'behold' and 7.7.5 on *wəhayâ* 'and it will happen'):

12   *"You will be a restless wanderer on the earth."*

13   *Cain said to the* LORD, *"My punishment is more than I can bear.* (14) *Hen today you are driving me from the land, & I will be hidden from your presence;* **I will be a restless wanderer on the earth** wəhayâ *whoever finds me will kill me."*

In 1 Thessalonians 5, the assertion *you are not in darkness* (4) is repeated in 5b immediately before the exhortations of 6. This has the effect of highlighting the exhortations. Similarly, the assertion *you are all sons of the light and sons of the day* (5a) is repeated in participial form in 8, immediately before the repetition of the hortatory THESIS *let us be self-controlled* (see 7.7.2):

4   *But you, brothers, are not in darkness so that this day should surprise you like a thief.*

5a   *For you are all sons of the light and sons of the day.*

5b   **We do not belong to the night or to the darkness.**

6   *So then, let us not be like others, who are asleep, but let us be alert and self-controlled ...*

8   *But* **since we belong to the day**, *let us be self-controlled,*

Supporting material in hortatory texts is background by its very nature, but it can be highlighted. In the following extract from a text in Somrai [sor], the exhortation of 1 is paraphrased in 2 to highlight the following reason (supporting material). This is because the reason becomes an expository THESIS which is developed in 3–4:

1   *Occupy yourself with your work.*

2   *Do your work because everything calls for money.*

3   *For clothing, and also for medicines, one needs money.*

4   *If your wife is ill/pregnant, one also needs money.*

Application to the Kalinga text

What is the effect of paraphrasing *nu an-singit-kayu ...* 'when you are looking for ...' (6a) in 6b?[23]

---

[22] Nida et al. (1983:36–37) and Wendland (2000:42–45) cite the preposing of focal constituents and "disjunction" (split constituents) as instances of highlighting in Greek. Since both involve highlighting *within* a proposition, they are not discussed here, but in 5.2 and 5.5.

[23] **Suggested answer** for the Kalinga text: The effect of paraphrasing *nu an-singit-kayu ...* 'when you are looking for ...' (6a) in 6b is to slow down the discourse and thus highlight the following details about a suitable boarding house

Application to the Bariai text

What is the effect of repeating *kado-nga toa bedane* 'behaviour like this' (4b) in 4c?[24]

Application to the Dungra Bhil text

What is the effect of paraphrasing *ekhūhū mahū?ū tuma-ha koj* 'someone may say to you' (19a) in 21?[25]

7.7.2 Repetitions or paraphrases of important THESES

Repeating or paraphrasing a THESIS typically highlights it. In 7.7.1, we noted that the repetition of established information immediately prior to the hortatory THESIS *let us be self-controlled* (1 Thessalonians 5:8) highlighted it. The fact that this exhortation is a repetition of one given in 6 also shows how important it is.

Application to the Bariai text

Which expository THESIS is repeated and paraphrased most frequently in this text?[26]

Application to the Dungra Bhil text

1. Which exhortation is repeated most frequently in the text? Which device listed at the beginning of 7.7 may have been used to further highlight some of the repetitions?
2. Which consequences of not obeying the exhortations are repeated?[27]

7.7.3 Presentative particles

Both Hebrew and Greek use a presentative particle traditionally translated *lo, behold* to highlight a following THESIS. In Acts 13:11, for instance, Greek ἰδού highlights the pronouncement that follows the supportive material of 10:

10   *You are a child of the devil and an enemy of everything that is right! You are full of all kinds of deceit and trickery. Will you never stop perverting the right ways of the Lord?*

11   *And now* ἰδού *the hand of the Lord is against you. You are going to be blind, and for a time you will be unable to see the light of the sun.*

See 7.7.1 for Hebrew *hen* used in Genesis 4:14 to highlight a following pronouncement.[28]

(*one where we pay a little, where the character of the house owner is good, where boys are not included and where it is near the school* – 6c–e).

[24] **Suggested answer** for the Bariai text: The effect of repeating *kado-nga toa bedane* 'behaviour like this' (4b) in 4c is to slow down the discourse and thus highlight the reason stated in 4d (*many people will be dying from such behaviour*).

[25] **Suggested answer** for the Dungra Bhil text: The effect of paraphrasing *ekhūhū mahū?ū tuma-ha koj* 'someone may say to you' (19a) in 21a is to slow down the discourse and thus highlight the exhortation of 21b and the important consequence described in 22 (*then you should accept his counsel. Then there will be peace in your house*).

[26] **Suggested answer** for the Bariai text: The expository THESIS that is repeated and paraphrased most frequently in this text is *Banana [beer] and marijuana is a bad thing* (1), which is repeated as a THESIS in 4b and 9b, as well as 2b.

[27] **Suggested answers** for the Dungra Bhil text:
1. The exhortation that is repeated most frequently in the text is the one to work (hard) (19b, 27a, 28b, 29, 34, 36; see also the exhortations not to roam around without working – 30, 35). The highlighting device that may have been used to further highlight some of these repetitions is the vocative *maa pujira* 'my children' (e.g. in 29 – sec. 7.5).
2. One consequence of not obeying the exhortations which is repeated is that dependants will die of hunger (8, 32–33a). The lack of clothing to wear is also repeated (15–16, 33b).

[28] Sim (2010) considers *hen* to be an interpretive use marker, used in Genesis 4:14 to mark what follows as an echo of what the LORD had just said.

7.7.4 Rhetorical questions that are answered immediately by the exhorter

Rhetorical questions are used for a variety of purposes (see Beekman 1972 on five functions of rhetorical questions in the New Testament; see 7.5 on *why* questions that rebuke exhortee(s) for inappropriate behaviour). This section concerns questions that the exhorter immediately answers. Such questions are a slowing-down device that highlights the answer.

In 1 Corinthians 11:22, for instance, the last of a series of rhetorical questions asks, ἐπαινέσω ὑμᾶς; 'Should I commend you?' Its presence highlights the answer that immediately follows, ἐν τούτῳ οὐκ ἐπαινῶ 'In this matter I do not commend you', which forms an *inclusio* with Τοῦτο δὲ παραγγέλλων οὐκ ἐπαινῶ 'Now in the following instructions I do not commend you' (17).

Although no rhetorical questions are found in the **Bariai** text, they are commonly used in the language. The following example from the beginning of another text is used to highlight the fact that our lives and those of our ancestors are not the same:

1   *I want to talk about our ancestors' lives and also ours today.*

2a *Are these two lifestyles the same?*

2b *No, not the same.*

Application to the Dungra Bhil text

Why, in 7 and 31, does the author ask a question that he answers immediately?[29]

7.7.5 Other marked patterns or structures

I conclude this chapter with a couple of additional devices that highlight the material that follows them.

The **Hebrew** verb *wəhayâ* 'and it will happen' may be used to point forward to "significant background or important events to follow" (Longacre 1994:84). For example, Cain uses *wəhayâ* to highlight the concluding THESIS of his speech of Genesis 4:13–14 (cited in 7.7.1).[30]

Theresa Heath (2000) finds that, in an expository text in Makaa [mcp], **cleft sentences** are "used to highlight a following conclusion". In the following extract, for instance, the reference in the first part of the cleft sentence to established information (*that wisdom*) has the effect of highlighting the second part (*we have today*) and, thereby, the whole proposition:

After that, when we used to walk together with our fathers, we were taking in the wisdom of our fathers.

It is that wisdom that we have today.

Application to the language you are analysing

Describe the devices used in your non-narrative texts to highlight propositions or groups of propositions. Distinguish their functions.

---

[29] **Suggested answer** for the Dungra Bhil text: In 7 and 31, the author asks a question that he answers immediately in order to highlight a consequence of not behaving in the way he wants.

[30] See Levinsohn 2006b, 3, for discussion of *wayhî* 'it happened' in Hebrew narrative.

8

Boundary Features

This chapter concerns criteria that enable a reader or hearer to recognise boundaries between paragraphs and larger units such as episodes of a narrative or sections of a book (8.2–12). These criteria are then applied to the four texts that we have been using (8.13–16).

8.1 Problems in identifying boundaries

Two problems arise when seeking to identify the boundaries of units:

1. The paragraph or section is a semantic unit characterised by having a single theme, not by the presence of certain surface features.[1]
2. The presence of any specific surface feature is seldom a sufficient criterion on which to identify a paragraph or section boundary.

8.1.1 The paragraph or section is a semantic unit

Tomlin (1987:458) claims that "episodes are defined ultimately by the sustaining of attention on a particular paragraph level theme." Beekman and Callow (1974:279) make a similar point:

> The basic criterion [for delineating a unit] is that a section or a paragraph deals with one theme. If the theme changes, then a new unit has started ... what gives a section or paragraph its overall coherence as a semantic unit is the fact that one subject matter is being dealt with.

As a semantic unit, then, the boundaries of a paragraph or section are defined on semantic grounds ("If the theme changes, then a new unit has started" – 1974:279), not with reference to surface features such as connectives and constituent order.

Although segmentation into paragraphs and sections is not determined by reference to surface features, there are many such features that occur at boundaries and can be taken as **supporting** evidence for the boundaries. These features are discussed in 8.2–8.12.

8.1.2 Surface features do not exclusively indicate boundaries

Although the presence of a surface feature can be taken as supporting evidence for a unit boundary, the presence of that feature is seldom a sufficient criterion on which to base a boundary. Rather, if one

---

[1] Randall Buth (p.c.) prefers to refer to the paragraph as a "pragmatic" unit.

of the reasons for the presence of a certain feature is because of a boundary between units, there will almost invariably be other reasons why the feature might be present.

The use of a seemingly redundant noun phrase to identify an active referent is a case in point. The default encoding of a subject is minimal when it is the same as in the previous clause, whereas a noun phrase is often used following a unit boundary. However, a noun phrase is employed also when the sentence concerned is highlighted (see Levinsohn 2015, 8.2.3). Thus, though the presence of a seemingly redundant noun phrase may provide supporting evidence for the existence of a boundary, it is not by itself sufficient evidence on which to posit the boundary.

Now, suppose we discover a feature that does seem to occur systematically at boundaries in some particular text. It would be wrong to assume on that basis that the same feature will always mark boundaries since different texts are arranged in different ways.

For example, Schooling (1985:21) observed that, in the Greek of Matthew, ἀπὸ τότε 'from that time' "appears to occur very near those points where the book can be divided into four major units". However, to argue from this observation that the presence of ἀπὸ τότε will always indicate a major boundary in Greek would be very foolish.

Another danger is to look for boundaries where they do not exist. For example, Luke has so designed the book of Acts that the major sections of the book are linked by **transitional** material. Commentators do not agree on where the sections begin and end, because the transitional material does not belong to one or the other; it bridges the gap.

As an example, consider Acts 8:25–26 (you will find the context in a Bible):

25 *They, then* (Οἱ μὲν οὖν), *having testified and proclaimed the word of the Lord, returned to Jerusalem, preaching the gospel in many Samaritan villages.*

26 *Now* (δέ) *an angel of the Lord spoke to Philip ...*

Commentators invariably recognise a boundary in this passage between 25 and 26. This is consistent with the use of the articular pronoun οἱ 'they' in 25 (implying that 25 belongs with the preceding material) and the change in the cast of participants in 26 (implying a boundary before 26). However, one of the connectives used in 25 is μέν, which may be glossed "On the one hand" (Arndt and Gingrich 1957:503). The English connective *On the one hand* anticipates a corresponding *On the other hand*, and has the effect of associating together the material that they introduce. Greek μέν is similar. It anticipates a corresponding δέ, and constrains the material concerned to be associated together.

In the case of Acts 8:25–26, μέν and its corresponding δέ occur on opposite sides of the proposed boundary. The effect is to constrain the reader to associate the material together. This is understandable, as both sets of events involve the same Christian leader (Philip). Consequently, 25 is to be interpreted not so much as the conclusion of an episode, but rather as transitional material uniting two related episodes.

Review questions

1. On what grounds are the boundaries of paragraphs or sections defined?
2. Is the presence of a particular surface feature usually a sufficient criterion on which to base a paragraph or section boundary?
3. When a pair of related connectives such as *On the one hand ... On the other hand* occurs on opposite sides of a proposed boundary, what does this indicate? What implications might this have for the use of a title at such a point?[2]

---

[2] **Suggested answers:**
1. The boundaries of paragraphs or sections are defined on semantic grounds ("If the theme changes, then a new unit has started" – Beekman and Callow 1974:279), not with reference to surface features such as connectives and constituent order.
2. No, the presence of a particular surface feature is seldom a sufficient criterion on which to base a paragraph or section boundary. Typically, there will be other reasons why the feature might be present.

The following subsections comment on surface features cited by Beekman and Callow (1974:279–280), Neeley (1987) and Guthrie (1998).

Application to the language you are analysing

Divide your texts into larger and smaller units on semantic grounds ("a section or a paragraph deals with one theme"). (Bear in mind, though, that, if you find no supportive features, then the author may not have intended a boundary to be perceived at that particular place.)

8.2 The presence of a point of departure

One useful piece of supportive evidence for a unit boundary is the presence of a point of departure, as it not only signals some sort of discontinuity, but also indicates the **primary basis** for relating what follows to the context. It thus gives some indication as to which of the potential supporting evidence is or is not valid.

In Philemon 22, for example, if the analyst perceives a change of theme between 8–21 and 22, then the temporal point of departure ἅμα 'at the same time, together' is appropriate support for that boundary, as situational points of departure involving renewal may be used to introduce different exhortations applicable to the same general setting (4.3.1).³

The same is true of 1 Thessalonians 4:9. If the analyst perceives a change of theme from sexual matters (3–8) to brotherly love (9–12), then the initial constituent Περὶ τῆς φιλαδελφίας 'Concerning [the] brotherly love' provides appropriate support for that boundary, as such points of departure are an appropriate way of signalling a change of theme (4.3.1).

However, the mere presence of a point of departure does not support the recognition of a boundary between units. This is illustrated by Philemon 11, where νυνὶ 'now' signals a switch of time from ποτέ 'once' in the middle of a sentence!

Similarly, 1 Thessalonians 4:14 begins with the conditional point of departure εἰ πιστεύομεν ὅτι Ἰησοῦς ἀπέθανεν καὶ ἀνέστη 'since we believe that Jesus died and rose again'. The connective γάρ 'for' indicates that the function of this sentence is to strengthen the previous one (13), and no commentator introduces a paragraph break at this point (see further in 8.3).

Furthermore, points of departure often indicate parallel or sequential progression **within** a paragraph (see 4.1).

Concerning boundaries in **narrative**, Beekman and Callow state that indications of change of time or location provide supporting evidence for boundaries. However, for a **temporal** change to be supporting evidence for a boundary, reference to it must be initial; i.e. it must be a point of departure. When a temporal expression is not initial, this consistently indicates that the basis for relating to the context is not temporal (see Levinsohn 2015, 3.3).

Spatial changes are most frequent in connection with travel. In the Greek of Acts, there is no evidence that such changes of location *per se* ever constitute grounds for an episode break. Rather, events at one location are usually separated from those at a second location because the two sets of events involve different casts of participants (see Levinsohn 2000:278–279). In fact, travel from the scene of one incident to the scene of the next is usually appended to the description of events at the one location or the other (compare Acts 13:51 and 18:1). In other words, whereas changes of location may coincide with the presence of a boundary, such changes should not normally be cited as supporting evidence independent of changes of cast or time.

---

3. When a pair of related connectives such as *On the one hand ... On the other hand* occurs on opposite sides of a proposed boundary, this constrains the material concerned to be associated together. This, in turn, may imply that it would be inappropriate to introduce a title between the two parts.

³ Philemon 17, 18 begin with conditional points of departure (see 8.13).

Review question

Why are points of departure useful supportive evidence for a unit boundary?[4]

Application to the Kalinga text

Section 4.3.3 suggested that the following sentences begin with an NP or nominalised clause to signal a switch of theme: 2, 5, 6, 8, 13, 16 and 18.

Question

Which other sentences begin with a point of departure? Which of these do NOT occur where you perceive a change of theme and, therefore, a paragraph boundary?[5]

Application to the Bariai text

Section 4.3.4 recognised the following points of departure:
- left-dislocated constituents at 1, 2b and, following orienters (8.10), 4b and 9b
- conditional clauses at 3, 4c and 8.

Questions

1. What additional point of departure occurs in this text?
2. Which of the above points of departure occur where you would insert a paragraph break because you perceive a change of theme?[6]

Application to the Dungra Bhil text

Section 4.3.5 recognised points of departure at 2, 10–12 and 19 (there may be others). Which of these occur where you would insert a paragraph break because you perceive a change of theme?[7]

Application to the language you are analysing

Check whether an appropriate point of departure has been used that would provide supporting evidence for boundaries that you have proposed.

8.3 Connectives and juxtaposition

Section 6.1 of Levinsohn 2015 differentiates between connectives that associate and those that introduce distinctive information, including development markers (often translated *then, so* or *but*). Markers of **distinctive** information are more likely to occur at perceived unit boundaries than those that **associate**

---

[4] **Suggested answer**: Points of departure are useful supportive evidence for a unit boundary because they signal some sort of discontinuity. In particular, they indicate the primary basis for relating what follows to the context. They thus give some indication as to which of the potential supporting evidence is or is not valid.

[5] **Suggested answer** for the Kalinga text: The other sentences that begin with a point of departure are 12, 14, 17 (following *Also, you children* – see 8.3 and 8.9) and 21; plus 20 (discussed in 8.11). Of these, the ones at 12, 14 and 21 do NOT occur where I perceive a change of theme and, therefore, a paragraph boundary.

[6] **Suggested answers** for the Bariai text: A conditional point of departure begins 10.
The only paragraph break that *I* would insert is at 9, which begins with an orienter and a left-dislocated constituent.

[7] **Suggested answer** for the Dungra Bhil text: I would insert a paragraph break because of a change of theme at 2 (from the exhortation not to drink liquor to an exposition of the THESIS that liquor is like a poison) and 19 (from the liquor-drinking person to *you*). A paragraph break is also possible at 10, because of a shift of theme from hunger to irrational behaviour; however, both themes are consequences of liquor addiction and the associative connective *ono* is used (8.3). There is no shift of theme within 10–12, which are united by parallel progression (4.1).

information together (often translated *and* or *also*). Thus, in **Greek**, developmental connectives such as δέ, οὖν 'then' and τότε 'then' are often found at perceived unit boundaries. In contrast, the associative and additive connectives, καί 'and' and τέ 'also', are less likely to occur at boundaries.

In **narrative**, for example, if καί is used to associate information at the beginning or end of an episode in which each new development in the story is marked by δέ, then new paragraphs will tend not to begin with such a καί.

Nevertheless, if introductory material united by καί extends over several sentences and the events described by them occur at different times, then they will naturally fall into distinct paragraphs. Such is the case even when the absence of δέ may imply that they only form the setting for what is to follow.

Furthermore, it is common in the Synoptic Gospels for καί to introduce episodes that do not build directly on the last episode, so the presence of καί in no way excludes a paragraph break.

Some connectives follow a THESIS and introduce material that **supports** it. Such material naturally belongs with the THESIS to which it relates. However, if the strengthening material extends over several sentences, it may well merit its own paragraph.

Thus, material in **Greek** that is introduced with γάρ 'for, after all' will tend not to occur at unit boundaries (see Philemon 7, 15, 22b). The exception is when such material extends over several sentences. Under such circumstances, the material may well merit its own paragraph (as is the case in Titus 1:10, where the supportive material continues to the end of the chapter).

We noted in 3.6 that inferential connectives such as Greek οὖν 'then' are used to mark the **resumption** of a theme line following supportive material (the same is true of Greek διὰ τοῦτο 'because of this'). When used in this way, they often occur at perceived unit boundaries (Neeley 1987:18).

First Timothy 2:8 (discussed in 3.6) provides an example. This verse resumes the hortatory theme line that was left six verses before (after v. 2), so οὖν provides good supportive evidence for a paragraph break proposed on the ground of a change of theme.

The longer the amount of material that separates the two parts of the theme line, the more major is the boundary likely to be. See, for example, the use of οὖν at Hebrews 4:14 to mark the resumption of the theme of Jesus as our high priest, which was last mentioned in 3:1 (see further in 8.12). If the digression is only one sentence long, in contrast, it will not lead to the introduction of a paragraph break unless a change of theme is perceived (see John 11:5).

Watch out for **reorientation** particles such as *Now* or *Well* which imply a discontinuity with the immediate context. They may well provide supportive evidence for a unit boundary proposed on the ground of a change of theme.

Juxtaposition is commonly found at the beginning of a new paragraph or section in Greek if that unit has its own nucleus (THESIS).[8] This is seen in the letter to Philemon. In 2.2.2, we divided the letter into three major sections: the introduction (Philemon 1–3), the main body (4–22) and the closure (23–25). Each of these sections begins without a conjunction, as does the benediction itself (v. 25).

However, juxtaposition is often found also in connection with restatements and other relations that would suggest an association of the proposition concerned with its nucleus. Therefore, the absence of a conjunction provides unambiguous support for a unit boundary only in connection with other of the potentially supportive features that we are discussing in these sections. In Philemon 4, 23, 25, for example, juxtaposition is accompanied by shifts of mood and person (8.11).

The value of taking the connectives into account when deciding where a boundary occurs is illustrated in Luke 6:35–37 (below). Verses 27–35 concern the theme "Love your enemies" (*NIV*), and parallel progression in 37–38 associates these two verses together. Marshall (1978) considers 36 to be a "bridging passage" between the two sets of verses. Editors therefore have to decide whether to attach 36 to 27–35 or to 37–38. The connectives help. Verse 36 has juxtaposition (Ø), whereas 37 begins with καί. As Creed (1930) observes, "These words in Lk. [36] introduce the subsequent teaching which forbids judgement upon others; note the conjunction kai ['and'] at the beginning of v. 37".

35 *But love your enemies and do good and lend, expecting nothing in return. And your reward will be great, and you will be children of the Most High, for he is kind to the ungrateful and the wicked.*

36 *Ø Be merciful, just as your Father is merciful.*

---

[8] Greek grammarians use the term **asyndeton** to refer to "the omission of a conjunction" (*OED*).

37 **Καί** *do not judge, and you will not be judged; and do not condemn, and you will not be condemned. (38) Give and it will be given to you ...*

Review question

Which connectives are most likely to occur at unit boundaries: those that signal new developments or those that associate information together?[9]

Application to the letter to Philemon

In the body of the letter (Philemon 4–22), the *NRSV* has paragraph breaks at 8, 17 and 22. Do the connectives used provide supporting evidence for boundaries at these places?[10]

Application to the Kalinga text

1. Does the strengthening connective *te* 'for' (3, 9, 15, 19, 21) provide supporting evidence for boundaries?
2. Does the developmental connective *kad* 'then' (4, 12, 14, 15, 19, 20) ever occur where you perceive a change of theme?
3. Does any other connective ever occur where you perceive a change of theme?[11]

Application to the Bariai text

Is the additive *be* (3) or the combination *ga pade* 'and also' (11) likely to provide supporting evidence for boundaries?[12]

Application to the Dungra Bhil text

1. Does the associative connective *ono* 'and' (4, 6, 9, 10, 13, 15, 16, 23) provide supporting evidence for boundaries?
2. Does the developmental connective *tahã* 'then' (7, 14, 22, 25) ever occur where you perceive a change of theme?
3. Is the countering connective *ga?ʈhehe* 'in contrast' (19) likely to provide supporting evidence for boundaries?[13]
   Note: The additive *ihĩkojite* 'likewise' is used at 17 to add a further consequence of liquor addiction.

---

[9] **Suggested answer**: The connectives that are most likely to occur at unit boundaries are those that signal new developments. Connectives that associate information together are only likely to occur at unit boundaries if the material concerned extends over several sentences.

[10] **Suggested answer** for Philemon: Yes, the connectives used at Philemon 8 (διό), 17 (οὖν) and 22 (δέ) are all developmental, so provide supporting evidence for boundaries at these places.
    Russell (1998:22–23) divides Philemon 8–22 at 14, 18 and 21. Each of these paragraphs also begins with an appropriate connective (δέ at 14 and 18, and juxtaposition at 21 – see also 8.13).

[11] **Suggested answers** for the Kalinga text:
1. No, *te* 'for' does not provide supporting evidence for boundaries, as it introduces material that supports a THESIS that was presented in the immediate context.
2. Although *kad* 'then' is a developmental connective, the only time it occurs where I perceive a change of theme is at 20, where it marks the resumption of the hortatory theme line (3.6).
3. The additive *(b)os* 'also' occurs in 7, 8 and 17 to add further hortatory units. Otherwise, no connective is used where I perceive a change of theme (2, 5, 6, 10, 13, 16, 17, 18 and 22).

[12] **Suggested answer** for the Bariai text: No, the additive *be* and the combination *ga pade* 'and also' are unlikely to provide supporting evidence for boundaries, as they appear to associate information together.

[13] **Suggested answers** for the Dungra Bhil text:
1. The connective *ono* 'and' does not provide supporting evidence for boundaries as it is associative.
2. Although *tahã* 'then' is a developmental connective, the only times it occurs where I perceive even a partial change of theme are at 7 and 14, where it introduces consequences of what has been stated in the immediate context.

Application to the language you are analysing

Check whether an appropriate connective (including juxtaposition) has been used that would provide supporting evidence for boundaries that you have proposed.

8.4 Summarising expressions and cataphoric demonstratives

By their nature, summarising expressions unite together the information to which they allude and thereby imply that the preceding material is to be treated as a block, over against what is to follow. Summarising expressions thus provide good supporting evidence for boundaries (Larsen 1991:51). In 1 Thessalonians 4:18, for example, ἐν τοῖς λόγοις τούτοις 'with these words' functions as a summarising expression, since it refers back to the teachings of 14–17.

Summarising expressions may occur, not at the end of the unit, but at the beginning of the next one. For example, the episode following the 'Sermon on the Plain' (Luke 6:20–49) is introduced by a point of departure which includes a summarising expression: *After he had finished all his sayings in the hearing of the people* (7:1).

Similarly, 1 Corinthians 10:6 and 10:11 (discussed in 7.1.2 and repeated below) begin with the summarising expression ταῦτα 'these things', the effect of which is to treat the preceding material (1–5, 7–10) as a block. Reflecting this fact, the *NIV* begins new paragraphs at 6 and 11.

6   *Now these things (ταῦτα) occurred as examples for us, so that we might not desire evil as they did.*

7   *Do not become idolaters as some of them did; as it is written, "The people sat down to eat and drink, and they rose up to play."*

8   *We must not indulge in sexual immorality as some of them did, and twenty-three thousand fell in a single day.*

9   *We must not test Christ, as some of them did, and were destroyed by serpents.*

10 *And do not complain as some of them did, and were destroyed by the destroyer.*

11 *These things (ταῦτα) happened to them to serve as an example, and they were written down to instruct us.*

When a demonstrative such as Greek τοῦτο 'this' is used **cataphorically** (5.2.1), the information to which it alludes will belong together if that information extends over more than one sentence. In this instance, it is the FOLLOWING material that should be treated as a block, over against what has preceded.

In 1 Thessalonians 4:15a, for instance, the referent of τοῦτο extends over more than one sentence (15b–17). Verses 15–17 therefore should be treated as a block. The presence of τοῦτο then provides support for the paragraph break inserted by some versions.[14]

Application to the letter to Philemon

Which expression in v. 21 implies that the preceding material should be treated as a block?[15]

Application to the Kalinga text

1. Which expression in 22 implies that the preceding material should be treated as a block?
2. Which expression in 1 implies that the following material should be treated as a block?[16]

---

3. Yes, the countering connective *æ?ţehe* 'in contrast' is likely to provide supporting evidence for boundaries, as it appears to signal a new development in the argument at 19.

[14] In Philemon 15, the referent of διὰ τοῦτο 'because of this' is only one sentence (15–16).

[15] **Suggested answer** for Philemon: In Philemon 21, ἃ λέγω 'what I say' implies that the preceding material (17–20) should be treated as a block. This does not tell us, though, whether a boundary should be placed at 21 or at 22 (see 8.13).

[16] **Suggested answers** for the Kalinga text:
1. In 22, *da sana' e mi-tuttudu* 'these teachings' implies that the preceding material (2–21) should be treated as a block.
2. In 1, *Annaya* 'this' implies that the following material (2–21) should be treated as a block.

Application to the Bariai text

Which expression in 15 implies that the preceding material should be treated as a block?[17]

Application to the Dungra Bhil text

Which expression in 18 implies that the preceding material should be treated as a block?[18]

Application to the language you are analysing

Look for summarising expressions and cataphoric expressions in your texts. Do any of them provide supporting evidence for boundaries that you have proposed?

8.5 *Inclusio* structures

We saw in section 4.1 that *inclusio* structures involve the bracketing of a section by making a statement at the beginning, an approximation of which is repeated at the end (see Guthrie 1998:14). *Inclusios* may thus imply that the enclosed material should be treated as a block.

The following extract from a Toussian (OV) text by Pierre Ouattara[19] illustrates an *inclusio* structure in which the THESIS is followed by supportive material and the reiteration of the THESIS. Such a structure suggests that the material should be treated as a block:

> THESIS
>> *Since you are already old, you should think of the future and leave things in order for your children. It must not be that you give birth to a feud that will last for ever between you and your children. That could become in the future – in your absence – that could become a feud that lasts for ever.*
>> **Supportive Material: Counterpoint to Main Point**
>> *Because I have said to you today that you are already old and approaching death, that could seem as though it isn't the truth that I am saying. I myself could die and leave you, even though you are old. The elders say, "The hide of the calf is in the market, while the old cow is still walking around." That could happen.*
>> **Supportive Material: Main Point**
>> *Nevertheless, if I ask you, you who are seated here, if I ask you, "Which is closer: the place from which you come and the place to which you are going?": you will say to me, "Yes, the place to which I am going is closer now, I have already travelled a long way, I have already covered the longest part of the journey."*
>
> Reiteration of THESIS
>> *That is why I said that, if you are already old, you must think of the future. Don't do anything that will give birth to an eternal feud among you. People would say, "Seeds of weeds have been put in a field." That would be a bad thing.*

Application to the Dungra Bhil text

Look for an *inclusio* in the second half of the body of the text (19–38) that might be cited as supporting evidence for a section boundary.[20]

---

[17] **Suggested answer** for the Bariai text: In 15, *gid kado-nga toa beda-oa* 'behaviour like that' implies that the preceding material (10–14) should be treated as a block.

[18] **Suggested answer** for the Dungra Bhil text: In 18, *ehnoho* 'like this' implies that the preceding material (5–17) is to be treated as a block.

[19] Hannes Wiesmann kindly provided the two examples from Toussian.

[20] **Suggested answer** for the Dungra Bhil text: An *inclusio* is formed by the repetition of *varuhu mer thi dʒi-va* 'live happily with love' (19d) in 38 and of *ek bidʒa ari viḍa* 'not fighting with one another' (20a) in 37. This *inclusio* may be cited as supporting evidence for a section extending from 19 to 38. (Some of the information in 19–20 is also repeated in 23–24, but 24 does not seem to end a unit – see 8.6.)

Application to the language you are analysing

Look for *inclusio* structures in your texts. Do any of them provide supporting evidence for boundaries that you have proposed?

8.6 Chiastic and parallel structures

A **chiastic** structure has two defining features:
   It involves two or more pairs of parallel elements.
   The second elements of the pairs occur in the inverse order to the ones they correspond to.
   For example, if the order of elements in the first part of a structure with two pairs of parallel elements is AB, then the second part will be ordered B'A', where A' corresponds to A, etc. The following is an extract from a Chadian Arabic text:

A (positive)   *Do good things.*
   B (negative)   *Don't do bad things, because they [the recipients] will do the same.*
   B' (negative)   *Stop doing bad things*
A' (positive)   *and do good deeds, so that ...* [consequences]

Like *inclusios*, chiastic structures may imply that the material concerned forms a unit (Neeley 1987:13–18). Neeley cites Hebrews 5:1–10 as an example in Greek of a chiastic structure. Superscript numbers and bolding mark the corresponding elements in each part.

A   *For every **high priest**[1] taken from among men **is appointed**[2] on behalf of men in relation to things of God, that he may offer gifts and sacrifices for sins,*
   B   *being able to deal gently with the ignorant and deceived, since he himself also is surrounded with weakness, and for this reason he ought, just as for the people, so also for himself, to offer for sins.*
      C   *And no one **takes this honour to himself**,[3] but **he who is called by God**,[4] just as Aaron was.*
      C'   *So also Christ **did not glorify himself to become a high priest**,[3] but the one who said to him, You are my son, today I have begotten you. Just as also in another place **he says, You are a priest forever** after the order of Melchizedek.*[4]
   B'   *who in the days of his flesh having offered up prayers and petitions with strong cries and tears to him who was able to save him from death and having been heard because of his fear of God, although he was a Son, learned obedience through what he suffered*
A'   *and having been perfected, he became the source of eternal salvation to those who obey him, **being designated by God**[2] **a high priest**[1] after the order of Melchizedek.*

Question

How might 1 Corinthians 10:6–11 (cited in 8.4) be said to have a chiastic structure? Does this mean that the material concerned forms a unit?[21]

Parallel structures may also imply that the material concerned forms a unit. The following example is from a text in a language of Burkina Faso:

---

[21] **Suggested answer**: 1 Corinthians 10:6–11 might be said to have a chiastic structure because 6 corresponds to 11 (A and A'), 7 corresponds to 10 in being in second person (B and B'), and 8 corresponds to 9 in being in first person (C and C'). However, as noted in 8.4 and 8.5, 11 (A') begins a new unit.

A   *One day, you are angry.*

B   *And your neighbour is happy.*

C   *(If) he asks you for pardon, you should then let the matter rest.*

D   *You let it lie, that day you (pl.) continue (with what you were doing).*

A' *Another day, then, your heart is light;*

B' *his stomach is hot (i.e. he is angry).*

C' *I again tell you to let the matter rest.*

D' *You let it lie, and you (pl.) continue again.*

CONCLUSION   *It is that which enables people to live peacefully together.*

The following parallel structure in Marba (VO) also forms a unit:

EXHORTATIONS

1 (A)   *I don't want you to keep company with thieves, lazy people, etc.*

   2 (reason)   *Such people don't respect their parents.*

  3 (B)   *Abandon them.*

negative consequences

4 (A')   *If you keep company with them, like them you will become the lowest of the people.*

  5 (B')   *If you don't abandon them, you will not have my ear.*[22]

Application to the Bariai text

Sentences 1–4 appear to form a thematic unit. Which type of structure discussed in this section might support this analysis?[23]

Application to the Dungra Bhil text

The consequences described in clauses 14–18 and in 22, 25–26 have a chiastic arrangement. 14–18 concern the consequences of drinking liquor: having no food (15), having no clothing (16) and enjoying no peace (17–18). The consequences of heeding good advice are described in the inverse order: enjoying peace (22), having food (26a) and having clothing (26b). However, the boundary at 19 is so heavily supported that this chiastic structure is spread over two units (see 8.16).

Note that certain languages prefer parallel structures to chiastic structures. Isaiah 6:10 (cited in Acts 28:27) has a chiastic structure in Hebrew and Greek. In other languages, a parallel structure would be more natural when translating this passage. The following table compares the chiastic structure of Acts 28:27 in Greek with two possible parallel structures.[24]

---

[22] The motivational section of a text in the Bhatri in which the writer rebukes the addressee for not following his advice and getting into trouble consists of two parallel sections, both ending with the rhetorical question, *How will you pay the fine?* The hortatory section, in contrast, has an *inclusio* structure.

[23] **Suggested answer** for the Bariai text: Parallel structures would provide support for the treatment of 1–4 as a thematic unit. Sentences 1, 2 and 4 each assert that *the behaviour with regard to drinking banana [beer] and consuming marijuana tobacco, this is bad*. Sentences 2, 3 and 4 each state consequences of such behaviour.

[24] John 12:40 uses a parallel structure (C A C' A') when citing this passage!

Table 8. Chiastic and parallel structures of Acts 28:27

	Chiastic structure		Parallel structure 1		Parallel structure 2
A	*For this people's heart has become calloused;*	A	*For this people's heart has become calloused;*	A	*For this people's heart has become calloused.*
B	*they hardly hear with their ears,*	B	*they hardly hear with their ears,*	A'	*Otherwise, they might understand with their hearts,*
C	*and they have closed their eyes.*	C	*and they have closed their eyes.*		
				B	*They hardly hear with their ears,*
C'	*Otherwise, they might see with their eyes,*	A'	*Otherwise, they might understand with their hearts,*	B'	*Otherwise, they might hear with their ears.*
B'	*hear with their ears,*	B'	*hear with their ears,*		
A'	*understand with their hearts*	C'	*see with their eyes*	C	*And they have closed their eyes.*
				C'	*Otherwise, they might see with their eyes*
	and turn, and I would heal them.		*and turn, and I would heal them.*		*and turn, and I would heal them.*

Application to the language you are analysing

Look for chiastic and parallel structures in your texts. Do any of them provide supporting evidence for boundaries that you have proposed?

8.7 Rhetorical questions

Previous sections have already discussed rhetorical questions that are used to rebuke inappropriate behaviour (7.5 – e.g. Dungra Bhil 30) and those that are posed by an exhorter in order to highlight the answer that he or she will immediately give (7.7.4 – e.g. Dungra Bhil 31). Rhetorical questions are also used in connection with the introduction of a new theme or some new aspect of the same theme (Beekman and Callow 1974:243). The following is an example from Romans 7:7:

7   *What shall we say, then* (οὖν)? *Is the law sin?*

An examination of the examples cited by Beekman and Callow and by Neeley (1987:10–11) suggests that those rhetorical questions that occur at generally recognised boundaries are usually accompanied by other supporting evidence (e.g. δέ or οὖν, in the case of Greek – 8.3). The question and connective **together** provide the supporting evidence for a boundary. See, for example, Luke 6:46:

46   *Why* δέ *do you call me "Lord, Lord," and do not do what I tell you?*

Application to the Kalinga text

Rhetorical questions occur in 3 and 9. What indicates that they do NOT provide supporting evidence for a boundary?[25]

Application to the language you are analysing

Look for rhetorical questions in your texts and determine their function (e.g. to rebuke, to highlight what follows, to introduce a new theme).

---

[25] **Suggested answer** for the Kalinga text: Sentences 3 and 9 do not provide supporting evidence for a boundary because the connective used is *te* 'for', which introduces supportive material.

8.8 Referent identification by means of a seemingly redundant NP

If an active referent seems to be identified 'redundantly' with a noun phrase (NP), the context should be examined to see why the NP is present. It may be there to highlight what follows. Alternatively (and, sometimes, in addition), it may mark the beginning of a unit.

The following passage from Psalm 103:1–9 illustrates the use of seemingly redundant NPs in **Hebrew** to refer to the LORD both for highlighting and at unit boundaries. In 2, the reference to the LORD is repeated in the structure that parallels 1, to highlight the exhortation to praise him. In 6 and 8, in contrast, the references to the LORD appear to signal the beginning of new units.

1   *Praise the LORD, O my soul; all my inmost being, praise his holy name.*
2–5 *Praise the LORD, O my soul, and forget not all his benefits – who forgives all your sins, who heals all your diseases, who redeems your life from the pit, who crowns you with love and compassion, who satisfies your desires with good things so that your youth is renewed like the eagle's.*
6   *The LORD works righteousness and justice for all the oppressed.*
7   *He made known his ways to Moses, his deeds to the people of Israel.*
8   *The LORD is compassionate and gracious, slow to anger, and abounding in love.*
9   *He will not always accuse, and he will not harbour his anger for ever.*

The **absence** of a seemingly redundant NP at what may otherwise seem to be a boundary may be useful counter-evidence for one. In Psalm 103:1–9 (above), the LORD is not referred to by an NP in 7. This suggests that the *NIV* is wrong to introduce a paragraph break at 7, rather than at 8.

Application to the letter to Philemon

Philemon 19 and 20 contain seemingly redundant references to ἐγὼ Παῦλος 'I, Paul' and ἐγώ 'I'. Are these references due to highlighting or do they mark the beginning of a new unit?[26]

Application to the Dungra Bhil text

Sentences 14 and 17 begin with seemingly redundant references to *that man's house* and *the house of a liquor-drinking person* (contrast *in his house* – 13b). Are these references due to highlighting or do they mark the beginning of a new unit?[27]

Application to the language you are analysing

Look for seemingly redundant noun phrases in your texts and determine their function (e.g. to highlight what follows, to mark the beginning of a new unit).

8.9 Vocatives

Like seemingly redundant NPs, some vocatives are found at the beginning of units, others highlight what follows (5.4 and 7.7) and still others seem to do both. Consequently, vocatives may provide supporting evidence for a boundary, but their presence does NOT automatically indicate a boundary.

Thus, Banker's (1984) treatment of the **Greek** vocative ἀδελφοί 'brothers' concludes that it acts with other features to signal the beginning of new units on various levels. It also reinforces conjunctions

---

[26] **Suggested answer** for Philemon: The seemingly redundant references in Philemon 19 and 20 to ἐγὼ Παῦλος 'I, Paul' and ἐγώ 'I' switch attention to or maintain attention on other than the default centre of attention (4.3.2) and are for highlighting.

[27] **Suggested answer** for the Dungra Bhil text: The seemingly redundant references to *that man's house* (14) and *the house of a liquor-drinking person* (17) mark the beginning of subunits in the list of consequences of liquor-addiction. These particular consequences contrast chiastically with the consequences of following good advice (8.6), so they may also be highlighted by the seemingly redundant references.

such as ὥστε 'so then' (as in 1 Corinthians 15:58) and ἄρα οὖν 'so then' (as in 2 Thessalonians 2:15) when they highlight important exhortations. (See also Longacre 1992 on vocatives in 1 John.)

Application to the letter to Philemon

1. The vocative ἀδελφέ 'brother' occurs at beginning of Philemon 20 (following the interjection ναί 'yes'). Does it provide supporting evidence for a boundary or highlight what follows?
2. Unusually, the vocative ἀδελφέ 'brother' occurs at the **end** of Philemon 7. Does it seem to provide supporting evidence for a following boundary or highlight what follows?[28]

Application to the Kalinga text

1. Vocatives occur at the beginning of 1 and 17. Vocative-like expressions such as *kan dikayu, e abeng' e um-adayu* 'to you children that go far' also occur in the points of departure for 5 and 18. Do they provide supporting evidence for a boundary or highlight what follows?
2. Do the vocative-like expressions that occur non-initially in 13 and 21 (see 5.5) and at the end of 22 provide supporting evidence for a boundary?[29]

Application to the Bariai text

Does the vocative *kapeipei ga kakau* 'Elders and young people' (2) provide supporting evidence for a boundary or highlight what follows?[30]

Application to the Dungra Bhil text

Vocatives such as *maa pujra* 'oh my children' occur in 1, 27, 29 and 39. Which ones provide supporting evidence for a boundary? Which ones highlight what follows?[31]

Application to the language you are analysing

Look for vocatives in your texts and determine their function (e.g. to highlight what follows, to provide supporting evidence for a boundary). In what ways is their function affected by their position in the sentence?

8.10 Orienters

Like seemingly redundant NPs and vocatives, some orienters such as *we ask you* or *we urge/appeal to you* are found at the beginning of units, others highlight what follows. In Greek, for example, *Now* (δέ) *we ask you, brothers* (1 Thessalonians 5:12) occurs at the beginning of a unit, whereas *But* (δέ) *we urge/ appeal to you, brothers* (1 Thessalonians 4:10b) introduces and highlights an important exhortation (7.2.1).

---

[28] **Suggested answers** for Philemon:
1. The vocative in Philemon 20 highlights the following exhortation.
2. The vocative at the **end** of Philemon 7 may well provide supporting evidence for a following boundary.

[29] **Suggested answers** for the Kalinga text:
1. The vocatives or vocative-like expressions in 1, 5, 17 and 18 provide supporting evidence for a boundary.
2. The vocative-like expressions that occur noninitially in 13 and 21 do not provide supporting evidence for a boundary. However, the expression at the end of 22 may well provide supporting evidence for a following boundary (compare Philemon 7).

[30] **Suggested answer** for the Bariai text: The vocative in 2 highlights the following expository THESIS (7.4).

[31] **Suggested answer** for the Dungra Bhil text: The vocatives in 1, 27 and 39 provide supporting evidence for a boundary. The vocative in 29 may also provide supporting evidence for a boundary. However, it may well be highlighting the following exhortation (7.5).

Application to the Kalinga text

1. In section 7.3, we noted that the following exhortations are introduced with an orienter: 5, 6, 7, 8, 13, 16, 18 and 20. Which of these appear to occur at the beginning of a unit?
2. The rhetorical question orienter *igammu-yu kamman* 'Don't you know ...?' does not occur at the beginning of a unit in 3 or 9 (see 8.7). What is its function?[32]

Application to the Bariai text

Orienters such as *gau na-keo tautaunga pa-gimi* 'I speak truly to you' occur in 2, 4 and 9. Which of these appear to occur at the beginning of a unit?[33]

Application to the Dungra Bhil text

Sentence 19 contains the speech orienter *ekhūhū mahū?ū tuma-ha koj* 'someone may tell you'. Does it occur at the beginning of a unit?[34]

Application to the language you are analysing

Distinguish the orienters in your texts that occur at the beginning of units from those that highlight what follows.

Review questions

1. Under what circumstances does a **rhetorical question** provide supporting evidence for a boundary?
2. What other factor must be considered before it is judged that the presence of a seemingly **redundant NP** provides supporting evidence for a unit boundary?
3. Name two other features that tend to have the same distribution as seemingly redundant NPs.
4. What three features discussed in 8.2–8.10 confirm that 2 Timothy 2:1 begins a new unit? (The immediately preceding sentence reads, *And you know very well how much service he rendered in Ephesus*.)

2:1 Σὺ   οὖν,   τέκνον   μου,   ἐνδυναμοῦ   ἐν τῇ χάριτι τῇ   ἐν   Χριστῷ   Ἰησοῦ,
    you   then   child   my   be empowered   in the grace   the in   Christ   Jesus

'You, then, my child, be empowered in the grace that is in Christ Jesus'[35]

---

[32] **Suggested answers** for the Kalinga text: All the orienters appear to occur at the beginning of a unit. In 3 and 8, the rhetorical question orienter *igammu-yu kamman* 'Don't you know ...?' highlights the supportive information that follows.

[33] **Suggested answer** for the Bariai text: The only orienter that appears to occur at the beginning of a unit is in 9. The others highlight what follows.

[34] **Suggested answer** for the Dungra Bhil text: Yes, the speech orienter of 19 occurs at the beginning of a unit.

[35] **Suggested answers**
1. A rhetorical question provides supporting evidence for a boundary when accompanied by other supporting evidence such as a developmental connective.
2. Before it is judged that the presence of a seemingly redundant NP provides supporting evidence for a boundary, the possibility that it is present to highlight an important THESIS must be considered.
3. Other features that tend to have the same distribution as seemingly redundant NPs are vocatives and orienters. Both tend to be found both at the beginning of units and in connection with important THESES.
4. Three features that confirm that 2 Timothy 2:1 begins a new unit are: the seemingly redundant preverbal pronoun Σύ 'you' (8.8 and 8.2), the developmental connective οὖν (8.3), and the vocative τέκνον μου 'my child' (8.9).

8.11 Shifts of verb tense-aspect, mood and person

Shifts of tense-aspect and mood may provide supporting evidence for a unit boundary (Porter 1992:301). Hebrews 3:12–18 (below) illustrates this for Greek; "at the break [between 15 and 16], the verbs change in person, tense and mood" (Neeley 1987:19).[36] First and second person change to third, while the mood changes from imperative to rhetorical questions.

12–15   *See to it, brothers, that none of you has a sinful, unbelieving heart that turns away from the living God. But encourage one another daily, as long as it is called Today, so that none of you may be hardened by sin's deceitfulness. For we have come to share in Christ if we hold firmly till the end the confidence we had at first; as has been said: "Today, if you hear his voice, do not harden your hearts as you did in the rebellion."*

16–18   *For who were they who heard and rebelled? Were they not all those Moses led out of Egypt? And with whom was he angry for forty years? Was it not with those who sinned, whose bodies fell in the desert? And to whom did God swear that they would never enter his rest if not to those who disobeyed?*

However, Nida et al. (1983:38–39) point out that, in Acts 1:4–5, there is a shift from indirect reporting of speech (with infinitives) to first and second person direct reporting: *He ordered them not to leave Jerusalem, but to wait there for the promise of the Father which* **you** *heard from* **me**. This shift does not occur at a unit boundary, but has the effect of highlighting what follows. So, once again, the same device may be used at unit boundaries and for highlighting.

Application to the letter to Philemon

The *NRSV* has paragraph breaks at Philemon 4, 8, 17, 22, 23, 25. For which of these would a shift of mood and person provide supporting evidence?[37]

Application to the Kalinga text

When hortatory material is followed by supportive material, at which places in the text is the beginning of the next hortatory unit accompanied by a shift of mood and person?[38]

Application to the Bariai text

Previous sections have proposed that 1–4 be treated as a unit, over against what follows, and that 9 begins a new unit. Are there any shifts of tense-aspect, mood or person at 5 and 9?[39]

Application to the Dungra Bhil text

In which sentences is a vocative (8.9) accompanied by a shift of tense-aspect, mood or person?[40]

---

[36] Campbell (2008:36–38, 41–44) considers the Greek aorist, imperfect and present verb forms not to indicate tense.

[37] **Suggested answer** for Philemon: Shifts of mood and person occur at Philemon 4, 17, 23, 25. At 4, the shift is from an implied third person optative (*May God our Father* [Allen 2000]) to a first person indicative (*I give thanks*). At 17, the shift between independent clauses is from third person indicative (*he was separated* – 15) to second person imperative (*receive*). At 23, the shift is from second person singular imperative (*prepare*) to third person indicative (*Epaphras greets you*). At 25, a change of third person subject is accompanied by a shift to an implied optative (*May our* [incl] *Lord Jesus Christ* [Allen 2000]).

[38] **Suggested answer** for the Kalinga text: The beginning of the next hortatory unit is accompanied by a shift from declarative to some sort of hortatory mood and from third to second person at 5 and 10.

[39] **Suggested answer** for the Bariai text: At both 5 and 9, there is a shift of mood (irrealis to realis) and of person. The shifts of person are from *I, you and many people* in 4 to *God* and first person inclusive in 5; and from first person inclusive in 8 to third person in 9.

[40] **Suggested answer** for the Dungra Bhil text: A vocative is accompanied by a shift of person at 27 (second to

Note that a shift of mood from future to jussive/gerund occurs at 34. In the absence of other confirming features, this suggests a minor boundary.

Application to the language you are analysing

Check whether shifts of tense-aspect, mood or person ever provide supporting evidence for boundaries in your texts.

8.12 Back reference

Neeley (1987:19) says **back reference** "involves reference to the preceding paragraph or paragraphs or to a point or points within preceding paragraphs. Back-reference often occurs at the beginning of a new paragraph."

In Koine Greek, for example, the participial clauses of Hebrews 4:14 refer back to the theme of Jesus as our high priest, which was last mentioned in Hebrews 3:1. This, together with the presence of the inferential connective οὖν 'then' (8.3), provides good evidence that a new unit is beginning.

3:1 *Therefore, holy brothers, who share in the heavenly calling, fix your thoughts on Jesus, the apostle and high priest of our confession.*

[3:2–4:13: expository material]

4:14 *Having, then (οὖν), a great high priest who has gone through the heavens, Jesus the Son of God, let us hold firmly to our confession. (15) For (γάρ) ...*

Note that languages that frequently use independent clauses to express time (e.g. *It became day*) are likely to use independent clauses for back reference where Greek uses a participle.

One type of back reference is **tail-head linkage**. Matthew 6:14 (below) provides an example. The 'tail' of 12 (*as we also have forgiven our debtors*) is repeated as the 'head' on 14 (*if you forgive men when they sin against you*):

12 *And forgive us our debts, as we also have forgiven our debtors.*
13 *And do not bring us to the time of trial, but rescue us from the evil one.*
14 *For if you forgive men when they sin against you, your heavenly Father will also forgive you;*

However, as with the devices discussed in 8.8–8.10, tail-head linkage may also be used to highlight what follows (see Levinsohn 2015, 3.2.3).

Like οὖν when used as a resumptive (8.3), the greater the distance between the back reference and the material to which it refers, the more major is the boundary likely to be. Compare, for example, the degree of discontinuity implied by the references back to Acts 8:1 in 8:4 and in 11:19 (*those who had been scattered*).

Application to the Kalinga text

What type of back reference occurs in 20? How major is the boundary likely to be?[41]

---

first person), 29 (first to second person) and 39 (first to third person). There is also a shift of tense or mood at 27 (the future marker -*dʒi* is translated 'must').

[41] **Suggested answer** for the Kalinga text: The type of back reference that occurs at 20 is tail-head linkage. *When you've finished* refers back to the exhortation *to finish your studies* (18). The boundary is likely to be minor, as only one sentence separates 20 from 18.

Application to the Dungra Bhil text

What type of back reference occurs in 10? What surface feature indicates that any boundary is not a major one?[42]

Application to the language you are analysing

Look for instances of back reference in your texts. Identify the sentence to which each instance relates.

8.13 Application to the letter to Philemon

In earlier sections, we noted several features that could be confirming a segmentation of the letter into larger and smaller units on semantic grounds. They are as follows:

- a point of departure at Philemon 17, 22 (8.2)
- connectives at 8, 17, 22; juxtaposition at 4, 23, 25 (8.3)
- a summarising expression at the end of 21, relating back to 17–20 (8.4)
- a vocative at the end of 7 (8.9)
- shifts of mood and person at 4, 17, 23, 25 (8.11).

We also noted in 8.3 that the material introduced with the strengthening connective γάρ 'for, after all' in 7, 15 and 22b naturally belongs with the material it supports.

The following table shows how the above features support the paragraph breaks in the *NRSV* at 4, 8, 17, 22, 23 and 25 (the section titles in quotation marks are from Allen 2000) (PoD = point of departure):[43]

Table 9. Features supporting paragraph breaks in the *NRSV*

Proposed section	Supportive features
Introduction "Paul and Timothy greet Philemon" (1–3)	
Body of text (4–22)	juxtaposition, shift of mood & person
"Paul thanks God for Philemon and prays for him" (4–7)	
"Paul asks Philemon to accept back Onesimus" (8–21)	
Supportive material (8–16)	vocative (end of 7), connective διό
The actual appeal (17–21)	PoD, connective οὖν, shift of mood & person
Additional request for guest room (22)	summary (end of 21), PoD by renewal, connective δέ
Closure (23–25)	juxtaposition, shift of mood & person
"Fellow believers greet Philemon" (23–24)	
"Goodbye" (25)	juxtaposition, shift of mood & person

In the above table, Philemon 8–16 and 17–21 are grouped together into a single section because both subsections concern Paul's appeal to Philemon on behalf of Onesimus. In contrast, there is no

---

[42] **Suggested answer** for the Dungra Bhil text: The type of back reference that occurs at 10 is tail-head linkage. *After drinking liquor* refers back to *he will drink liquor* (6). The surface feature that indicates that the boundary is not a major one is the associative connective *ono* (8.3).

[43] I do not discuss the *NIV* paragraph break at 12, as it falls in the middle of a Greek sentence. Russell (1998:12–13) divides 8–22 at 14, 18 and 21, each of which begins with an appropriate connective (δέ in 14 and 18, juxtaposition in 21). Of these, 14 could constitute an additional break in the supportive material of 8ff. Even though 18 also begins with a conditional point of departure, Russell seems to be alone in proposing a paragraph break at 18 rather than 17. In contrast, several commentators and editors begin a new section at 21, rather than at 22 (the summarising expression in 21 could be cited for either boundary, though the initial participle Πεποιθώς 'having confidence' suggests continuity with the context – Levinsohn 2000, 11.1.3).

particular reason why 23–24 and 25 should be grouped together, as there is good supportive evidence for a break at 25.

8.14 Application to the Kalinga text

In earlier sections, we noted several features that could be confirming a segmentation of the text into larger and smaller units on semantic grounds. List them, then prepare a table that shows the sections you propose together with the supporting features. The suggested answer is below.

Suggested answer

The features we noted in earlier sections are as follows:
- points of departure at 2, 5, 6, 8, 13, 16, 17 and 18 (8.2)
- additives at 7, 8 and 17; juxtaposition at 2, 5, 6, 10, 13, 16, 17, 18 and 22 (8.3)
- a cataphoric demonstrative at 1 and a summarising expression at 22, both relating to 2–21 (8.4)
- vocatives at 1, 5, 17, 18 and the end of 22 (8.9)
- orienters at 5, 6, 7, 8, 13, 16, 18 and 20 (8.10)
- shifts of mood and person at 5 and 10 (8.11)
- back reference with the developmental connective *kad* at 20 (8.12 and 8.3).

We also noted in 8.3 that the material introduced with the strengthening connective *te* 'for' at 3, 9, 19 and 21 naturally belongs with the material it supports.

The following table indicates a way of segmenting and grouping the text, based on the above supportive features.

Table 10. Features supporting section breaks in the Kalinga text

Proposed section	Supportive features (except for juxtaposition)
Body of text (1–22)	
Opening of Body (1)	Cataphoric demonstrative (introducing 2–21)
Exhortation 1 Enrol in right courses (2–4)	PoD
Exhortation 2 on homesickness (5)	PoD with orienter, vocative, shift of mood/person
Exhortation 3 on boarding house (6)	PoDs with orienter, additional PoDs
Exhortation 4 on hardship (7)	Additive, orienter
Exhortation 5 on friends (8–9)	Additive, PoD with orienter, additional PoD
Exhortations 6 on money (10–12)	Shift of mood/person
Exhortation 7 on sex (13–15)	PoD with orienter
Exhortation 8 if sick (16)	PoD with orienter
Exhortation 9 on working (17)	Vocative with additive, PoD
Exhortations 10–11 on completing studies and finding work (18–21)	
Exhortation 10 (18–19)	PoD with orienter
Exhortation 11 (20–21)	Back reference and *kad*, orienter
Conclusion of Body (22)	Summarising expression (relating back to 2–21)
Closure (23)	Vocative (end of 22)

In the above table, clauses 18–19 and 20–21 are grouped together into a single section because the back reference and the developmental connective *kad* at 20 probably imply that the same theme is being resumed and advanced (see 3.6).

8.15 Application to the Bariai text

In earlier sections, we noted several features that could be confirming a segmentation of the text into larger and smaller units on semantic grounds. List them, then prepare a table that shows the sections you propose together with the supporting features. The suggested answer is below.

Suggested answer

The features we noted in earlier sections are as follows:
- the left-dislocated point of departure at 9 (8.2)
- a summarising expression at 15, relating back to 10–14 (8.4)
- parallel structures in 1–4 (8.6)
- an orienter at 9 (8.10)
- shifts of mood and person at 5 and 9 (8.11).

We also noted in 8.3 that the material introduced with the additive *be* (3) and the combination *ga pade* 'and also' (11) naturally belongs with the material to which it is added.

The following table indicates a way of segmenting and grouping the text, based on the above supportive features.

Table 11. Features supporting section breaks in the Bariai text

Proposed section	Supportive features
Reasons for not taking banana beer & marijuana (1–4)	Parallel structures
Consequences of obeying God's talk (5–8)	Shift of mood/person
Consequences of taking banana beer & marijuana plus Exhortation (9–16)	PoD, summary (15), orienter, shift of mood/person

8.16 Application to the Dungra Bhil text

In earlier sections, we noted several features that could be confirming a segmentation of the text into larger and smaller units on semantic grounds. List them, then prepare a table that shows the sections you propose together with the supporting features. The suggested answer is below.

Suggested answer

The features we noted in earlier sections are as follows:
- the points of departure at 2, 19 and, possibly, 10 (8.2)
- developmental connectives at 7, 14 and 19; plus the additive at 17 (8.3)
- a summarising expression in 18, referring back to 5–17 (8.4)
- an *inclusio* between 19–20 and 37–38 (8.5)
- seemingly redundant noun phrases at 14 and 17 (8.8)
- vocatives at 1, 27, 39 and, possibly, 29 (8.9)
- an orienter at 19 (8.10)
- shifts of person at 27, 29 and 39; plus a shift of mood at 34 (8.11)
- back reference at 10 (8.12).

We also noted in 8.3 that the material introduced with the associative connective *ono* 'and' (4, 6, 9, 10, 13, 15, 16 and 23) naturally belongs with the material with which it is associated. Furthermore, parallel progression unites 10–12 (4.1).

The following table indicates a way of segmenting and grouping the text, based on the above supportive features.

Table 12. Features supporting section breaks in the Dungra Bhil text

Proposed section	Supportive features
Introductory exhortation: *Don't drink liquor!* (1)	Vocative
Motivational section (2–18)	PoD
Liquor is a poison, with evidence (2–6)	
Consequences of addiction (7–13)	Connective
hunger (7–9)	
irrational behaviour (10–13)	PoD, back reference, but *ono*
Consequences of 10–13 (14–18)	Connective, NP
A/B: No clothing or food (14–16)	
C: No peace (17–18)	Additive, NP
Hortatory section (19–38)	PoD, connective, summary (18), *inclusio* to 38, orienter
Heed good advice, plus consequences (19–26)	
C': Peace (19–22)	
B'/A': Food & clothing (23–26)	(*ono*)
Work in farming (27–28)	Vocative, shift of person
Consequences of not working (29–33)	Vocative, shift of person
Work, don't drink liquor, live at peace (34–38)	Shift of mood
Conclusion (39)	*Inclusio* ends at 38, vocative, shift of person

In the above table, clauses 7–9 and 10–13 are grouped together into a single section because of the associative connective *ono*. The same is true of 19–22 and 23–26. Clauses 14–16 and 17–18 are grouped together because of the additive *ihĩkojite* 'likewise'.

Application to the language you are analysing

1. List the features that you identified in earlier sections which could be confirming a segmentation of your texts into larger and smaller units on semantic grounds.
2. Prepare tables that show the sections you propose along with the supporting features.
3. Which supporting features occur in more than one text?

Appendix A: Letter to Philemon in Koine Greek
ΠΡΟΣ ΦΙΛΗΜΟΝΑ

Appendix A: Letter to Philemon in Koine Greek

Ref.	Con.	Prenuclear-V	Nucleus	Postnuclear
1		Παῦλος Paul	δέσμιος Χριστοῦ prisoner of.Christ	Ἰησοῦ καὶ Τιμόθεος ὁ ἀδελφὸς Jesus and Timothy the brother
		Φιλήμονι τῷ ἀγαπητῷ to.Philemon the beloved		
2		καὶ Ἀπφίᾳ τῇ ἀδελφῇ καὶ Ἀρχίππῳ and Apphia the sister and Archippus		τῷ συστρατιώτῃ ἡμῶν καὶ τῇ κατ' οἶκόν σου ἐκκλησίᾳ the fellow-soldier our and to.the in house your church
3		χάρις ὑμῖν καὶ εἰρήνη grace to.you and peace		ἀπὸ θεοῦ πατρὸς ἡμῶν καὶ κυρίου Ἰησοῦ Χριστοῦ from God Father our and Lord Jesus Christ

'Paul, a prisoner of Christ Jesus, and Timothy our brother, to Philemon our dear friend and coworker, to Apphia our sister, to Archippus our fellow soldier, and to the church in your house: Grace to you and peace from God our Father and the Lord Jesus Christ.'

Ref.	Con.	Prenuclear-V	Nucleus	Postnuclear
4a			Εὐχαριστῶ τῷ θεῷ I.give.thanks to.the God	μου my
4b				πάντοτε μνείαν σου ποιούμενος ἐπὶ τῶν προσευχῶν μου always mention of.you making at the prayers my
5a				ἀκούων σου τὴν ἀγάπην καὶ τὴν πίστιν hearing your the love and the faith
5b				ἣν ἔχεις πρὸς τὸν κύριον Ἰησοῦν καὶ εἰς πάντας τοὺς ἁγίους which you.have for the Lord Jesus and for all the saints
6a				ὅπως ἡ κοινωνία τῆς πίστεώς σου ἐνεργὴς γένηται so.that the fellowship of.the faith your effective may.become
6b				ἐν ἐπιγνώσει παντὸς ἀγαθοῦ τοῦ ἐν ἡμῖν εἰς Χριστόν in acknowledgment of.every good.thing of.the in us for Christ

'I always thank my God when I remember you in my prayers,
because I hear of your love for all the saints and your faith toward the Lord Jesus.
I pray that the sharing of your faith may become effective
when you perceive all the good that we may do for Christ.'

Ref.	Con.	Prenuclear-V	Nucleus	Postnuclear
7a	[γὰρ]	χαρὰν γὰρ πολλὴν ἔσχον καὶ παράκλησιν joy for much I.had and encouragement		ἐπὶ τῇ ἀγάπῃ σου at the love your
7b				ὅτι τὰ σπλάγχνα τῶν ἁγίων ἀναπέπαυται διὰ σοῦ, ἀδελφέ because the inward.parts of.the saints have.been.refreshed thru you brother

'I indeed received much joy and encouragement from your love,
because the hearts of the saints have been refreshed through you, my brother.'

Ref.	Con.	Prenuclear-V	Nucleus	Postnuclear
8a	Διὸ therefore	πολλὴν ἐν Χριστῷ παρρησίαν much in Christ boldness	ἔχων having	
8b			ἐπιτάσσειν σοι τὸ ἀνῆκον to.order to.you the required	

Appendix A: Letter to Philemon in Koine Greek

Ref.	Con.	Prenuclear-V	Nucleus			Postnuclear					
9a	διὰ because.of	τὴν the	ἀγάπην love	μᾶλλον rather	παρακαλῶ I.appeal						
9b						τοιοῦτος such	ὢν being	ὡς Παῦλος as Paul	πρεσβύτης old.man		
9c	[δέ]					νυνὶ now	δὲ DM	καὶ ADD	δέσμιος prisoner	Χριστοῦ of.Christ	Ἰησοῦ Jesus

'Therefore, though I am bold enough in Christ to command you to do your duty, yet I would rather appeal to you on the basis of love – such a one being Paul, an old man, and now also a prisoner of Christ Jesus.'

10a			παρακαλῶ I.appeal	σε to.you		περὶ concerning	τοῦ the	ἐμοῦ my	τέκνου child		
10b						ὃν whom	ἐγέννησα I.gave.birth	ἐν τοῖς in the	δεσμοῖς, bonds	Ὀνήσιμον Onesimus	
11a						τόν the.one	ποτέ once	σοι to.you	ἄχρηστον useless		
11b	[δέ]					νυνὶ now	δὲ DM	[καὶ] ADD	σοὶ to.you	καὶ ἐμοὶ and to.me	εὔχρηστον useful
12a						ὃν whom	ἀνέπεμψά I.sent.back	σοι to.you			
12b		αὐτόν, τοῦτ' him this	ἔστιν is	τὰ the	ἐμά my	σπλάγχνα inward.parts					
13a						ὃν whom	ἐγὼ I	ἐβουλόμην I.was.desiring	πρὸς ἐμαυτὸν with myself	κατέχειν to.keep	
13b						ἵνα that	ὑπὲρ σοῦ μοι διακονῇ for you me he.might.serve	ἐν τοῖς in the	δεσμοῖς bonds	τοῦ of.the	εὐαγγελίου good.news

'I am appealing to you for my child, Onesimus, to whom I became a father while in bonds; the one formerly useless to you, but now indeed useful both to you and to me; whom I am sending, that is, my own heart, back to you; whom I was wanting to keep with me so that he might be of service to me in your place during my imprisonment for the gospel;'

14a	[δέ]	χωρὶς without	δὲ DM	τῆς σῆς the your	γνώμης consent	οὐδὲν nothing	ἠθέλησα I.wanted	ποιῆσαι to.do			
14b						ἵνα μὴ ὡς that not as	κατὰ according.to	ἀνάγκην necessity	τὸ ἀγαθόν the goodness	σου your	
14c	ἀλλὰ but					κατὰ according.to	ἑκούσιον willingness				ᾖ might be

'but I preferred to do nothing without your consent, in order that your good deed might not be something forced but voluntary.'

122 Appendix A: Letter to Philemon in Koine Greek

Ref.	Con.	Prenuclear-V	Nucleus	Postnuclear
15a	[γὰρ]	τάχα γὰρ perhaps for	διὰ because.of	τοῦτο ἐχωρίσθη πρὸς ὥραν this he.was.separated for hour
15b				ἵνα αἰώνιον αὐτὸν ἀπέχῃς that eternally him you.might.have
16a				οὐκέτι ὡς δοῦλον no.longer as slave
16b	ἀλλ' but			ὑπὲρ δοῦλον, ἀδελφὸν ἀγαπητόν more.than slave brother beloved
16c				μάλιστα ἐμοί especially to.me
16d	[δὲ]			πόσῳ δὲ μᾶλλον σοὶ καὶ ἐν σαρκὶ καὶ ἐν κυρίῳ how.much DM more to.you ADD in flesh and in Lord

'Perhaps this is the reason he was separated from you for a while, so that you might have him back forever, no longer as a slave but more than a slave, a beloved brother – especially to me but how much more to you, both in the flesh and in the Lord.'

Ref.	Con.	Prenuclear-V	Nucleus	Postnuclear
17a	[οὖν]	Εἰ οὖν if then	με ἔχεις me you.hold	κοινωνόν partner
17b			προσλαβοῦ αὐτὸν ὡς ἐμέ receive him as me	

'If, then, you consider me your partner, welcome him as you would welcome me.'

Ref.	Con.	Prenuclear-V	Nucleus	Postnuclear
18a	[δὲ]	εἰ δέ if DM	τι anything	ἠδίκησέν σε ἢ ὀφείλει he.wronged you or he.owes
18b		τοῦτο ἐμοὶ this to.me	ἐλλόγα charge.to.account	τῇ ἐμῇ χειρί with.the my hand

'And if he has wronged you in any way or owes you anything, charge this to my account.'

Ref.	Con.	Prenuclear-V	Nucleus	Postnuclear
19a		ἐγὼ I	Παῦλος ἔγραψα Paul wrote	τῇ ἐμῇ χειρί with.the my hand
19b		ἐγὼ I	ἀποτίσω· I.will.repay	
19c				ἵνα μὴ that not
19d				ὅτι καὶ σεαυτόν μοι προσοφείλεις that ADD yourself to.me you.owe

'I, Paul, am writing this with my own hand: I will repay it – to say nothing about your owing me even your own self.'

Appendix A: Letter to Philemon in Koine Greek

Ref.	Con.	Prenuclear-V	Nucleus	Postnuclear
20a	ναὶ yes 'Yes,	ἀδελφέ, ἐγώ brother I brother, let me benefit from you in the Lord!'	σου ὀναίμην of.you I.may.have.profit	ἐν κυρίῳ in Lord
20b			ἀνάπαυσόν μου τὰ σπλάγχνα refresh my the inward.parts 'Refresh my heart in Christ.'	ἐν Χριστῷ in Christ
21a		Πεποιθὼς having.confidence	τῇ ὑπακοῇ in.the obedience	σου your
21b			ἔγραψά σοι I.wrote to.you	
21c		εἰδὼς knowing		
21d				ὅτι καὶ ὑπὲρ ἃ λέγω ποιήσεις that ADD above what I.say you.will.do 'Confident of your obedience, I am writing to you, knowing that you will do even more than I say.'
22a	[δὲ]	ἅμα at.same.time	δὲ καὶ ἑτοίμαζέ μοι ξενίαν DM ADD prepare for.me lodging	
22b	[γάρ]		ἐλπίζω γὰρ I.hope for	
22c				ὅτι διὰ τῶν προσευχῶν ὑμῶν χαρισθήσομαι ὑμῖν that through the prayers your° I.will.be.restored to.you 'One thing more – prepare a guest room for me, for I am hoping through your prayers to be restored to you.'
23			Ἀσπάζεταί σε Ἐπαφρᾶς ὁ συναιχμάλωτός μου ἐν Χριστῷ Ἰησοῦ greets you Epaphras the fellow.prisoner my in Christ Jesus	
24			Μᾶρκος, Ἀρίσταρχος, Δημᾶς, Λουκᾶς, οἱ συνεργοί μου Mark Aristarchus Demas Luke the co.workers my 'Epaphras, my fellow prisoner in Christ Jesus, sends greetings to you, and so do Mark, Aristarchus, Demas, and Luke, my fellow workers.'	
25			Ἡ χάρις τοῦ κυρίου Ἰησοῦ Χριστοῦ μετὰ τοῦ πνεύματος ὑμῶν the grace of.the Lord Jesus Christ with the spirit your° 'The grace of the Lord Jesus Christ be with your spirit.'	

Appendix B: Advice to a Student in Lower Tanudan Kalinga

by Mary Duno

126 Appendix B: Advice to a Student in Lower Tanudan Kalinga

Ref.	Con.	Prenuclear-V	Nucleus	Postnuclear						
01[1]		Abeng,	annaya	[ma-sapul'	e	ko-on-yu	e	um-oy	an-uswila	si	adayu]
		child	this.EMP	PASS.IMPF-need	LK	do-TH.IMPF-2p.GEN	LK	AG-go	AG-study	LOC	far
		'Children, this (is) what you need to do when you go to school in a far place.'

02		Sa	um-una,	sosomk-on-yu
		the	AG-first	DUR.think-TH.IMPF-2p.GEN

b					ta	siya	iy-enrol-yu	de	makwa	e	pion-yu
					PUR	that.which	TH-enrol-2p.GEN	ABS	POT.know	LK	like-2p.GEN

c					kan	ma-kaya-yu	e	courso
					and	PASS-carry-2p.GEN	LK	course

'so that what you enrol in is a course you know you like and one you can afford.'

03	Te		igammu-yu	kamman
	for		know-2p.GEN	QUES

'The first thing (is) to think hard,'

b			ka-adu-wan'	e	maka-taktak	si	an-uswila,
			REC-many-REC	LK	POT-delay	OBL	AG-study

c			adi-na	pun	kad	pion	awa	illus-na	iy-enrol
			NEG-3s	NEG	when	want	EXIS	TH.start-3s	TH-enrol

d			i-kasin-na	bos	ang-ala	'k	osa	courso
			TH-repeat-3s	also	AG-take	OBL	one	course

'After all, don't you know, there are many who are delayed in their studies when they don't like what it is they enrolled in and so take another course.'

04	Kad	sadi	osa	e	ma-gastu	lawa	pilak
	then	that	one	LK	PASS.IMPF-spend	no.reason	money

'Then that is one way money is spent for nothing/senselessly.'

05		[Sa osa e	mi-baga	kan	dikayu,	e	abeng'	e	um-adayu]
		the one LK	PASS-tell	OBL	2p.TOP	LK	CHILD	LK	AG-far

b			adi-kayu	okyan	al-lasu	e	um-ayu
			NEG-2p.ABS	should	AJR-easy	LK	AG-homesickness

c				[te	sadi	osa	e	angi-agay-an	da	udum'	e	an-uswila
				for	that	one	LK	OCC-stop-OCC	PL	other	LK	AG-study

d				adi-da	pun	maka-kwa	si	ayu-da]				
				NEG-3p	NEG	POT-do	OBL	homesickness-3p

'The one thing I'm telling you, children that go far, you should not easily be homesick, because that is one thing that stops others that go away to school, not being able to bear their homesickness.'

---

[1] This text began with the title *Sa tuttudu atta abeng e um-oy an-uswila si adayu* 'the lesson OBL.PL child LK AG-go AG-study LOC far'. Mary had just sent her daughter, Florida, off to school in Vigan.

Appendix B: Advice to a Student in Lower Tanudan Kalinga

Ref.	Con.	Prenuclear-V	Nucleus		Postnuclear				
06			Sa osa e	ma-sapul'	e	ko-on-yu,	nu	an-singit-kayu	'k boardinghouse-yu
			the one LK	PASS.IMPF-need	LK	do-TH.IMPF-2p.GEN	if	AG.IMPF-look.for-2p.ABS	OBL boardinghouse-2p.GEN
b		[siya	singt-on-yu]		poos am-bayad-ta				
		that.which	look.for-TH.IMPF-2p.GEN		little AG-payment-1d				
c			sa	am-baʔu	kadauyan	da	simbo¹oy		
			the	AJR-good	character	PL	house.owner		
d			sa	adi	mi-doga	da	laʔaki		
			the	NEG	PASS.include	PL	boy		
e			kan sa adani	si	uswila-an,	ta	adi-kayu	ma-gastu-wan	si puliti
			and the near	LOC	student-LOC	PUR	NEG-2p.ABS	PASS.IMPF-spend-LOC	OBL fare
6.		'The one thing you need to do, when you are looking for a boarding house, what you are looking for is one where we pay a little, where the character of the house owner is good, where boys are not included and where it is near the school so that you won't have to spend the fare.'							
07		i-baga-k	os	kan	dikayu				
		TH-tell-1s.ABS	also	OBL	2p				
b			ma-sapul¹		man',	e	i-sasaggana-yu	e	an-rigat
			PASS.IMPF-need		surely	LK	TH-DUR.prepare-2p.GEN LK		AG-hardship
c					te	siguradu	e	awad	da ang-kurang-an
					for	assured	LK	EXIS	PL AG-lacking-LOC
d					atta	ka-sapul-an-ta	e	an-uswila,	kamaʔta pilak, binayu
					OBL.PL	REC-need-REC-1d	LK	AG-study	like.OBL.PL money uncooked.rice
e					te	sillalabi	kad	an-sigab	an-singit-an-ni 'k pilak
					for	sometimes	then/when	AJR-difficulty	AG.IMPF-look.for-LOC-1ex OBL money
f					kan	na-ip.pun	makwa	'k	angi-paw-it-an-ni
					and	ST.PF-NEG.EXIS	POT.do	OBL	person.who-send.with-LOC-1ex
7.		'I also tell you, it is surely necessary that you prepare for hardship, as it is sure that there will be lacking for our school needs, like money & rice, because sometimes, then, we have difficulty finding money and there may be no one for us to send it with.'							
08		Sa	mi-baga	bos					
		what	PASS-tell	also					
b		nu	inggaw-kayu	si	adayu				
		if	stay-2p.ABS	LOC	far				
c			adi-kayu	ang-gakagakay	kan	pat	si	barkada	
			NEG-2p.ABS	AG.IMPF-DUR.roam	and	fond.of	OBL	peers	
8.		'What I'm also saying is, if you stay far (away), don't be fond of roaming and (going out) with your peers.'							

Ref.	Con.	Prenuclear-V	Nucleus	Postnuclear				
09	Te for	igammu-yu know-2p.GEN	kamman QUES	sadi that	osa one	e LK	maka-dadail POT-destroy	si uswila de bungbunggoy. OBL student ABS DUR.group
9.				'After all, don't you know, that is one of the things that can destroy a student, the group one always goes around with?'				
10				Umma-nyu be.careful-2p.GEN		ila-n see-LK	ang-gastu-wan-yu-'tta AG.IMPF-spend-LOC-2p.GEN-OBL.PL	pilak-yu money-2p.GEN
10.				Be careful (and) watch how you spend your money.'				
11				Ma-sapu¹' PASS.IMPF-need	e LK	[siya that.which	okyan um-una e ang-gastu-wan-yu should AG-first LK AG.IMPF-spend-LOC-2p.GEN	da ka-patg-an] PL REC-important-REC
b				um-una AG-first	e LK	bayad-an-yu payment-LOC-2p.GEN	tuitionfee tuition.fee	ya da uniform-yu and PL uniform-2p.GEN
11.				You need to … what you should spend first is on the most important, first for your tuition fee and your uniform.'				
12	[kad]	Sillalabi-na sometimes-3s	kad then/when	anus-an-yu patience-LOC-2p.GEN			ngoswal meatless.meal	
12.		'There will be times, then, when a meal that is just rice will be your lot.'						
13	Sa the	importante important		kad then/when	pagay really.EMP	e LK	mi-baga TH-tell	
b				umma-nyu be.careful-2p.GEN		da PL	long-ag-yu one's.body-2p.GEN	amod ay dikayu e bubai especially.EMP 2p LK girl
c						te sana for this	ka-adu-wan os' e maka-dadail atta an-uswila REC-many-REC also LK POT-destroy OBL.PL AG-study
13.		'The really important thing I'm saying is be careful of your body, especially you girls, because this is how many students may be destroyed;'						
14	[kad] nowadays	sinsana then/when	kad many	[adu PL	da	ma-bugi ST.IMPF-pregnancy	kan bumugi] and AG.pregnancy	
b						te for	ko-on-yu do-TH.IMPF-2p.GEN	gay' e abeng pinion-yu EMP LK child TH.want-2p.GEN
14.		'nowadays, as a consequence, those who are pregnant and cause pregnancy are many; after all, you children do just whatever you want.'						
15	Kad then	adi-yu NEG-2p.GEN		pun NEG	dongo-n listen-TH.IMPF	i-baga-n TH-tell-LK	da ama-yu PL father-2p.GEN	kan i-tuttudu-da and TH-lesson-3p
15.	'And then you don't listen to what your parents tell you or their teaching.'							

Appendix B: Advice to a Student in Lower Tanudan Kalinga

Ref.	Con.	Prenuclear-V	Nucleus	Postnuclear
16			*Sa osa e mi-baga* the one LK TH-tell	
b		*nu awad kappay* if EXIS whenever		*ma-sakit-an-yu* ST.IMPF-sickness-LOC-2p.GEN
c			*ma-sapul' e i-baga-yu atta ama-yu kan ina-yu* PASS.IMPF-need LK TH-tell-2p.GEN OBL.PL father-2p.GEN and mother-2p.GEN	
16.				'The one/other thing I'm saying is that, if you ever become really sick, it is necessary for you to tell your mother and father.'
17			*Dikayu bos abeng* 2p.TOP also child	
b		*nu dumatong okyan duwa-n bulan'* if AG.arrive should two-LK month		*e bakasyun* LK vacation
c			*in-kayu an-singit ak* go-2p.ABS AG-look.for ABS	*an-kewaal-an-yu* AG.IMPF-work-LOC-2p.GEN
d				*ta ma-tulung-an da ama-yu kan ina-yu si gastu* PUR PASS.IMPF-help-LOC PL father-2p.GEN and mother-2p.GEN OBL spend
17.				'Also you children, when your 2-month vacation arrives, you should look for work, so that your parents will be helped with expenses.'
18			[*Siya okyan somsomk-on-yu e abeng' e an-uswila*] that.which should think-TH.IMPF-2p.GEN LK child LK AG-study	
b			*ma-sapul' e i-gangput-yu da uswila-yu* PASS.IMPF-need LK TH-finish-2p.GEN PL study-2p.GEN	
c				*te igammu-yu siya mi-lak.sun si sana adal* for know-2p.GEN that.which PASS.IMPF-inheritance OBL this learn
18.				'What you children who are studying should think about, is the need for you to finish your studies, because you know, it is education that is the inheritance at this time.'
19	[kad]	*Te* for	*ila-nyu kad* see-2p.GEN then/when	
		dikani e ama-yu 1ex LK father-2p.GEN	*kan ina-yu* and mother-2p.GEN	*anna e am-pa-rigat-kani e pumamilya* this LK AG-CAUS*-suffering-1p.ABS LK AG.family
b				*te an-sigab an-singit-an-ni 'k pilak' e farmer* for AJR-difficulty AG.IMPF-look.for-LOC-1ex ABS money LK farmer
19.				'For you see, then, we, your father and mother, these difficulties we are having in having a family, (*CAUS = causative) (they are) because it's hard to find money being farmers.'

Ref.	Con.	Prenuclear-V	Nucleus	Postnuclear					
20	*Kad*	*nu awad*	*i-gangput-yu*						
	then	if EXIS	TH-finish-2P.GEN						
b			*ila-nyu*	*ta*	*asi-kayu*	*ang-asawa*	*nu*	*ang-das-kayu*	*'k kewaal-yu*
			see-2p.GEN	PUR	will-2p.ABS	AG-spouse	if	AG.IMPF-find-2p.ABS	OBL work-2p.GEN
20.	'When you've finished, then, see that you get married, provided you find your work/job.'								
21	*Te*	*nu*	*um-anak-kayu*						
	for	if	AG-child-2p.ABS						
b			*na-ip.pun*	*agon*	*inon-ta e*	*um-oy an-singit*	*ak*	*kewaal, amod ay*	*dikayu e bubai*
			ST.PF-NEG.EXIS	no.longer	way-1d LK	AG-go AG-look.for	OBL	work	especially.EMP 2p.TOP LK girl
21.	'After all, if you have children, there will no longer be the time to go look for work,								especially you girls.'
22			*Am-balu*		*nu*	*[da sana' e*	*mi-tuttudu]*,	*dongng-on-yu*	*okyan'*
b			AJR-good		if	this PL LK	PASS.IMPF-lesson	listen-TH.IMPF-2p.GEN	should
						e abeng' e	*an-uswila*		
						LK CHILD LK	AG-study		
22.			'It's good		if you children who are studying listen to these teachings as you ought.'				
23			*Abus-na*						
			finish-3s						
23.			'The end.'						

Appendix C: Banana Beer and Marijuana in Bariai
by Peter Biriu

Ref.	Con.	Prenuclear	Nucleus	Postnuclear
1		[Iaba ga mariuana] ein danga paeamao banana.sp & marijuana this thing bad 'Banana [beer] and marijuana, this is a bad thing.'		
2a	Kapeipei ga kakau, elders & youth		gau na-keo I 1s-speak	tautaunga pa-gimi truly at-you.PL
2b		[kado-nga do-NOM	ngan iaba ga mariuana] ein GP banana.sp & marijuana this	ga ean-nga guas mariuana consume-NOM tobacco marijuana
2c			ngan le-da mado-nga GP AG-1lin sit-NOM	ngansa i-paeabu because 3s-destroy
		'Elders and young people, I speak truly to you, the behaviour with regard to drinking banana [beer] and consuming marijuana tobacco, this is a bad thing, because it destroys our living in the village.'		
3a	be ADD		sai i-longo linge-g who 3s-hear voice-1s	mao NEG
3b	be ADD	i-an 3s.consume	guas paeamao tobacco bad	
3c	ga &	i-un 3s-drink	iaba] banana.sp	
3d	eine ga this IRR		i-paeabu 3s-destroy	ngan i-uae ede pade GP 3s-companion one ADD
3e				ga i-mate IRR 3s-die
	'Yes, then	if anyone doesn't listen to my voice, but consumes bad tobacco and drinks banana [beer], he will destroy his fellow companion so that he dies.'		
4a			Na-keo tautaunga 1s-speak truly	pa-gimi at-you.PL
4b		[kado-nga do-NOM	toa bedane] eine REL like.this this	paeamao bad
4c				[ngansa {oangga kado-nga toa bedane i-uotot somisomi tuanga-i} because if do-NOM REL like.this 3s-happen.IMPF always village-LOC
4d	eine ga this IRR			panua busa ga ti-matemate ngan kado-nga toa beda-oa] people many IRR 3p-die.IMPF GP do-NOM REL like.that
	then	'I speak truly to you, behaviour like this is bad because, if behaviour like this is always coming about in the village, many people will be dying from such behaviour.'		

Appendix C: Banana Beer and Marijuana in Bariai

Ref.	Con.	Prenuclear	Nucleus	Postnuclear
5a			Deo i-kado gita God 3s-do 1in	
5b				ga ta-ot IRR 1in-happen
				'God made us so that we came about.'
6a			I-uangga 3s-want	ta-mate somisomi mao 1in-die always NEG
6b				ngansa kado-nga toa bedane -nasi ei e-le kim-nga mao] because do-NOM REL like.this 3s-follow 3s 3s-AG want-NOM NEG
			'He intends [that] we never die, because behaviour like this doesn't follow his desire.'
7			Eine i-nasi Satan e-le kim-nga. this 3s-follow Satan 3s-AG want-NOM	
			'This here follows Satan's desire.'	
8a	eine	[Oangga	gita toa ngada ne ta-bada oatai-nga ngan Deo e-le laulau ae-a posa-nga] 1in REL all here 1in-get know-NOM GP God 3s-AG leaf 3s-EXP talk-NOM	
8b	this	ga IRR	le-da mado-nga tuanga-i ga i-uot kemi AG-1in sit-NOM village-LOC IRR 3s-become good	
8c	ta &.so		tini-da i-gelgel somisomi exterior-1in 3s-be.happy always	
8d	ga &		i-lalala 3s-walk	
8e	ga &		i-la 3s-go	
	then	'If all of us here get knowledge about God's book's talk our living in the village will become good, and so we will be happy always and it will continue and go on.'		
9a			gau na-keo pade I 1s-speak ADD	
9b		[mariuana marijuana	ga iaba] eine danga paeamao & banana.sp this thing bad	
		'I say again, marijuana and banana [beer] is a bad thing.'		
10a		[Oangga if	eao un iaba you 2s.drink banana.sp	
10b		mao ean or 2s.consume	mariuana] marijuana	
10c	eine this		i-kado go 2s.GP 3s-do	

Ref.	Con.	Prenuclear	Nucleus	Postnuclear					
10d				ga IRR	le-m AG-2s	tub-nga grow-NOM	i-uot 3s-become	paeamao bad	

'If you(sg) drink banana [beer] or consume marijuana, then it makes you so that your growth becomes bad.'

11	ga pade, & ADD 'And also,'		oatai 2s.know	naurata work	ae-a 3s-EXP	kado-nga do-NOM	mao NEG		

'you won't experience the doing of work.'

| 12a | | | Mado
2s.sit | | | | | | |
| 12b | be
ADD | | melengleng
2s.wander | alele
around | | | | | |

'You(sg) sit and also wander around.'

| 13 | | | Oatai
2s.know | ngan
GP | earum-nga
plant-NOM | le-m
AG-2s | kaokao
sweet.potato | eta
one.IRR | mao
NEG |

'You(sg) won't experience the planting of any sweet potato.'

| 14 | | | Oatai
2s.know | ngan
GP | earum-nga
plant-NOM | le-m
AG-2s | niu
coconut | eta
one.IRR | mao
NEG |

'You(sg) won't experience the planting of any coconuts.'

15a			gimi manta a-tnan you.PL must 2p-leave			[gid 3p	kado-nga do-NOM	toa REL	beda-oa] like.that
15b	ta &.so		a-nasi gid kado-nga 2p-follow 3p do-NOM			kemikemi good.PL			
15c	ta &.so		a-nasi 2p-follow			[mambe like	Deo God	i-kim] 3s-want	

'You(pl.) must leave behaviour like that, and so follow good behaviour as God desires.'

16a	[Ngan GP	kado] 2s.do							
16b	ta &.so		a-nasi 2p-follow	Satan Satan	e-le 3s-AG	kim-nga want-NOM			
16c	ta &.so		a-unun 2p-drink.IMPF	iaba banana.sp					
16d	ga &		a-eanean 2p-consume.IMPF	guas tobacco	mariuana marijuana	somisomi always			
16e	ta &.so		i-paeabu 3s-destroy	ngan GP	gimi you.PL				

'Otherwise, you follow Satan's desire and so be always drinking banana [beer] and consuming marijuana tobacco, and so he destroys you(pl.).'

Appendix D: Liquor Text in Dungra Bhil

Appendix D: Liquor Text in Dungra Bhil

Ref.	Con.	Pre-S	Nucleus	(Post-V)
1		o maa pujra oh my children	tumi horu ma 2p liquor PRO	piha drink.be.PL
		'Oh, my children, you should not be drinking liquor.'		
2		horu to liquor SPACER	ek dʒer hudu one poison like	hoje be
		'Liquor is like a poison.'		
3a		[horu pi-nara liquor drink-AG	mahõ-õ man-POS	dua eye.OBL	tumi pala 2p see.IMP
3b		tijaa 3ms.POS	dua ekdom rata rata eye.OBL complete red red	dekh-a see-PASS
		'Look at the eyes of a liquor-drinking person; his eyes appear completely red.'		
4	ono &	[tijaa 3ms.POS	dʒĩgi] life	tumi pala 2p see.IMP
		'And look at his life;'		
5a	tahã then	tuʔu ek 3ms one	vaʔa horu pit-neje time liquor drink-COMP	
5b		tija-ha 3ms.OBL-ACC	horu liquor	pi-va drink-INF	nag-e feel-FUT
		'(if) he liquor-drinks all at one go, then he will acquire a desire for liquor-drinking.'		
6a	ono &	[tuʔu tijaa 3ms 3ms.POS	phaje dʒetihi with how.much	modʒuri work	koʔ-e do-FUT
6b		tetaha that.much	horu pi liquor drink	dʒa-je go-FUT
		'And whatever work he may do, he will drink liquor with it (that will be completed in liquor-drinking).'		
7	tahã then 'Then	[tuʔu tijaa 3ms 3ms.POS	bujeʔẽ ono pujre] lady & children	kihĩ koʔ-e? what do-FUT
		what will his wife and children do?'		
8		phuko hunger.OBL		moʔ-e die-FUT
		'They will die of hunger.'		
9a	ono &	tija-ha 3ms.OBL-ACC	koda pojsa no.one money	naj NEG	ap-e give-FUT
9b	kihĩke because	[tuʔu 3ms	daruju] drunkard	hoje] be

Appendix D: Liquor Text in Dungra Bhil

Ref.	Con.	Pre-S	Nucleus	(Post-V)
9c		ehnoho like.this	maʔhe tija-ha ko-je people 3ms.OBL-ACC say-FUT	
		'And no one will give him money, because people will say to him, "You're a drunkard."'		
10a	ono &	horu pi-t liquor drink-PTC	pohõʔõ after	
10b			tijaa okole akhi vihra dʒa-he 3ms.POS wisdom all forget go-be	
		'And, after drinking liquor, he will forget all his wisdom.'		
11a		horu pi-t liquor drink-PTC	pohõʔõ after	
11b			tuʔu mahõ-hõ dʒemtem bun-e 3ms man.OBL-ACC babbling say-FUT	
		'After drinking liquor, he will babble to other people.'		
12a		horu pi-t liquor drink-PTC	pohõʔõ after	
12b			[ekhahũ-hũ maʔi tak-unoʔo naj taha suri koʔ-unoʔo] someone-ACC kill.LK AUX-GER NEG then theft do-GER	
12c		tijaa 3ms.POS	mono-mẽ ehnaha kajbi visare av-ja koʔ-taha heart.OBL-in like.these some thoughts come-mp.PER do-mp.be	
		'After drinking liquor, thoughts like killing someone or stealing something will keep on coming to his mind.'		
13a	ono &	tija 3ms.OBL	phaje pojasa sena dʒaj with money finish go.FUT	
13b	tahã then	[koʔ mẽ kaj that house in any tõʔo ves-i that sell-LK	kha-noʔo de-je hoje] eat-GER AUX-FUT be	
13c	pohõʔõ after	horu liquor	pi-je drink-FUT	
		'And, (when) all his money is finished, then any food that is in his house – that he will sell, and afterwards he will drink (more) liquor.'		
14	tahã then	[tija mahõ-õ that man-POS	koʔ-mẽ] kaj dʒato ro naje house-in any kind stay NEG	
		'Then in that person's house will remain nothing of any kind.'		
15	ono &		[tijaa koreʔe ke pujre bi] ugdana dino phir-e 3ms.POS household or children also open body.OBL roam-FUT	
		'And the people of his house and his children will roam naked.'		

Ref.	Con.	Pre-S	Nucleus					(Post-V)					
16	ono	tija-ha	[kaj	ud-uno?o	ke	pe?-uno?o	ke	kha-no?o	ru?u	bi]	dʒoɽ-e	naj	
	&	3ms.OBL-ACC	any	cover-GER	or	wear-GER	or	eat-GER	bread	also	accrue-FUT	NEG	
	'And		he will not get anything to cover or to wear or any bread to eat.'										
17	ihikojite		[horu	pi-nara-a		ko?-mẽ]	kedihi	sāti	naj	uve			
	likewise		liquor	drink-AG-POS		house-in	never	peace	NEG	become			
	'Similarly,		in the house of a liquor-drinking person there will never be any peace.'										
18a			moj	dʒaj		ta?hũ	dʒā?a						
			die	go.FUT		then	till						
18b				i?i		akho		ehnoho-dʒ	uve				
				these		all		like.this-EXC	become				
18c	pe?e	tija-ha			sāti	dʒoɽ-e	naje						
	but	3ms.OBL-ACC			peace	accrue-FUT	NEG						
	'Till he dies,		all these things will happen just like this, but he will not get peace.'										
19a	pe?e	tumi	ga?thehe	ekhũhũ		mahũ?ũ		tuma-ha	koj				
	but	2p	in.contrast	someone		person		2p.OBL-ACC	say.FUT				
19b	ke	[tumi		modʒuri		ko?-a							
	that	2p		work		do-IMP							
19c	ono	tumaa		gomto	kahage	khano?o	kha-ja						
	&	2p.POS		like	some	food	eat-IMP						
19d	ono	tumi		bada	yaruhũ	mer thi	dʒi-ya						
	&	2p		all	happily	love with	live-IMP						
	'As for you, in contrast, someone may tell you that you should work and eat the food you like, and all live happily with love,'													
20a	ono		ek	bidʒa	ari	vid-ha	ma						
	&		one	another	with	fight-be.PL	PRO						
20b	ono		ek	bidʒa	guthi mẽ	ma	pod-ha]						
	&		one	another	speech in	PRO	fall-be.PL						
	'(If) this is what that person says to you, then you should accept his counsel.'													
21a	ehnoho		to?o	tuma-ha		ko-je							
	like.this		that	2p.OBL-ACC		say-FUT							
21b	tahã		tumi	tijaa	guthi	manu-hũ	dʒuve						
	then		2p	3ms.POS	speech	accept-INF	obligation						
22	tahã	tumaa	ko?-mẽ		sāti	uve							
	then	2p.pos	house-in		peace	become							
	'Then		there will be peace in your house.'											

Appendix D: Liquor Text in Dungra Bhil

Ref.	Con.	Pre-S	Nucleus			(Post-V)		
23	ono & 'And		tumi 2p	varuhu happily 'live happily with love,'	mer love	thi with	dʒi-va live-IMP	
24a			kha-ha eat-be.PL					
24b			pi-ha drink-be.PL					
24c			modʒ modʒa enjoyment 'Be eating, drinking and enjoying yourselves;'	koʔ-ha do-be.PL				
25	tahã then 'then	tuma-ha 2p.OBL-ACC	ketoho how.much how good it is for you!'	hadʒo good				
26a			tumaa 2p.POS	kha-ʔno eat-ing		pi-ʔno drink-ing	mẽ in	naj NEG	tuṭ short	poṛe fall
26b	ke or		nugṛasibara clothes	me in	naj NEG	tuṭ short	poṛe fall	
26c	ke or		kaj any	bi also	dʒatiʔi kind	huh anxiety	tuma-ha 2p.OBL-ACC	av-e come-FUT	naje NEG
			'You will not become short of food and drink, you will not become short of clothing, and no kind of anxiety will come upon you.'					
27a		maa my	pujra children	apũ 1in	modʒri work	koʔ-dʒi do-1p.FUT		
27b	ono &		pojasa money	ekṭa gather	koʔ-dʒi do-1p.FUT			
27c	ono &		khet field	ne-dʒi bring-1p.FUT				
			'My children, we must work, gather money and buy fields.'					
28a	naj NEG	tahã then	bolod cattle	ne-dʒi bring-1p.FUT				
28b	ono &		apũ 1in	kheto-mẽ field.OBL-in	kam work	dõdu business	koʔ-dʒi do-1p.FUT	
			'If not, then we must buy cattle and make a business in the fields.'					
29		maa my	pujra children	tumi 2p	kheto-mẽ field.OBL-in	kam work	koʔ-dʒi do-1p.FUT	
			'My children, you must work in the fields.'					

Ref.	Con.	Pre-S	Nucleus						(Post-V)			
30			tumi 2p	[kaha why	kote] for/saying	[ija these	kamo-o work-POS	diho-me] day.OBL-in	nevru workless	phir-tnu roam-ms.IMPF
			'Why, in these days for working, are you roaming about without working?'									
31a		tumi 2p	kamo-o work-POS	diho-me day.OBL-in	kheto-o field-POS	kaj any	kam work	naj NEG	koʔ-ho do-be			
31b	tahã then		apũ 1in	kag what	kha-hũ eat-be.1p.FUT							
			'If you don't do any work in the fields in these days for working, what will there be for us to eat?'									
32a			apũ 1in	to-me SPACER-?	phuko hunger.OBL	moj die	dʒa-hũ go-be.1p.FUT					
32b	ono &		apũ-ũ 1in-POS	pujre children	bi also	phuko hunger.OBL	moj die	dʒa-je go-FUT				
			'Not only will we die from hunger, but our children also will die from hunger.'									
33a	ihikojite likewise		apũ 1in	akha-ha all-ACC	kaj any	khanoʔo food	naj NEG					
33b	ke or		pevunoʔo wear.GER	nugɽe clothes	naj NEG							
33c	ke or		kaj any	bi also	dʒoʈe accrue-FUT	naje NEG						
	'Likewise,		none of us will get any food to eat, any clothes to wear or anything at all.'									
34			apũ 1in	borabor very.well	kam work	koʔ-unoʔo work do-GER						
			'We need to work hard.'									
35a			apũ 1in	[bidʒe other	maʔhẽ people	nevre workless	kaj any	kam work	koʔ-te do-IMPF.PTC	nahĩ NEG	tĩjaa 3p.POS	hõs] like
35b			nevro workless	naj NEG	phir-unoʔo roam-GER							
			'We should not roam about without working like other people who make no effort to work.'									
36	peʔe but		apũ 1in	kam work	koʔ-unoʔo do-GER							
	'Rather,		we need to work.'									
37a			apũ 1in	horu liquor	naj NEG	pi-vunoʔo drink-GER						
37b	ono &		ek one	bidʒa another	ari with	vidɑ-noʔo fight-GER	naje NEG					
			'We should not drink liquor and we should not fight with one another.'									

Appendix D: Liquor Text in Dungra Bhil

Ref.	Con.	Pre-S	Nucleus				(Post-V)			
38			apũ	bada	maʔhõ	ari	varuhũ		mer thi	dʒi-vunoʔo
			1in	all	man.OBL	with	happily		love with	live-GER
			'We need to live happily with love with all people.'							
39		maa pujra	[horu	pi-noʔo	viʈa-noʔo	suri		koʔ-unoʔo]		
		my children	liquor	drink-GER	fight-GER	theft		do-GER		
			ĩʔĩ	akho	kaj	kamo-o	naje			
			these	all	any	work-POS	NEG			
		'My children, liquor-drinking, fighting and stealing: none of these is of any use.'								

References

Alford, Henry. 1863. *The Greek testament*, 4 vols. Fifth edition. London: Rivingtons.
Allen, Jerry. 2000. *Translator's notes on Philemon*. Dallas, TX: SIL International.
Arndt, William F., and F. Wilbur Gingrich. 1957. *A Greek-English lexicon of the New Testament and other early Christian literature*. Chicago: University of Chicago Press and Cambridge: Cambridge University Press.
Andrews, Avery. 1985. The major functions of the noun phrase. In Timothy Shopen (ed.), *Language typology and syntactic description,* 1:62–154. Cambridge: Cambridge University Press.
Banker, John. 1984. The position of the vocative *adelphoi* in the clause. *START* 11:29–36.
Banker, John. 1996. *A semantic structural analysis of Philippians*. Semantic and structural analysis series. Dallas, TX: Summer Institute of Linguistics.
Banker, John. 1999. *A semantic structural analysis of Philemon*. Semantic and structural analysis series. Dallas, TX: Summer Institute of Linguistics.
Beekman, John. 1972. Analyzing and translating the questions of the New Testament. *Notes on Translation* 44:3–21.
Beekman, John, and John C. Callow. 1974. *Translating the Word of God*. Grand Rapids, MI: Zondervan.
Blakemore, Diane. 1987. *Semantic constraints on relevance*. Oxford: Blackwell.
Breeze, Mary. 1992. Hortatory discourse in Ephesians. *Journal of Translation and Textlinguistics* 5(4):313–347.
Borchard, T. H. 1991. Discourse level functional equivalence translation. PhD dissertation. Fuller Theological Seminary, Pasadena, CA.
Callow, Kathleen. 1974. *Discourse considerations in translating the Word of God*. Grand Rapids, MI: Zondervan.
Callow, Kathleen. 1992. The disappearing *de* in 1 Corinthians. In David Alan Black, Katherine Barnwell, and Stephen Levinsohn (eds.), *Linguistics and New Testament interpretation: Essays on discourse analysis,* 183–193. Nashville: Broadman.
Campbell, Constantine R. 2008. *Basics of verbal aspect in Biblical Greek*. Grand Rapids, MI: Zondervan.
Comrie, Bernard. 1989. *Language universals and linguistic typology*. Second edition. Chicago: University of Chicago Press.
Connor, Ulla. 1996. *Contrastive rhetoric*. Cambridge: Cambridge University Press.
Creed, John Martin. 1930. *The Gospel according to St. Luke*. London: MacMillan.
Crystal, David. 1997. *A dictionary of linguistics and phonetics*. Fourth edition. Oxford: Basil Blackwell.
Dallaire, Hélène. 2004. Social dynamics and the Biblical Hebrew volitives. Paper read at the Society of Biblical Literature International Meeting, San Antonio, TX, November 20–23, 2004.

Diessel, Holger. 2001. The ordering distribution of main and adverbial clauses: A typological study. *Language* 77(3):433–455.

Dik, Simon. 1978. *Functional grammar*. Amsterdam: North-Holland.

Dik, Simon. 1989. *The theory of functional grammar. Part I: The structure of the clause*. Dordrecht: Foris.

Dooley, Robert A., and Stephen H. Levinsohn. 2001. *Analyzing discourse: A manual of basic concepts*. Dallas, TX: SIL International.

Dryer, Matthew S. 1997. On the six-way word order typology. *Studies in Language* 21(1):69–103.

Ellingworth, Paul, and Eugene A. Nida. 1976. *A translator's handbook on Paul's letters to the Thessalonians*. Helps for Translators. New York: United Bible Societies.

Fee, Gordon D. 1987. *The First Epistle to the Corinthians*. The New International Commentary on the New Testament. Grand Rapids, MI: Zondervan.

Greenberg, Joseph H. 1963. Some universals of grammar with particular reference to the order of meaningful elements. In Joseph H. Greenberg (ed.), *Universals of language*, 73–113. Cambridge, MA: MIT Press.

Greenlee, J. Harold. 1998. *An exegetical summary of Hebrews*. Exegetical summary series. Dallas, TX: Summer Institute of Linguistics.

Guthrie, George H. 1998. *The structure of Hebrews: A text-linguistic analysis*. Grand Rapids, MI: Baker Books.

Harro, Gretchen, and Nancy Haynes. 2002. *Features of paragraph and section breaks in Yemba expository and hortatory discourse*. Yaoundé, Cameroon: Société Internationale de Linguistique. http://www.sil.org/resources/archives/47944.

Heath, Theresa. 2000. Life these days and in days past: An expository text in Makaa. Ms.

Heimerdinger, Jean-Marc. 1999. Topic, focus and foreground in Ancient Hebrew narratives. *JSOTSS* 295. Sheffield: Sheffield Academic Press.

Kelly, J. N. D. 1963. *A commentary on the pastoral epistles*. Harper's New Testament Commentaries. New York: Harper & Row.

Kiss, Katalin É. 1998. Identificational focus versus information focus. *Language* 74(2):245–273.

Kompaoré, Anne E. Garber. 2004. Discourse analysis of directive texts: The case of biblical law. MA thesis. Associated Mennonite Biblical Seminary, Elkhart, IN.

König, Ekkehard. 1991. *The meaning of focus particles: A comparative perspective*. London: Routledge.

Lambrecht, Knud. 1994. *Information structure and sentence form: Topic, focus, and the mental representation of discourse referents*. Cambridge Studies in Linguistics 71. New York: Cambridge University Press.

Larsen, I. 1991. Boundary features. *Notes on Translation* 5(1):48–54.

Lautamatti, L. 1987. Observations in the development of the topic in simplified discourse. In Ulla Connor and Robert B. Kaplan (eds.), *Writing across languages: Analysis of L2 text*, 87–114. Reading, MA: Addison-Wesley.

Levinsohn, Stephen H. 1999. Ordering of propositions in OV languages of Brazil. *Notes on Translation* 13(1):54–56.

Levinsohn, Stephen H. 2000. *Discourse features of New Testament Greek: A coursebook on the information structure of New Testament Greek*. Second edition. Dallas, TX: SIL International.

Levinsohn, Stephen H. 2003a. Is Ὅτι an interpretive marker? Paper read at the Society of Biblical Literature International Meeting, Cambridge, England, July 2003.

Levinsohn, Stephen H. 2003b. Towards a unified linguistic description of οὗτος and ἐκεῖνος. Paper read at the Society of Biblical Literature Meeting, Atlanta, GA, November 2003.

Levinsohn, Stephen H. 2006a. Reasoning styles and types of hortatory discourse. *Journal of Translation* 2(2):1–10.

Levinsohn, Stephen H. 2006b. Towards a typology of story development marking. (Repeatedly naming the subject: The Hebrew equivalent of Greek Δέ). *Journal of Translation* 2(2):31–42.

Levinsohn, Stephen H. 2015. *Self-instruction materials on narrative discourse analysis*. Dallas, TX: SIL International.

Levinsohn, Stephen H., 2021. The infinitive absolute in Hebrew as a substitute for a finite verb. *Journal of Language, Culture, and Religion* 2(2):19–34. https://diu.edu/documents/jlcr/jlcr-2.2-2021.pdf.

Levinsohn, Stephen H., and Mark Dubis. 2019. The use of the Greek article in 1 Peter: A case study. In Daniel King (ed.), *The article in Post-Classical Greek*, 101–125. Dallas, TX: SIL International.

Longacre, Robert E. 1983. Exhortation and mitigation in First John. *START* 9:3–44.

Longacre, Robert E. 1992. Towards an exegesis of 1 John based on the discourse analysis of the Greek text. In David Alan Black, Katherine Barnwell, and Stephen Levinsohn (eds.), *Linguistics and New Testament interpretation: Essays on discourse analysis*, 271–286. Nashville: Broadman.

Longacre, Robert E. 1994. *Weqatal* forms in Biblical Hebrew prose. In Robert D. Bergen (ed.), *Biblical Hebrew and discourse linguistics*, 50–98. Dallas, TX: Summer Institute of Linguistics.

Longacre, Robert E. 1995. Building for the worship of God: Exodus 25:1–30:10. In Walter R. Bodine (ed.), *Discourse analysis of biblical literature: What it is and what it offers*, 21–49. Atlanta: Scholars Press.

Longacre, Robert E. 1996. *The grammar of discourse*. Second edition. Topics in Language and Linguistics. New York: Plenum.

Lowe, Ivan. 1998. Why translators need to study the grammar of the receptor language. *Notes on Translation* 12(1):36–43.

Marshall, I. Howard, 1978. *The Gospel of Luke: A commentary on the Greek text*. Exeter, England: The Paternoster Press.

Martin, D. Michael. 2001. *1, 2 Thessalonians: An exegetical and theological exposition of Holy Scripture*. The New American Commentary 33. Bellingham, WA: Broadman & Holman Publishers.

Mathew, Sunil K. 2004. Some characteristics of hortatory texts in Dungra Bhil. MA/MTh thesis. TAFTEE, Bangalore, India.

McLachlin, Betty, and Barbara Blackburn. 1971. An outline of Sarangani Bilaan discourse and paragraph structure. In Robert E. Longacre (ed.), *Philippine discourse studies in memory of Betty McLachlin*, 1–83. Pacific Linguistics C 22. Canberra: Australian National University.

Miller, Neva F. 1992. The imperativals of Romans 12. In David Alan Black, Katherine Barnwell, and Stephen Levinsohn (eds.), *Linguistics and New Testament interpretation: Essays on discourse analysis*, 162–182. Nashville: Broadman.

Miller, Neva F., and Michael Martens. 1998. *Translator's notes on 1 Corinthians 1–7*. Preliminary version. Dallas, TX: Summer Institute of Linguistics.

Minor, Eugene E. 1992. *An exegetical summary of 2 Timothy*. Exegetical summary series. Dallas, TX: Summer Institute of Linguistics.

Mithun, Marianne. 1984. The evolution of noun incorporation. *Language* 62:56–119.

Neeley, Linda Lloyd. 1987. A discourse analysis of Hebrews. *OPTAT* 1(3-4):1–146.

Nida, Eugene A., J. P. Louw, A. H. Snyman, and J. V. W. Cronje. 1983. *Style and discourse: With special reference to the text of the Greek New Testament*. Cape Town, South Africa: The Bible Society.

Oxford English Dictionary (OED). 1989. Second edition. 20 vols. Oxford: Oxford University Press. Continually updated at http://www.oed.com/.

Porter, Stanley E. 1992. *Idioms of the Greek New Testament*. Biblical Languages: Greek 2. Sheffield: JSOT Press.

Richard, Earl J. 1995. *First and Second Thessalonians*. Sacra Pagina Series 11. Collegeville, MN: Liturgical Press.

Roberts, John R. 1997. The syntax of discourse structure. *Notes on Translation* 11(2):15–34.

Russell, David M. 1998. The strategy of a first-century appeals letter: A discourse reading of Paul's epistle to Philemon. *Journal of Translation and Textlinguistics* 11:1–25.

Schooling, S. 1985. More on Matthew's brackets: a study of the function of time references in Matthew's Gospel. *START* 13:14–27.

Schmidt, Ruth Laila. 1999. *Urdu: An essential grammar*. Routledge Essential Grammars. London: Routledge.

Sim, Roland J. 2010. *Lo and Behold!* Revisiting Hebrew presentative particles. Paper presented at the Bible Translation 2010 (BT2010) Conference, Horsleys Green, England, 4–6 July 2010.

Terry, Ralph Bruce. 1995. *A discourse analysis of First Corinthians*. Summer Institute of Linguistics and the University of Texas at Arlington Publications in Linguistics 120. Dallas, TX.

Tomlin, Russell S. 1987. *Coherence and grounding in discourse*. Typological Studies in Language 11. Philadelphia: Benjamins.

Wallace, Daniel B. 1996. *Greek grammar beyond the basics: An exegetical syntax of the New Testament*. Grand Rapids, MI: Zondervan.

Wendland, Ernst R. 2000. "Stand fast in the true grace of God!" A study of 1 Peter. *Journal of Translation and Textlinguistics* 13:25–102.

Werth, Paul. 1984. *Focus, coherence and emphasis*. London: Croom Helm.

White, Newport J. D. 1970 (1909). The first and second epistles to Timothy and the epistle to Titus. *The Expositor's Greek Testament*, vol. 4. Grand Rapids, MI: Eerdmans.

Wiesmann, Hannes. 2000. Éléments du discours narratif dans les textes win (toussian du sud) [Elements of narrative discourse in Win texts (Southern Toussian)]. *Cahiers Voltaïques – Hors Série* 2. Bayreuth, Germany: Universität Bayreuth.

Zeynali Dastuyi, Seddigheh. 2018. An investigation and comparison of some discourse features in Persian general practitioners' books and online medical journals. PhD dissertation. University of Sistan and Baluchestan, Zahedan, Iran.

Index of Languages

Agta, Palanan [apf] 93, 94
Amele [aey] 35
Amharic [amh] 22, 31
Arabic, Chadian Kangri [shu] 39, 107
Arabic, Standard [arb] 45
Awara [awx] 68

Bafut [bfd] 77
Bariai [bch] 6, 9, 10, 15, 17, 18, 20, 23, 28, 32, 40, 46, 53, 59, 69, 74, 91, 94, 96, 97, 102, 104, 106, 108, 111, 112, 113, 117, 131–134
Bhatri [bgw] 65–66, 108
Bilaan, Sarangani [bps] 90

Dungra Bhil [duh] 6, 11, 13, 14, 15, 16, 17, 20, 23, 28, 32, 34, 40, 46, 53, 54, 55, 57, 58, 62, 63, 64, 65, 69, 74, 75, 82, 83, 86, 91, 92, 94, 96, 97, 102, 104, 106, 108, 109, 110, 111, 112, 113, 115, 117–118, 135–141

English [eng] 19, 26n, 31, 32n, 34, 35, 37, 38, 41, 43, 45, 46, 55, 58, 59, 60, 65, 67, 81n, 82, 100

French [fra] 39, 55

Greek, Koine [grc] 1, 2, 13, 14, 19, 20, 22, 23n, 28, 29, 31, 33, 34, 35, 36, 39, 40, 41, 45, 47, 55, 56, 63, 65, 68, 69, 72, 75, 82, 84, 93, 94n, 95n, 96, 100, 101, 103, 105, 107, 110, 111, 113, 114. *See also* sections referring to Koine Greek

Hebrew, Ancient [hbo] 1, 3, 14, 15, 18, 19, 24, 27, 29, 45, 49, 55, 71, 77, 82, 85, 95, 96, 97, 108, 110
Hindi [hin] 62n

Inga [inb] 14, 24, 33, 55, 75, 76, 84

Kalinga, Lower Tanudon [kml] 1, 2, 6, 7, 8, 13, 15, 17, 18, 20, 22, 28, 29, 32, 40, 41, 46, 49, 52, 61, 62, 67, 69, 73, 74, 83, 90, 91, 93, 94, 95, 102, 104, 105, 109, 111, 112, 113, 114, 116, 125–130
Kambaata [ktb] 37, 65, 76
Kangri [xnr] 40n, 41
Konso [kxc] 31
Konzime [ozm] 76
Koorete 38 [kqy]

Makaa [mcp] 97
Makonde [kde] 64
Marba [mpg] 38, 108
Maria, Hill [mrr] 21
Me'en [mym] 67
Menya [mer] 19–20, 26
Mixtec, Southeastern Nochixtlán [mxy] 1

Oromo [orm] 37

Persian [pes] 81n

Sangil [snl] 67
Somrai [sor] 95
Suri [suq] 63

Tharu, Rana [thr] 20
Toussian, Southern [wib] 76, 106

Yemba [ybb] 66, 76

Index of Scripture References

Old Testament

Genesis
  3:11 77
  4:13–14 95, 97
  4:14 96

Exodus
  3:7–10 19
  20:2 21
  20:2–17 19, 27, 45n3
  20:4 77
  20:4–5 26
  20:5 18, 29n9
  20:5–7 24
  24:8 72n6
  32:1 19

Numbers
  27:3–4 18

Deuteronomy
  25:4 85n8

1 Chronicles
  22:7–10 22
  22:7–16 19, 21

Psalm
  54:1–3 18, 19n18, 20
  54:2–3 30
  54:3 29
  103:1–9 110
  130:7–8 29

Isaiah
  6:10 108

New Testament

Matthew
  6:10 37
  6:13 31
  6:14 114
  7:3–5 92
  7:16–20 45
  9:37–38 39
  26:26 36
  28:19 89

Mark
  4:3 85, 94

Luke
  1:52 31
  2:19 30
  6:8 38
  6:20–49 105
  6:35–37 103
  6:46 109
  7:7–8 39
  15:16 77
  18:16 31, 36, 37
  24:35 36

John
- 11:5 103
- 12:40 108n24

Acts
- 1:4–5 113
- 1:5 49, 54
- 1:11 35, 77, 78n16
- 2:6 36
- 2:36 86
- 8:1, 4 114
- 8:25–26 100
- 11:19 114
- 13:11 96
- 13:51 101
- 16:30 36
- 17:22–31 19, 86
- 17:30 86n9
- 18:1 101
- 23:21 85
- 27:25 40n27
- 28:27 108–109

Romans
- 7:7 109
- 8:29–30 44, 47
- 8:30 48
- 11:30 52n22
- 12:15 86

1 Corinthians
- 1:10 83, 86n11
- 1:12 55
- 1:13 14, 58, 59
- 1:27–28 51n18
- 3:18 85
- 7:25 22
- 10:6–10 94
- 10:6–11 83, 105, 107
- 10:7–10 85
- 11:22 97
- 15:58 111
- 16:11 85, 86

2 Corinthians
- 13:5 49

Galatians
- 3:1–4 30

Ephesians
- 1:1–2 15
- 1:3–14 16

Ephesians, continued
- 2:1–3 21
- 3:14–21 21
- 6:21–24 15n6
- 6:23–24 15

Philippians
- 2:12, 14 25

Colossians
- 1:23 50, 51n19

1 Thessalonians
- 1:1, 2 73
- 1:9 735n9
- 2:1 65
- 2:4, 5 73
- 2:9 83n
- 2:13 73
- 2:14 65n18, 68
- 2:15 73
- 4:1 73, 87, 94
- 4:3–4 51
- 4:6 56
- 4:7 51
- 4:8 73n9
- 4:9 48, 101
- 4:10 111
- 4:11 63
- 4:13 86, 87, 90n15
- 4:14 101
- 4:15 54, 105
- 4:16 73n9
- 4:18 90n15, 105
- 4:18–5:27 82
- 5 95
- 5:6 31
- 5:6–22 85
- 5:7 58, 59
- 5:8 59, 88, 89, 94n21, 96
- 5:12 111
- 5:14 87
- 5:14–22 82
- 5:15 88
- 5:18 73n11
- 5:20–21 31

2 Thessalonians
- 2:15 111

1 Timothy
- 2:1–8 41
- 2:7 33
- 2:8 41, 103

1 Timothy, continued
  2:12 87
  2:13–14 29
  3:2 41n31, 87
  3:12 87
  3:15 86
  4:6 68
  4:7 72, 85
  4:8 31, 34, 94
  4:11 47
  5:1 85
  5:3 83
  5:14 87
  5:16 84
  5:18 85n8
  5:21 84, 86n11, 88
  6:8 85
  6:13–14 87, 94
  6:20 88

2 Timothy
  2:1 112
  4:17–18 30

Titus
  1:10 103
  1:12, 15 51n19

Philemon
  1–3 15n7, 103, 115
  3 73
  4 28, 73, 103, 113, 115
  4–5 45n4
  4–7 22, 115
  4–16 18, 22
  4–18 18, 20, 89
  4–22 15, 103, 104
  5 73, 78
  5–6 45
  6 50, 60
  7 28, 40, 50, 60, 68n25, 103, 111, 115
  8 28, 60, 104, 113, 115
  8–14 22
  8–16 115
  8–22 104n10
  9 22, 29, 49, 59, 89
  10 28, 78, 89
  10–13 44, 50
  10–14 22
  11 29n7, 32, 47, 48, 101
  12 72n4, 78
  13 32, 50, 59, 78
  14 28, 32, 33, 60
  15 28, 40, 59, 61, 72, 103, 105n14

Philemon, continued
  15–16 22
  16 29n, 32
  17 28, 41, 81, 83, 84, 89, 101n3, 104n10, 113, 115
  17–18 18, 22, 32
  17–21 115
  18 22, 28, 46, 48, 60, 72, 89, 101, 104
  19 22, 28, 50, 59, 110
  19–22 20n23, 22, 89
  20 28, 89, 110, 111
  21 22, 28, 29n7, 60, 104n10, 105, 115
  22 18, 22, 28, 29n7, 40, 48, 61, 89, 101, 103, 104, 113, 115
  23 28, 103, 113, 115
  23–24 49, 56, 115, 116
  23–25 15n7, 103
  25 28, 103, 113, 115, 116

Hebrews
  3:1 103, 114
  3:3 72
  3:12–18 113
  4:2 72
  4:14 103, 114
  5:1–10 107
  7:1, 4, 27 72
  8:3, 7 72
  9:20 72n6
  10:12 72
  10:22 88
  11:12, 13, 15, 39 72
  11:13 75

James
  1:7 51n20
  1:9 34, 51n19
  1:9–10 33
  1:11 51n19
  2:2 56

1 Peter
  1–5 72
  3:18–22 44

1 John
  1:5 72n6
  2:6 72
  3:3, 5, 7 72
  3:16 72
  4:17 72
  5:6, 16, 20 72n5

2 John
7 40

Revelation
1:14 35

Stephen H. Levinsohn is a senior linguistics consultant with SIL International. He has a doctorate in Linguistic Sciences from the University of Reading, England, on the topic, "Relationships Between Constituents Beyond the Clause in the Acts of the Apostles" (1980), parts of which were published in 1987 by the Society of Biblical Literature under the title *Textual Connections in Acts* (1987). He and his wife, Nessie, became members of SIL International in 1965. They worked with the Inga (Quechuan) people in Colombia from 1968 to 1997. Since 1997 Stephen has run "Discourse for Translation" workshops in 20 countries for linguist-translators working with over 400 languages. National and expatriate participants in the workshops first learn how to analyse texts in the languages they are studying (the receptor languages), while learning how the source languages handle the same discourse tasks. They then apply their discoveries to draft translations into the receptor languages.

Academic website
sil.org/biography/stephen-levinsohn

Works by this author in SIL Language & Culture Archives
sil.org/resources/search/contributor/levinsohn-stephen-h

Works by this author in Google Scholar
scholar.google.com/citations?user=RpsBdtsAAAAJ&hl=en

www.ingramcontent.com/pod-product-compliance
Lightning Source LLC
Chambersburg PA
CBHW060420300426
44111CB00018B/2914